P L A C E W

Placeways

A THEORY OF THE

HUMAN ENVIRONMENT

EUGENE VICTOR WALTER

The University of North Carolina Press

Chapel Hill and London

92 91 90 89 88   5 4 3 2 1

Library of Congress Cataloging-in-Publication Data
Walter, E. V. (Eugene Victor), 1925–
Placeways: a theory of the human environment.
Bibliography: p.
Includes index.
1. Environmental psychology. 2. Space perception.
3. Thought and thinking. 4. Knowledge, Theory of.
5. Philosophy. I. Title.
BF353.W35   1988   155.9   87-13952
ISBN 0-8078-1758-9 (alk. paper)
ISBN 0-8078-4200-1 (pbk.: alk. paper)

For Lucille and Herbert, and

to the memory of my mother

The things of the world

cannot be known except

through a knowledge of the

places in which they are

contained.

Roger Bacon

CONTENTS

I L L U S T R A T I O N S

ACKNOWLEDGMENTS

Places as well as people helped to shape this book—places in Boston, northern England, and Greece.

In Boston, my fieldwork from 1969 to 1972 was made possible by the Metropolitan Studies Unit, under the supportive leadership of Robert Weiss. The unit was in the Laboratory of Community Psychiatry, Harvard University, which was directed by Gerald Caplan. The core of my research team included Rachel Forman and June Austin, sociologists, and Barbara Wolf, a psychologist. Bodil Bjerring, a Danish anthropologist, joined us for the summer of 1972. We mourn the loss of June Austin, who died of cancer in 1985. She was a brilliant fieldworker, a profoundly humane person, a loyal colleague, and a warm friend.

From 1974 to 1976 a Simon Senior Research Fellowship at the University of Manchester in England provided the opportunity to explore the first industrial city. My wife, Ruth, and my daughters, Natasha, Jenia, and Alexandra, shared with me the experience of place change. We are grateful for the warm friendship of Mancunians who taught us to feel at home in their city: Peter and Sheila Worsley, Norman and Caroline Burkhardt, and the Hartshorne family. Tomas Kabdebo helped me with library resources. I hope he will add this volume to his list of "books that change the mind."

I am grateful to the University Professors Program at Boston University for enabling me to teach the subject of topistics in 1981.

For many years, Lowell Edmunds has been my guide to ancient Greek language and literature. In 1985 I explored Greece, following several paths, including the route of Oedipus from Corinth to Colonus. My guide to the topography of Athens and to the sites of Plato's Academy and Sophocles' Colonus was Judith Binder.

I am grateful to people who commented on drafts of chapters or helped in other ways: Tzvi Abusch, Judith Binder, Joseph Boskin, David Cooperman, Kendall Dudley, Lowell Edmunds, Robert Erwin, Natasha Walter Fisk, Neil Friedman, Gene Green, Charles Herberger, Ruth Ice, David Kettler, Philip Kubzansky, Herbert Mason, Michael V. Miller, Clyde Mitchell, Mary Nash, Chris and Tim O'Reilly, Michael Palencia-

Roth, Amos Rapoport, Meyer Reinhold, Miriam Rothschild, Joseph Rykwert, Morris Schwartz, Cecelia Tichi, Yi-Fu Tuan, Alexandra Walter, Sam
Bass Warner, Bill Williams, and Kurt H. Wolff. None of them should be
held responsible for my interpretations.

I thank Adelle Robinson for impeccable typing and for organizing the
bibliography.

Anita Stauffer invited me to address the Inter-Lutheran Consultation
on Environment and Art in Worship Space in 1984, where I presented
the material of chapter 4, "Sacred Places." An early version of material in
chapter 6 appeared as "The Places of Experience," in *Philosophical Forum*
12, no. 2 (Winter 1980–81): 159–81.

Above all, my wife, Ruth Ice, has supported my work with her lively
interest, reading successive drafts and sharing thoughts, walks, and
conversations.

PLACEWAYS

I N T R O D U C T I O N

The Places of Experience

In everyday life, people keep track of places. They talk about how the neighborhood has changed; when that building went up; what it was like in the old days; how it feels to live here now. These comments are spontaneous. They belong to the vital obscurities of life in common—to the lore of places, composed from statements that are always heeded but seldom recorded. The reports continue from one generation to the next, proceeding by observation and reflection, by question and answer, by memory and anecdote.

We recognize different kinds of place change. Cities grow larger or smaller, feel more lively or run down, appear more beautiful or more ugly to the senses. We feel that they get better or worse. We talk about ruin and renewal, urban decay and restoration, decline and recovery. Jane Jacobs put it tersely as the "death and life" of cities. Nevertheless, civic identity endures despite vast changes of place. We continue to identify Rome, for example, as the "same" place over time—even though we recognize the enormous changes distinguishing the historical cities of Caesar, Petrarch, and Mussolini. No city is what it used to be. The same place does not remain the same. Yet, despite great changes, some places continue to make sense.

In popular writing about architecture and geography, "sense of place" has degenerated into a cliché, often suggesting little more than superfi- .

1

cial impressions. Nevertheless, a place with integrity does make sense—
it conveys meaning. The real "sense" of a place, therefore, is twofold. On
the one hand, people feel it; on the other hand, they grasp its meaning.
Today, the experience of place is often out of balance. Preoccupations
with the logic of space tend to suppress the feeling of place. There is a
tendency in modern Western thinking to separate the feelings, symbolic
meanings, moral sentiments, and intuitions of a place from the intellectual, rational features. The expressive dimension gets lost in systems of
design and management. Places, therefore, tend to lose an old kind of
meaning: *expressive intelligibility*.

In ordinary life, some people still do grasp a place as a whole through
a balanced experience of intellect, common sense, feeling, and imagination. Our technical languages, however, do not express the unity and
coherence of this holistic experience, which gets factored away by geography, local history, architecture, city planning, sociology, environmental psychology, and so forth. Fragmenting the experience of place in the
abstractions of the special disciplines reinforces the split between our
methods of feeling and our methods of thinking. It also spoils the
human environment, vitiating our ability to build and inhabit good
houses, communities, and cities, because the conventional ways of
thinking about housing and urban spaces do not grasp the reality of
places as wholes.

The integrity of a place suffers when what we learn by ear gets
disconnected from what we perceive with the eye—still more when
what we imagine seems irrelevant. The imagination makes sense. It is,
moreover, an organ of perception—like our eyes, ears, and legs. We get
to know a place when we participate in the local imagination. The whole
synthesis of located experience—including what we imagine as well as
the sights, stories, feelings, and concepts—gives us the sense of a place.

We are threatened today by two kinds of environmental degradation:
one is pollution—a menace that we all acknowledge; the other is loss of
meaning. For the first time in human history, people are systematically
building meaningless places. However, we are living through the end of
an era, experiencing the demise of modern architecture, a revulsion
from "futurism," scepticism about planning, and a reaction against urban renewal programs. As we contemplate the ruins and dislocations of
our cities, another way of understanding the built environment and the
natural landscape is struggling to emerge. Today, everyone yearns for
renewal, but from a holistic perspective, what does the renewal of a city

mean? It is not merely physical reconstruction, as many people think—demolishing slums and replacing them with new buildings. Historically, the renewal of a city was experienced as a mental and emotional transformation, an improvement of the spirit, a rebirth of psychic energies.

The purpose of this book is to provide theoretical resources for readers who want to rescue the obvious world from the degradation of feeling and meaning. A growing number of thoughtful and concerned people want to recover an environmental awareness that is not lost but driven underground. They are also looking for new ideas to change the world—but those new ideas, I believe, must include some old perspectives to grasp things whole and entire. We need to recover a way of thinking that ancient people took for granted. The renewal of consciousness implies a restitution of grounded intelligence. We need to experience the world in a radically old way.

When we are very young, the keepers of the obvious world encourage us to erect barriers segregating features of experience. We learn to build a mental life that separates thinking from feeling, and fact from fantasy. We settle reality, imagination, emotion, and reason in separate chambers of the psyche. When we follow fancy, we expect to step out of reality, and when we indulge our feelings, we exclude the intellect. Archaic people sought meaningful ways to fit the two together, "to combine empirical facts with imaginative fancies and to think in rhythm with their feeling and feel in rhythm with their thinking."[1] They wanted to build bridges in experience. They learned to represent their participation in cosmic processes—to identify the center of energy in themselves with the external energy of which nature is the image.[2] It is possible to recover this integrity of experience and to relearn what ancient people took for granted. To modify a phrase from the work of a forgotten antiquary, we need a "restitution of decayed intelligence."[3]

In some ways, the diet of the mind resembles the diet of the body. Abstraction refines theory from the grain of experience, but the process may grind up our thoughts until they turn into such highly refined abstractions, so remote from the whole grain of experience, and rendered so thin, that they keep no energy to nourish the mind. William Blake identified this mental grind as the "dark Satanic mill" that transformed factory towns in the nineteenth century.

To reverse this way of thinking, let us return to holistic theory—to the archaic *theoria* that grasped the whole experience of a place. Originally, *theoria* meant seeing the sights, seeing for yourself, and getting a worldview, but it involved all the senses and feelings. Disintegrating this whole experience degrades the intangible, nonphysical, human energies of a place, and true renewal depends on some recovery of its integrity. Archaic *theoria* survives hidden in dimly remembered ways of thinking. Therefore, several chapters in this book explore the language and thinking of ancient Greeks. Alfred North Whitehead observed:

> Greece was the mother of Europe; and it is to Greece that we must look in order to find the origin of our modern ideas. . . . The Greek genius was philosophical, lucid and logical. . . . Their minds were infected with an eager generality. They demanded clear, bold ideas, and strict reasoning from them. . . . They were lucid thinkers and bold reasoners.[4]

The connection between Greek thinking and modern ideas is well known. This book explores the connection of Greek thinking to the archaic past. In philosophy and in drama, some Greek thinkers such as Plato and Sophocles wanted to unite the domain of lucid thought with the older and darker realm of obscure intimations. They wanted a union of sight with insight.

It has been said that the history of Western philosophy is a long series of footnotes to Plato and Aristotle. The statement is too extreme to take literally, but as a metaphor it suggests that those Greek philosophers clarified many issues that are still important to us. In the course of this inquiry, we shall return to Plato and Aristotle because a metaphysical difference between them on the concept of place expressed for the first time the presuppositions underlying crucial alternatives. We know how Greek language and concepts have shaped our science and technology. However, we are less familiar with the full range and harmony of Greek thought. In Plato's doctrine of place we may recover an ancient balance of intellect and grounded experience. Nevertheless, Plato's thinking moved in two directions. The Socratic side of Plato stayed close to the earth, but Plato's invention of the "problem" was a turning point in the history of expressive intelligibility.

I argue that a place is not a problem but a riddle, and I explore the experiential difference between problems and riddles. Therefore, I do not investigate the modern crisis of places by offering solutions to their problems. Some readers may require more attention to our own era— more examples from the modern world—and in subsequent studies I hope to satisfy that demand. But for now let us explore historical changes in the structure of experience. This book is a theoretical rediscovery as well as a philosophical reinterpretation of the experience and meaning of place.

Our quest for archaic shapes of experience passes through "strange seas of thought," exploring the lost work of periegetes, antiquaries, and chorographers, where sometimes it is possible to find holistic, integrated *theoria*. This voyage retronavigates the course of Blake's enemy, Newton, who made the principal journey—now well charted in the modern mind—from magic to science. In Book 3 of his *Prelude*, William Wordsworth called the statue of Isaac Newton, beheld on bright nights from his college pillow,

> The marble index of a mind for ever
> Voyaging through strange seas of Thought, alone.

I risk a voyage in the opposite direction, through stranger seas of thought, in the company of readers who are discontented with Newton's way of experiencing the world. The frame of mind that makes holistic *theoria* possible is a form of inquiry I call "topistics," or the study of placeways.

Today, conventional thinking associates the city with problems, and countless books are written about the crisis of urban society. Yet, as the volume of talk and writing about the subject expands, ideas about the city diminish, and we live with an abundance of discussion but a poverty of discourse. A great deal of thinking remains confined to mechanistic, economic, or other abstract models, which may be useful as far as they go, but they scarcely exhaust the many features of urban life, and they are remote from the human experience of cities. Even preservationists, sensitive to the historic meanings of the city, express the need for new theoretical resources. Civic authorities, city planners, and social scientists fail to view the city as a whole—as an order that carries meanings other than the maxims of zoning, amenity, and circulation.[5] If the present trend continues, the city as a symbolic pattern—which is the way the ancients regarded it—may become unthinkable.

The following chapters explore the energies of places, modes of experiencing them, and the meaning of good and bad places. The main point of the entire argument is that our places will not improve until we change our form of topistic experience, and that it is humanly possible to change it. I describe some archaic kinds of grounded experience to suggest what may be recovered. We have not lost, in a mere century or two, a way of living in the world that belongs to the roots of humanity.

Appearance is built. . . .

Xenophanes

O N E

Road to Topistics

This book started when I moved to Boston in 1958, at the height of the urban renewal program, and watched them tearing down the West End. The passion for "the new Boston" not only dismantled the disreputable Scollay Square, which I remembered from my days as a sailor, but also demolished the respectable West End, a poor but comfortable neighborhood "objectively" identified as a slum. I tried to understand my own subjective response as I viewed the wrecking machines turning the place into a ruin. The demolition seemed to take a long time, revealing to the world expressive energies in those lost households by exposing the myriad wallpaper in rows of living rooms, bedrooms, and kitchens. Could my feelings be dismissed as nostalgia, even though I never lived in the West End or in any place like it? Or was I merely another bleeding heart, soft on slums because I never had to live in one? I wondered about the quality of life in that place, and what would happen to it now. How do people change their lives when they have to change their place? Eventually, I met the exiles and began to learn for myself. A decade later, I experienced unexpected, involuntary place change when an accidental fire burned down my home and forced me and my family to move somewhere else. We decided to stay in the same neighborhood because we were deeply attached to the place. We were poor enough, by middle-class standards, but I imagined what our experience would have been like if extreme poverty had determined our fate and driven us out of the beloved neighborhood to live in a slum. Something drove me to test the fantasy in my mind by experience in the world.

In 1969, I joined a research program devoted to urban populations at risk.[1] I wanted to do research on the slum, the location of urban poverty, and from the research to design a program conceived as the theory and therapy of bad places. I completed an ethnographic study of two housing projects in a district selected by objective indexes as a poverty zone. The social agencies, the neighbors, and even some of the residents defined one housing project as the worst place in the neighborhood—the slum within a slum. They warned me that research there was impossible, and that I would get my head bashed in. I moved in and lived there for a time, in an apartment I used as a field station, and grew to feel at home in the place. I met some exiles from the West End and learned about the changes in their lives. My research assistants lived in an apartment in the other housing project, located in another neighborhood of the same district. Three of them abandoned their middle-class, academic locations to move into the neighborhood near the "bad" housing project after they completed their research. More than twelve years later, when the idea of poverty had lost all fashion and resumed its invidious image in the public imagination, two of them still lived there.

In the midst of my study of public housing, some people in the Boston Housing Authority who were conducting their own research turned to me for advice. These were serious, responsible, well-educated housing therapists, devoted to improving the quality of places occupied by the poor. They wanted to learn what made the difference between a good place and a bad place, and they were puzzled by the remarkable differences between two adjacent entryways in "my" housing project, which I knew intimately. (An entryway held a common stairwell that served twelve apartments distributed symmetrically on three floors.) The two entryways were identical units from a physical and architectural point of view. But one was continually disturbed by fights, police calls, ambulance arrivals, and similar emergencies, while the neighboring unit was peaceful. The research folk at the Boston Housing Authority were also good Aristotelians: they believed that the "place" could be separated from its contents, and they wanted to understand the contents. They tried computer analysis of all the objective parameters, examining every bit of demographic and social information and sorting all the variables they could abstract from the tenant record cards, without finding any significant differences. The contrast between the two places could not be explained by abstracting the objective characteristics of the people who lived there. I asked if they had thought of going directly to the places, talking to the people, and seeing for themselves. No one had left the office, not because they were lazy or because they shrank from meeting the people, but because they continued to believe that an explanation must be sought in objective, lawlike regularities discovered from the analysis of aggregate data.

In the housing project, people said the two entryways felt different. One felt calm, while the other erupted with noise and anger from one day to the next. Life in the quiet place was boring, I discovered—an uneventful routine of households getting through the day, coping with poverty. In the other place, trouble poured out of the households to meet rage seething in the hallways. On my first visit to that building, I walked through the hall on the ground floor and heard a woman screaming at the top of her voice. She was standing barefoot on her threshold, an enormous woman without teeth, long hair falling about her round face, dressed in a garment that hung like a giant sack, addressing the empty hallway. "Fight, fight! I hate peace," she shrieked.

There is not enough space here adequately to describe the drama of violence, fear, and hatred in that cluster of twelve households—an intricate record of who did what to whom and how they retaliated. Trouble bred in the history of their relationships, in the stories of what people actually said and did, and in their fantasies about one another. I believe that the deepest source of conflict emerged from the imagination of the place. There was no way to grasp the sense of both entryways, I was convinced, without exploring the local imagination. Even basic facts about the housing projects, such as the number of people in a household, were shaped by imagination. One day I was sitting with my major informant, a man who lived in a different building—not one of the two entryways mentioned above. We watched a neighbor leave the building. She was a Micmac Indian. I asked where she lived, and my informant said, "Oh, she lives upstairs with a whole lot of Indians." It was 1970, a census year, and by coincidence one of my students was working as an enumerator, making the rounds of this building. I asked him how many people lived in her apartment, and he said three. The tenant record card in the office said that only two people, a widow and her child, occupied that apartment. My informant, however, told me, "There are fourteen Indians in that household, including one who sleeps in the bathtub. They pitch a tepee in the living room, and a whole village is living in the apartment." After I got to know the members of the household, I learned that the place contained the widow and her son, her boyfriend, her two brothers, and sometimes her sister. I never saw a tepee, and no one slept in the bathtub. In over two years of acquaintance, I never counted more than six people in the apartment.

In the case of the two entryways, I felt that I knew why the places were different. They contained different feelings, and everyone around there agreed about that. The reasons were to be found in the specific locations of daily sensory, moral, and emotional experience—not in the kind of information that goes into aggregate data. The difference between them was expressively intelligible. The reasons were in the structure of morale, in the expressive energies, in the passions, myths, and fantasies of each housing unit. They grew out of the biographies and local histories, and the drama of dwelling together. They were intimately connected with the local imagination, with the spirit of the place. I formulate these qualities as *expressive space*, defined and discussed in this book.

As a research team, my assistants and I searched for theory that would clarify our experience; we remained discontented with the prevailing abstractions. The idiom of "social problems" as well as the intellectual framework of social science seemed to us as graveyards of inert ideas. Yet our research seethed with life, excitement, and moments of insight. Our experience refused to climb into the open coffins that sociology had prepared for it. We began to develop another kind of "theory" that remained attached to our immediate experience, and we insisted on new abstractions, adjusted to our reality, which did not leave out important parts of the truth. Sitting out in front of one of the buildings on a hot summer night, eating slush or drinking beer together, we would expose one of our "theories" to the criticism of our friends and informants, and it was gratifying to hear, sometimes, "Whaddayamean theory? That's no theory, that's a fact!"

My research drove me to reinterpret the pregnant remark of R. H. Tawney that "the history of social theory is strewn with the wrecks of proposals which took account of everything except the obvious."[2] We need a theory that renders sufficient account of the obvious, and by the obvious world, I mean literally the original Latin sense of the words *ob viam*, the things that stand in the way, the world that confronts us in our most immediate experience of living: elements of the city, buildings, streets, neighborhoods, the phenomena of urban life. I think it is important to discover the forces that make and break this ob-vious world, to render the obvious scrutable, and to give a true account of obvious experience. The demon who holds the fibers of my life kept whispering, "How is it possible to understand it as a whole?" In my own homely voyage, before I could grasp the whole experience of life in a public housing project as well as the urban meaning of remedial housing, I had to understand the process of slum clearance, which led me still another interval back in time to historical questions about the birth of the slum. I took my research to Manchester, the first industrial city in the history of the world, and the location of the first industrial slum.

I moved to England in 1974 with my wife and three youngest children, and we lived in Manchester for two years.[3] At first, I intended to study English housing estates (housing projects) with the idea of incorporating the Boston experience in a comparative study of public housing.[4] Besides gathering ethnographic information, I kept thinking about the genesis of remedial housing and its historical relation to slum clearance. One of our informants in the English housing estate made a statement that kept ringing in my ears. "We are here at the end of a process," he said. I kept asking myself, "What is the process as a whole, and how did it begin?" This search uncovered the dynamics of place change and the meaning of topomorphic revolutions (the subject of the next chapter).

Soon after I arrived in Manchester, I tuned in to civic energies that distracted attention from the research on public housing. Manchester seized me by the scruff of the mind, and I have never been the same after the two years I lived there. The ancient Greeks, who had a word for everything, would have called me a chorophiliac, meaning a place-lover. Socrates explains the madness, describing the forces that seize victims with topolepsy. In Plato's *Phaedrus*, Socrates talks about the emotional effect of a lovely site—the kind of expressive space that is discussed in chapter 8—but my experience of Manchester proves that the power of a place to move the soul does not depend on its being attractive to the senses.

I walked totally absorbed in contemplation of the city's experience, sometimes staying in certain locations to let my imagination travel to another when. And I did hear voices—in the libraries, in the lifts, in the bookstores, and in the streets—but they were the voices of embodied people in everyday life, telling me precisely what I wanted to know about the city. But sometimes anonymous voices triggered an explosion of meaning in my head. Once, standing in a crowded lift inside the Manchester Central Reference Library, I heard one passenger ask another, "What is Crimble?" The other replied, "Crimble is a place—a place in the world." The world and its places, I mused. I never did discover Crimble, but the fragment of conversation served as a catalyst. What could one say about Crimble, I wondered, or about any other place, to describe it, capture its qualities, and reveal its meaning? The dialogue in the lift set me thinking about the world and its places, and how we represent them. For some reason that still puzzles me, my whole self tuned in to the whole experience of Manchester, communicated by the living and the dead, expressed in its streets, buildings, and people, as well as in the old books, maps, and pictures. The images of Manchester that flooded my consciousness are not private fantasies. I did not invent them. They inhabit the collective imagination.

An eighteenth-century French observer of placeways, Louis Sébastien Mercier, wrote that he walked around the city so much to complete his *Tableau de Paris* that he felt he drew the tableau with his legs. Similarly, I feel that I studied Manchester with my legs. I walked endlessly, especially around the Old Town, the medieval nucleus of Manchester, which turned, at the end of the eighteenth century, into the world's first industrial slum. I talked to old-timers about their memories, collected old maps and photographs, and read about the history of those streets. I pursued a mental, visionary archaeology, reconstructing layers of experience in the important locations. As St. Paul's conversion struck him down on the road to Damascus and made him blind, I confess to being struck by some intangible lightning more than once—on the road to Cheetham Hill, on Longmillgate, in Castlefield, in Albert Square, on Angel Meadow, and on the banks of the Irk, the Medlock, and the Rochdale Canal—and made to "see." The reader, therefore, will understand my sympathy for visionary antiquaries.

Incessant walking, reading, thinking, and talking about the city drew the suspicion of colleagues and other friends that I was turning into a local expert on Manchester. Even members of the university's history department sent visitors around to find the American chap who was studying the place. I conducted tours and lectured about the urban experience of Manchester. From a visiting American sociologist, I changed into a periegete or cicerone—the local guide who shows people around and interprets places. Seán Damer, who walked the Engels Trail with me once or twice, said that the French would call my interest in the lost slum *nostalgie de la boue*, and together we named my inquiry *la recherche de la boue perdue*. I enjoyed the tours because people who walked along helped me to "see," but sometimes I apologized for the presumptuous irony of my role. Showing Manchester to the Mancunians felt as redundant as bringing owls to Athens or coals to Newcastle. Each walk, however, raised new questions, causing me to reformulate my inquiry. The problematic of the slum is not a matter of "housing," as I originally thought. To formulate it as "housing," as most people do, moves the inquiry in a false direction and makes it a question of physique—fabric, amenities, and sanitation. I learned that the *riddle* of the slum is in the structure of places. Manchester taught me that energies of a place flow through its meanings. Tuning in to them, I felt the whole sense of the place, connecting the eye, the ear, and the imagination. Exploring the feelings that make the place, I also learned *theoria*, a way of seeing for myself and grasping as a whole the nature of cities.

After I returned to Boston from Manchester and resumed life in my own house and my old neighborhood, I went out one evening, as I did almost every day about the same time, to walk the dog in the park. This homely occasion rushed me out to the frontier of my inquiry, for I heard voices carrying on a dialogue that set me thinking again about the whole meaning of dwelling. I overheard two women talking about buying a house. One said to the other, "You have to stop being an idealist and be realistic about a house. You need four walls and a roof and space." The other woman replied, "That's not enough. A house has got to feel right for me to live in it. I need to find just the right place." She was protesting that her intangible needs were just as real as four walls and a roof.

I reflected that their disagreement about the "reality" or the "realism" of feelings represented two different frames of mind. The first woman believed that physical shelter was important, but feelings irrelevant. The second woman gave the feeling of a house—and probably the symbolic value as well—central importance. It was not a debate between a "realist" and an "idealist," but an encounter between Aristotelian assumptions about the nature of place and the doctrine of "grounded Platonism." The Aristotelian believes that "place" is a neutral container into which you move all the independent contents of your experience. The grounded Platonist understands that "place" is an active receptacle of shapes, powers, and feelings that energizes and nourishes its contents.

This difference between frames of mind may be detected in another homely encounter reported to me by David Cooperman, who carried on sociological research in Cedar-Riverside, a large housing complex in Minneapolis planned in the early 1970s to hold a mixed population with a wide range of income groups. Because federal money helped to finance construction, government regulations specified that the tenants must include a quota of families with incomes below the poverty line, and that the tenant community must participate in the design. In a meeting with the tenants, one of the architects showed some modifications of the design, explaining their intention to make a public enclosure that was meant to be seen but not occupied. The architect spoke about the meaning and the elegance of this unused space. A woman representing some of the poor families spoke up critically, expressing her grounded Platonism. "Space ain't nothing," she said, "if nothing don't happen in it."

I wish I had asked the woman I overheard in the park, who wanted more than mere physical shelter, what she expected of a house. The French philosopher Gaston Bachelard writes that the home gathers images, cementing memory to imagination, and that the essential benefit of a house is to shelter daydreams. According to Bachelard, "the house protects the dreamer, the house allows one to dream in peace. . . . The values that belong to daydreaming mark humanity in its depths. . . . Therefore, the places in which we have *experienced daydreaming* reconstitute themselves in a new daydream, and it is because our memories of former dwelling-places are relived as daydreams that these dwelling-places of the past remain in us for all time."[5]

The modern frame of mind, with slim patience for nonsense, encourages sweeping daydreams aside to stay unacknowledged as the rubbish of experience. This kind of treatment, however, renders no justice to the energies of daydreams. We spend a great portion of each waking day making daydreams. Psychologist Jean Houston carried out an informal experiment, asking volunteers (students, for the most part) to keep track, by means of special watches, of the time they spent at different activities. The average time spent daydreaming amounted to about 75 percent. Moreover, a surprising discovery of industrial researchers revealed that many workers prefer routine, assembly-line jobs—not because they enjoy the work, but because the repetitive, mechanical tasks free their minds for daydreaming. The major unacknowledged activity in classrooms and factories, then, is daydreaming.

According to Bachelard, we build houses to support daydreaming, and the home acknowledges our daydreams. Here I want to introduce the doctrine of selective support. We build a structure of consciousness by supporting the features of experience that we acknowledge. We make the obvious world by building it, and in constructing the world, we build ourselves, including our structure of consciousness. We build to support certain features of experience and to suppress others, and these decisions to acknowledge or deny them give form to the dominant structure of consciousness. The way in which people habitually and consciously combine or orchestrate three worlds of the mind—the domain of common sense, the intellect, and the imagination—gives form to their structure of consciousness. For example, archaic people lived with a magical structure of consciousness, and their worldview was dominated by the mythical imagination.[6] In contrast, modern people live with a rational structure of consciousness, a frame of mind dominated by the intellect. The designers who shape the obvious world of modernity enjoy giving expression to the intellect but are reluctant to build up the mythical imagination. It does not mean that modernity stamps out myths. On the contrary, mythical thinking continues to flourish, but it moves to another level of expression and recognition.

Today, we do not credibly populate the environment with spirits, ghosts, and demons because we claim expressive energies as part of our own mental experience. An image or a memory, even though it does not have the independent existence of a ghost or demon, nevertheless causes feelings and thoughts. We know it exists because it has the power to affect us. As Plato wrote, "anything which possesses any sort of power to affect another, or be affected by another, if only for a single moment, however trifling the cause and however slight the effect, has real existence; and I hold that the definition of being is simply power." Anything exists if it causes things to happen and in turn is subject to the exertion of power. For Plato, the essence of being is to be implicated with other beings in causal actions—experiencing change and causing change as well.[7]

In the archaic world, people endowed expressive energies with independent existences, imagining them as gods, demons, and so forth. We call that frame of mind "animism." For example, the ancient Romans built their obvious world to support a rich and complex imagination. They did not separate (as we do) the physical qualities from the expressive energies of objects, and they nourished the invisible spirits of things. They designed the Roman household as the sacred, local habitation of divine and human beings. An image of the *Lar familiaris*, clad in a toga, stood between two *Penates* in a shrine beside the hearth. The Latin word for the hearth is *focus*, and it was constructed as the center of worship as well as the seat of Vesta, the spirit of the sacred fire. On a table before it stood the materials of ritual, including the sacred salt cake. Behind the hearth, the storage place was built to house the *Penates*, spirits who guarded the food and possessions of the family—the spiritual side of their material needs. The *genius* of the *pater*, a guardian spirit, represented the continuity of the family. The doorway was a special location because dangerous spirits as well as people and animals could get in through it. Similarly, gates and walls had *religio*, or sacromagical qualities. The Romans honored Janus, the god of transitions who presided over all goings and comings, as their first and oldest divinity. Every object and activity claimed a spiritual representation: *Forculus*, god of the door; *Cardea*, goddess of the hinge; *Limentinus* and *Limentina*, deities of the threshold. The floor was the haunt of the *lares*, benevolent ancestral spirits. Loneliness was scarcely possible in the Roman household because the place was crowded with invisible dwellers. The house was constructed as a sacred place and the abode of household spirits. Some of this feeling remains in Bachelard's statement that the house "is the environment in which the protective beings live."[8]

Outside the household, to picture the character of a place, the Romans imagined a spirit who owned it, the *genius loci*. In the ancient world, when people grasped qualities, functions, or principles of activity, they often represented these intangible realities in a concrete image. The *genius loci*, which first appeared in Italy as a snake and later in human form, stood for the independent reality of a place. Above all, it symbolized the place's generative energy, and it pictured a specific, personal, spiritual presence who animated and protected a place.[9] On the deepest level, the image of a guardian spirit provided a way of representing the energy, definition, unifying principle, and continuity of place. The Roman conquerors dominated people and seized property, but in religious principle they respected the independent spiritual sovereignty of the places they occupied. Where they camped they often erected a votive tablet to the spirit of the place. For example, an inscription found in 1771 in Scotland at the Antonine Wall, the frontier of Roman domination, devotes a stone altar "*Genio Terrae Britannicae*"—to the spirit of the British land.[10]

Ancient and medieval builders expected imagination to animate the objects of human surroundings. Our traditional forms of ornament, such as the egg-and-dart patterns and serpentine motifs, store forgotten magical ideas. Archaic people expected to fill the human world with decoration as well as with structures to support their bodies. Decoration and ornament, supporting the imagination, gave shape to expressive energies. Familiar decorative figures, such as geometric shapes or patterns of interlaced leaves, belong to a world of forms in which we participate. This region of vitality expresses the motion and breath of life and it speaks to us in different languages, inviting the imagination to enter, explore, and thrive. Art historian Henri Focillon claims, "It prolongs and diffuses itself throughout our dreams and fancies: we regard it, as it were, as a kind of fissure through which crowds of images aspiring to birth may be introduced into some indefinite realm." The forms are metamorphic, expressing a life with no other aim than to come into view, to move and to change, and to renew themselves. In the life of ornament, then, the mind participates in the experience of renewal.[11] By engaging the mind to play with forms and colors, decoration animates the built environment. A city that does not support the imagination is a dead environment.

In some cases, the modern world continues to support the mythical imagination in an ancient way: by building wonders. Erected in 1883 and hailed as the Eighth Wonder of the World, the Brooklyn Bridge has been experienced as a psychological landscape, a clue to the meaning of American society, and a vehicle for emotions about the city and about modern civilization.[12] Built in the same decade as the Brooklyn Bridge, the Eiffel Tower is another place that supports the imagination. Roland Barthes observes that the tower attracts meaning as a lightning rod attracts thunderbolts. All the purposes or excuses for its presence "seem quite ridiculous alongside the overwhelming myth of the Tower, of the human meaning which it has assumed throughout the world." Nothing compares "to the great imaginary function which enables men to be strictly human."[13]

Any theory of the city that omits feelings, symbols, memories, dreams, myths, and all the subtle energies that go into the expressive dimension ignores the most human region of urban life. It is important to explore old and new ways of representing this region of life, for the familiar categories of science, designed for the features of experience that lend themselves to precise determination, must leave them aside. As Martin Heidegger observes, "Science always encounters only what *its* kind of representation has admitted beforehand as an object possible for science."[14]

To think in new ways requires some novel concepts expressed in words that are new—or, if not new, revived—to avoid habits of thought that lead in unprofitable directions. A new concept or a refreshed idea should take up the connections already established in the language but also open the search for new and unknown connections. However, my new terms—the neologisms in this book—are drawn from old meanings discovered in the roots and ruins of language and are intended to recover forgotten connections; I often return to the ancient Greeks because the clarity and wisdom of their language worked not to eliminate ambiguity but to illuminate it. The reader may keep track of new terms by referring to the glossary at the end of the book.

Modern theories of place and space have been influenced by the movement of scientific thought identified with Galileo, adapting observation to calculation, reducing the physical world to mathematical analysis, transforming the concrete into the abstract. But the newest trends in theoretical physics and in biology are moving scientific reflection away from analysis, which splits and fragments experience, toward wholeness—a movement that requires holistic thinking. According to physicist David Bohm, "science itself is demanding a new non-fragmentary world view, in the sense that the present approach of analysis of the world into independently existent parts does not work very well in modern physics." The new movement carries wide implications, for, as Bohm says:

> the proper order of operation of the mind requires an overall grasp of what is generally known, not only in formal, logical, mathematical terms, but also intuitively, in images, feelings, poetic usage of language, etc. (Perhaps we could say that this is what is involved in harmony between the "left brain" and the "right brain.") This kind of overall way of thinking is not only a fertile source of new theoretical ideas: it is needed for the human mind to function in a generally harmonious way, which could in turn help to make possible an orderly and stable society.[15]

The program of the following chapters, then, while critical of old-fashioned scientism, which confines experience to objective analysis and to fatigued abstractions, should not be construed as an attack on science. On the contrary, the quest for *theoria* past Galileo and Copernicus, retracing the progress of science, is a regression in the service of rethinking. It is an exploratory voyage looking for the passage to a new region of thought. To shift the metaphor to another sense, we are listening for the harmony of experience, expressed by a new ensemble, which includes science as one principal instrument.

Bachelard makes up terms such as "topoanalysis" and "topophilia" for certain perspectives that capture poetic features of space.[16] I intend topistics to serve a wider purpose as a nonfragmentary, theoretical framework to grasp the whole experience of place and space. Topistic inquiry seeks theories that represent and explain forces that make or break the integrity of located experience. To find the roots of integrated theory—not the objective, detached theory of conventional natural science and social science—let us explore archaic *theoria*, a frame of mind that made sense even before the birth of prose.

Originally, *theoria* meant seeing the sights, seeing for yourself, and getting a worldview. The first theorists were "tourists"—the wise men who traveled to inspect the obvious world. Solon, the Greek sage whose political reforms around 590 B.C. renewed the city of Athens, is the first "theorist" in Western history. Herodotus, a traveler and theorist in his own right, wrote a book around 430 B.C. which remains the earliest complete prose work in our literary tradition. He referred to it as his *Inquiries*, using the Greek word that we now translate as "histories." In recent years, the fashion of nineteenth-century historians to claim the superiority of Thucydides over Herodotus has changed. Today, scholars appreciate them both as the two greatest ancient historians and understand that the work of each is based on entirely different presuppositions.[17]

Herodotus is called the father of geography and ethnography as well as history, but because his book also explores the whole nature of places in Greece, Asia, and Egypt, I claim him as the father of topistics as well. The first chapter of the *Inquiries* describes the visit of Solon to the court of Croesus, the ruler of Lydia. Herodotus says that Solon traveled to Egypt and Asia partly for political reasons, but also for the sake of *theoria*.

In the generation before Herodotus, Hecataeus of Miletus traveled through Europe, Asia, and Egypt and wrote a description of the world. Bruno Snell says about Hecataeus, "The ardour with which he devotes his life to *theory* surpasses even that of Solon."[18] *Theoria* did not mean the kind of vision that is restricted to the sense of sight. The Greek word for exclusively optic perception is *opsis*. The term *theoria* originally implied a complex but organic mode of active observation—a perceptual system that included asking questions, listening to stories and local myths, and feeling as well as hearing and seeing. It encouraged an open reception to every kind of emotional, cognitive, symbolic, imaginative, and sensory experience—a holistic practice of thoughtful awareness that engaged all the senses and feelings.[19]

Active observers, the world theorists who traveled around 600 B.C., exercised an integrated "seeing," talking and listening to local residents, staying in places of interest, and searching for things to "see." They were spectators who responded to the expressive energies of places, stopping to contemplate what the guides called "the things worth seeing."[20] They left no record of their observations. Therefore, the experience and meaning of archaic places before the classical era must be sought in early poetic literature: in *The Iliad*, *The Odyssey*, and works of Hesiod, as well as in hymns, elegies, lyrics, and the drama. Apart from poetry, an oral tradition of topistic lore may be inferred from fragments of prose writing in the fifth century B.C.

There is more than "history" in the work of Herodotus. As a "theorist," Herodotus gathered different kinds of information about places—putting together what he saw with his own eyes, what he heard, and what was "known," as well as recording the memory and the "words" or stories of a place. Local guides—the men who knew the stories—helped visiting theorists to "see." Almost every town had periegetes, expert local guides who showed people around, pointed out notable sights, described the local rituals, explained the customs, and told traditional stories of historical and mythical events. They were living archives of placeways, as well as the first antiquaries.

A "periegete" was a tour guide who led people around, giving commentaries on whatever was worth seeing. A written commentary describing places—a travel guide—was known as a "periegesis." Unfortunately, no complete periegesis survives from the ancient world any earlier than the work of Pausanias, which was published during the reign of Hadrian at the high point of the Roman Empire, in the second century A.D. Nevertheless, the *Guide to Greece* written by Pausanias tells us a great deal about the program of civic renewal in the Hadrianic renascence. The best guides represented the whole integrity of places. They would describe a place not "objectively" but holistically, in a pattern that included the elements that Plato identified as shapes, powers, and feelings. They did not discard subjective collective experience. Their view, like the vision of the theorists, did not departmentalize or dissociate the unity of topistic experience. In the archaic world, the theorists who traveled to view strange places, the local guides who showed people around, and the chorophiliacs (also known as philochoriacs), or place-lovers, who simply stayed home, may reasonably be called the *therapeutae*, the close attendants of places—which brings us to another concept close to *theoria*, namely *therapeia*.

Since the principal connection explored in this book is the relation between the therapy and the theory of cities, let us set out to discover their inner connection. Our voyage of discovery reverses the historical journey of linguistic refinement and returns to the earlier Greek words, *therapeia* as well as *theoria*. In our idiom, "therapy" usually means some kind of medical or physical treatment, although the idea of psychotherapy has gathered wider meanings. The Greek word *therapeia* is much broader and more ambiguous. Ambiguity means that a word holds several possible meanings, and poetry depends on the musical delight evoked by different but simultaneous responses to a word. The range of meanings in *therapeia*, however, is not the same as poetic ambiguity because each meaning of the word is relevant to a special context. In general, *therapeia* means "close attendance" or "caring" for something, but the precise nature of the specific action is defined by the situation. Applied to farming, *therapeia* means "cultivation"; in reference to children, it means acting as a parent; in the case of lovers, "courtship"; regarding a rich man, "flattery"; speaking of the gods, "worship." Plato, for example, calls worship *therapeia* of the gods. Sometimes philosophy is called *therapeia* of the self, reflecting the maxim "know thyself." In the work of a physician, *therapeia* of a person who is ill means "healing." What, then, is the *therapeia* of cities? In the old sense of the word, the *therapeutae* of cities are the ones who "care" for it with "close attendance"—a category that includes theorists, guides, and place-lovers.

Today, in the idiom of our renewal programs, urban therapy is a surgical metaphor. Healing, in this frame of mind, prescribes the excision of "blighted" neighborhoods, often called "cancers" of the city. The frame of mind is not open to the whole experience of the city, and its slim logic proceeds from the fallacy of subjective exclusion. This kind of "therapy" requires objectivity because few surgeons want to operate on their own parts. The people who clear the slums never dwell in the regions they clear. Objectivity means that the "surgeon" may view a place marked out for amputation and think, "there is nothing of me in there." Moreover, objective "therapy" presupposes the irrelevance of feelings that make the place.

Unfortunately, our language needs an adjective derived from the noun "place." Not until the nineteenth century did the Middle-English word "space" generate the adjective "spatial," but it is too late and too awkward to hatch "platial" from "place." Preferring neologism to barbarism, I use "topistic," derived from the Greek word *topos*, as an adjective associated with "place," and the noun "topistics" for the study of place-ways. This is a new name by which I hope to renew the context of an old inquiry, but I did not invent a new field. It belongs to ancient wisdom, with intimations in the work of great writers such as Herodotus and Plato as well as some obscure periegetes. In my adventures in Boston and Manchester I began to recover methods and ideas of a holistic form of inquiry designed to render the identity, character, and experience of a place intelligible. The full range of meaning located as a "place"— sensory perceptions, moral judgments, passions, feelings, ideas, and orientations—belong to an order of intelligibility that I call "topistic reality."

My claim that feeling and imagination are at the core of topistic reality may be misunderstood, but I am not joining the forces of anti-intellectualism. I believe that mental integrity requires a balance of intellect, common sense, and imagination. I criticize detached intellect, but my quest for *theoria* is a search for grounded intelligence. Thales, one of the Seven Sages, while observing the stars fell into a well. A Thracian slave woman laughed at him, saying he wanted to know what happened in the heavens, but failed to observe what was in front of his own feet. In this simple way, she exposed the predicament of a theorist who lost his ground.

Moreover, when I write about the feelings of place, I am not committing what logicians call the "pathetic fallacy"—a mental error that projects feelings on a thing, a relationship, or some "external" state of affairs. A place has no feelings apart from human experience there. But a place is a location of experience. It evokes and organizes memories, images, feelings, sentiments, meanings, and the work of imagination. The feelings of a place are indeed the mental projections of individuals, but they come from collective experience and they do not happen anywhere else. They belong to the place.

Some readers may object that most of the population of Rome or Athens, for example, may be oblivious to the feelings and meanings evoked by their cities. True enough, but their insensitivity does not destroy the reality of topistic experience. If most people in Paris and Boston are oblivious to the feelings and meanings evoked by the contents of the Louvre and the Museum of Fine Arts, that does not prove the nonexistence of art or the unreality of aesthetic experience. The distribution of topistic awareness is not universal or symmetric. Indeed, the lack of this awareness is an issue discussed in this book.

Finally, no one should expect that images, feelings, and meanings experienced in places remain immutable. It is a matter of record that they change from one period to another. Like any kind of human experience, they have a history. To change the present theory and therapy of cities requires a renewal of consciousness that makes holistic thinking possible. It follows the new course of science mentioned above, represented in the work of David Bohm. It demands a mental change as large as the Copernican revolution. True renewal of places requires a change in our structure of experience and a different paradigm for understanding both the natural land and the built environment. One tradition of Western thought has led to the modern crisis of places. This book explores the other tradition.

> *Let us just compare the condition of the free*
> *Englishman in 1845 with the servile Saxon*
> *under the lash of the Norman baron in 1145.*
>
> Friedrich Engels,
> *The Condition of the Working Class in England*

T W O

Topomorphic Revolutions

A place is a unity of experience, organizing the intercommunication and mutual influence of all beings within it. Every place, then, implies a form of dwelling together, and all the realities in a place—living people, images, memories, animals, plants, as well as bacteria and other hidden forces—make a group of effective presences dwelling together. Even though we rarely acknowledge them all, they participate in one another's natures and constitute a topistic structure, the system of mutual immanence. People—with their complex ways of dwelling together and apart —are the most vivid and significant presences in a local system of immanence. The relations in a topistic structure are not necessarily simple or continuous. The modern city is full of barriers, both material and intangible, which conceal or deny that segregated people with different social identities, defined by class or by ethnic characteristics, dwell in the same town. A topomorphic revolution is a radical shift of topistic structure, a fundamental change in the form of dwelling together. Such revolutions conceal, interrupt, or break the old forms, causing new structures by patterns of exclusion, enclosure, and dissociation.

Modern changes associated with the industrial revolution of the eighteenth century caused great dislocations and relocations, rearranging the structure of places in the city. In the nineteenth century, these changes generated a new topistic ideal—to segregate good and bad experience, locating wealth and illth in separate spaces. The new ideal denied the old nature of a town—formerly a common place of shared experience, including com-passion (meaning shared feelings), shared expressive space, and a common diet of symbols. Instead, the town became a system of differentiated places separating the extremes of experience. Slums and suburbs today are historic products of this topistic differentiation.

At the end of the eighteenth century, the slum was a new kind of place in the world—a place within a place, distinct and bounded, a dissociated "cacotope" occupied exclusively by the poor. Beginning in Manchester, it spread through Britain, transforming Birmingham, Dublin, Edinburgh, Glasgow, Leeds, Liverpool, London, Sheffield. The list grew long and fast, extending beyond Britain and eventually including New York, Boston, Chicago, Los Angeles, and Houston. In 1915, Patrick Geddes called the slums "squalid Kakotopias."[1] Let us expand his term. We need a generic name for the kind of place that means the opposite of "utopia," and "cacotope" is derived from the Greek *kakos topos*, which means a place that is bad, foul, or evil. Geddes may have invented the term, but in 1829 Robert Southey, the poet laureate of England, while reflecting on the slums of industrial towns, came close to finding a word for the bad place that was everywhere to match Thomas More's good place that was nowhere.

When Thomas More invented "utopia," three centuries before Southey's time, he made a double play on the Greek words that inspired it, for *eu topos* means "good place," while *ou topos* means "no place." Utopia, therefore, is the good place that is no place. Southey imagined a dialogue with the ghost of Thomas More. He observed that More had introduced into our language a term understood by tens of thousands who would never read the work of fiction from which it was derived. In his dialogue with More's spirit, Southey questioned the idea of progress along with the notion of utopia. The ghost served as a guide to historical changes, explaining the transformations of England from the demise of the feudal system to the industrial revolution. Both Southey and the ghost deplored "these portentous and monster-breeding times," and they shuddered at the condition of factory towns. Thomas More wondered, "What if your manufactures . . . were to generate for you new physical plagues, as they have already produced a moral pestilence unknown to all preceding ages?" The decay of the feudal system, he said, produced a huge population of rootless, placeless victims, evolving from outcasts in More's day to a caste in Southey's time, "numerous to infest society, yet not so large as to threaten its subversion."

In Saxon times, the spirit of Thomas More explained, "every person had his place," but now a large part of the population was "unowned, unbroken to any useful purpose, subsisting by chance or by prey, living in filth, mischief and wretchedness."[2]

On the surface, Southey's dialogue seems to be the nostalgic rumination of a conservative gentleman lamenting feudalism and shrinking from the industrial age. Yet some themes, working under the surface, draw attention to issues that are not merely ideological reflexes. The idea that the human condition had deteriorated since feudal times was not exclusively a reactionary sentiment, for it anticipated the revolutionary Friedrich Engels as well as the conservative Thomas Carlyle. Both Engels and Carlyle, writing independently in 1843–44, stressed the placelessness as well as the helpless insecurity of the industrial workers.[3] Southey, Engels, and Carlyle all drew on medieval images to understand the industrial revolution. Evoking the past, we shall see, was a familiar way in the nineteenth century to examine or to live with the defects of the present.

"Nostalgia," a term derived from Greek words meaning a painful return home, signifies to us a sentimental, useless longing for places and situations no longer available. For some Victorians, however, the wistful view of the way we used to live expanded their topistic consciousness and modified their orientation to the environment. They turned old buildings and ancient places into material supports for mythical place change. Their sense of place, then, reached deeper than the experience of the moment, stretching beyond the industrial cacotope of their own time. As new choices transformed old places, the industrial environment was haunted by images that represented the rejected alternatives. Southey's ghost of Thomas More was not alone. When Marx and Engels wrote, in *The Communist Manifesto*, that a specter was haunting Europe, they underestimated the spectral population. Carlyle counted "troops and populations of Phantasms," and wondered, "Is our poor English Existence wholly becoming a Nightmare; full of mere Phantasms?"

Crowds of ghosts attended the European imagination, and in England a regiment of specters marching out of that mythical country that Peter

Laslett names "The World We Have Lost" obsessed the Victorian mind. One of them repeatedly materialized in Victorian picture books, taking the form of an illustration from the Harley Psalter, a medieval manuscript kept in the British Library.[4] Figure 2-1 shows the illustration both as it appears in the manuscript and with the words removed to make the details easier to see.

This image illustrates Psalm 111, *Beatus Vir*, of the Vulgate Bible (Psalm 112 in the Protestant version), which begins, "Blessed is the man that feareth the Lord, that delighteth greatly in his commandments." The Victorians saw in the illustration the courtyard of a great house in which a Saxon lord and lady are carrying out works of mercy. According to the psalm, "Wealth and riches shall be in his house . . . he is gracious, and full of compassion, and righteous. . . . He hath dispersed, he hath given to the poor." Over the great house in the picture, the hand of God makes the sign of benediction. The antlers of a stag's head on the roof represent the phrase, "his horn shall be exalted with honor." The men standing in the portals on the left, armed with spears and shields, show that "his seed shall be mighty upon earth." In the lower left corner, a troop of armed men shrinking from the scene, commanded by a wicked angel, tells that "The wicked shall see it, and be grieved . . . gnash his teeth, and melt away: The desire of the wicked shall perish." The lord and lady in the doorway of the house are presiding over hospitality to the poor within the gates. Within the house, behind the lady, the sick are being healed; she distributes loaves to women and their children at the doorstep while the master, seated by her side, hands bread to three men leaning on staves. On the right, the open chapel displays the piety of the great house; at the far left, an almoner is clothing the naked, while other servants in the foreground pour wine, and a kneeling cripple waits his turn, leaning on tiny, archaic crutches.

The illustration suggests that if a visitor from another time or another planet had appeared in England a thousand years ago and demanded "Take me to the poor so that I may see their place," a medieval guide might have proceeded to the enclosure of a great household as the ideal place to find them. This vision of hospitality, drawn from the Middle Ages, idealized the place of the rich as the proper location of the poor.

Modern Englishmen used the picture to imagine the physical and moral character of life before the Norman Conquest. For example, in the middle of the Victorian period Thomas Wright, in his *History of Domestic*

2-1. Beatus Vir *in the Harley Psalter*
(By permission of the British Library)

Manners and Sentiments, chose the *Beatus Vir* to describe details of what he believed to be "Anglo-Saxon domestic architecture," but he also noted the social relationships it revealed, claiming that the illustration gave "the description of the just and righteous chieftain: the beggars are admitted within the inclosure (where the scene is laid), to receive the alms of the lord; and he and his lady are occupied in distributing bread to them, while his servants are bringing out of one of the bowers raiment to clothe the naked."[5]

The image continued to appear in the Edwardian decade. In 1901 J. S. Mann brought out an illustrated edition of *Social England*, an influential six-volume set of historical sources. He used the picture from the Harley Psalter to describe the homestead of a typical "gentleman's house" before the Norman Conquest.[6] In Manchester a few years later, Joseph Phelps, a local antiquarian, displayed the image to represent his idea of the baron's hall and yard, the nucleus of the Old Town, in Saxon times.[7]

The pictures in the Harley Psalter evoke a strange, fascinating, beautiful world. As Francis Wormald described the style: "The characteristics are marked. The figures, and the whole compositions, have the appearance of violent and agitated activity. Animals leap about, tearing winds blow, draperies and veils are tossed about, and the eyes of the men and women caught in this tornado roll with wild and ecstatic glances. The general effect is highly dramatic."[8] I remember vividly the excitement and wonder I felt as I examined the original manuscript in the British Library, absorbed by the intensely animated little figures in the drawings. The tinted outlines, finely sketched, lose some of their energy in printed reproductions, but this technique of expressionist drawing remained a powerful tradition in the history of English art, culminating in the work of William Blake, whose spiritual imagination sometimes recalls the world of the Harley Psalter.

Drawn in England around 1000 A.D., the Harley manuscript was copied from an earlier Continental masterpiece, the Utrecht Psalter, in which the miniatures are drawn in uniform brown ink. Although the colorful Harley version renders the lines in delicate red, green, blue, and sepia, it replicates the illustration of the Utrecht Psalter, which was made in Reims, a great medieval city of northeastern France, in the second quarter of the ninth century. Therefore, the imagery of the Psalter does not represent the actual social life of Saxon England. Indeed, the images are much older than medieval Reims. Dmitri Tselos has demonstrated persuasively (and to my mind, conclusively) that the Utrecht Psalter comes from an earlier Greco-Italian model, derived in turn from Greek sources that reach back to the fourth century.[9] Nevertheless, the English will not let it go. The Victorians believed they had discovered the world of their ancestors, but even today writers will still exhibit illustrations from the Utrecht Psalter to represent scenes from Saxon life.[10]

It was not the aesthetic qualities, but the moral and social ideals perceived in the illustrations of the Utrecht Psalter that captivated the Victorians. Psalm 112 (King James Version) haunted their topistic imagination and dramatized the topomorphic revolution that had shaped the industrial town—a fundamental change in the form of mutual immanence. When Engels described Manchester in 1844, the city had passed through the industrial revolution with its topomorphic changes, drawing the lines of slum and suburb, erecting both physical and subjective barriers between mutually exclusive zones. The middle classes, running before the smoke, ascended the breezy heights of Ardwick, while the lower classes, rushing to the mills, sank into the old courts, cellar dwellings, and back-to-back houses of the seven urban slums. The places of the rich excluded the poor, while the places of the poor repulsed the rich. The spontaneous development of the town, Engels showed, shaped bad streets behind good facades, beguiling the sensory experience of the comfortable classes. A merchant could ride home to the edge of town from the Royal Exchange at the heart of the city without seeing or smelling a slum. The first industrial city distributed good and bad experience to rich and poor through the structure of places.

Thomas Malthus formulated the new ideal in his powerful image of a banquet. In an inflammatory passage in the second edition of his *Essay on the Principle of Population*, he wrote:

> A man who is born into a world already possessed, if he cannot get subsistence from his parents on whom he has a just demand, and if the society do not want his labour, has no claim of *right* to the smallest portion of food, and, in fact, has no business to be where he is. At nature's mighty feast there is no vacant cover for him. She tells him to be gone, and will quickly execute her own orders, if he do not work upon the compassion of some of her guests. If these guests get up and make room for him, other intruders immediately appear demanding the same favour. The report of a provision for all

that come, fills the hall with numerous claimants. The order and
harmony of the feast is disturbed, the plenty that before reigned is
changed into scarcity; and the happiness of the guests is destroyed
by the spectacle of misery and dependence in every part of the hall,
and by the clamorous importunity of those who are justly enraged
at not finding the provision which they had been taught to expect.
The guests learn too late their error, in counteracting those strict
orders to all intruders, issued by the great mistress of the feast,
who, wishing that all her guests should have plenty, and knowing
that she could not provide for unlimited numbers, humanely refused to admit fresh comers when her table was already full.[11]

This image of the invidious banquet—suggesting not merely a distribution of food, but the whole diet of experience—squarely contradicts the
picture from the Harley Psalter. According to Malthus, the presence of
the poor in the place of the rich disturbs the order and harmony of the
feast; the spectacle of misery and dependence also destroys the happiness of the guests. Therefore, the image supports an ideal of segregated
places.

In the Harleian illustration of the psalm, *Beatus Vir*, rich and poor
turn toward each other and share a common place. The image locates
poverty in the environment of the rich. The ideal supports a common
ground of experience and the personal relief of distress. You are hungry,
but I am not—I give you some of my bread. You are homeless—I share
my house. You are naked—I clothe you. In legend, St. Martin of Tours
cut his cloak in twain and gave half to a beggar. He kept the rest for
himself. This image remained so powerful throughout the Middle Ages
because it expressed the ideal of unmediated personal participation in
the experience of sharing resources. The illustration of the psalm and
the literary image of Malthus express contrary topistic imperatives. The
psalm pictures an enclosure devoted to the intimate connection of rich
and poor. The Malthus principle demands exclusion, dissociation, and
separate enclosures.

In his initial chapter on the shaping of modern England, the Victorian
historian, James Anthony Froude, marked the decline of hospitality as
one of the conditions of the modern age:

We hear of "the glory of hospitality," England's preëminent boast,—
by the rules of which all tables, from the table of the twenty-shilling

freeholder to the table in the baron's hall and abbey refectory, were open at the dinner-hour to all comers, without stint or reserve, or question asked: to every man according to his degree, who chose to ask for it, there was free fare and free lodging; bread, beef, and beer for his dinner; for his lodging, perhaps, only a mat of rushes in a spare corner of the hall, with a billet of wood for a pillow, but freely offered and freely taken, the guest probably faring much as his host fared, neither worse nor better.[12]

Although this sort of hospitality began to decline centuries before the industrial era, the idea and image of the medieval poor at the gate dramatized the segregation of the industrial poor. Victorian writers such as Froude explored the defects of their time by gazing at pictures of the past. Medieval imagery appealed to both defenders and critics of industrial society. William Irwin Thompson has observed:

> The medieval *image* has always appealed to intellectuals recoiling from the savagery of industrialization. After the first wave of the Industrial Revolution from 1770 to 1851, England itself seemed to be in a mood for consolidation; and in "The Medieval Court" designed by Pugin for the Crystal Palace of the Great Exhibition of 1851, it took a nostalgic look at the European civilization it helped to destroy. With Pugin, William Morris, Matthew Arnold, and Cardinal Newman, medievalism became one of the first counter-cultures to industrialism.[13]

Nevertheless, most of the people who enjoyed Pugin's Medieval Court in the Crystal Palace were not recoiling from industrialism, but on the contrary remained devoted to the myth of progress. For them, the dramatic contrasts made by Pugin and others expressed their sense of a fundamental change in the form of mutual immanence.

In his book, *Contrasts*, an important work of topistic imagination, A. W. N. Pugin—the apostle of the Gothic revival in England—compared architecture and urban space in the modern and medieval worlds through a series of pictures. One pair of illustrations shows the difference in principle between the two kinds of poor space: the workhouse of his own time and a medieval almshouse (Figs. 2-2 and 2-3). His fantasy modern poor house looks like a prison designed from Bentham's panopticon, expressing a sense of torment, while its imagined medieval

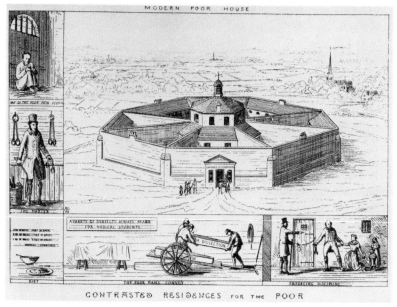

2-2. *Pugin's Contrasts: Modern Poor House*
(From Pugin, *Contrasts*)

counterpart shows picturesque buildings embracing the poor in a wholesome religious community. Pugin felt urged to show pictorially the topistic difference between the regulations of the Poor Law and the old rule of hospitality.[14]

Thomas Carlyle drew a similar contrast of worlds in a literary picture. *Past and Present* begins with scenes of destitution, with descriptions of unemployed men, with millions sitting in poor-law prisons, workhouse Bastilles filled to bursting. "In the midst of plethoric plenty, the people perish." Then, book 2 portrays a wholesome monastic world of Bury St. Edmunds in the twelfth century, drawn from a chronicle of the abbey. Carlyle leads the reader "into a somewhat remote Century . . . to look face to face on it, in hope of perhaps illustrating our own poor Century thereby. . . . Another world, truly: and this present poor distressed world might get some profit by looking wisely into it, instead of foolishly."[15]

According to Carlyle, the medieval world held rich and poor together in meaningful connection, in contrast to the isolation, false dissocia-

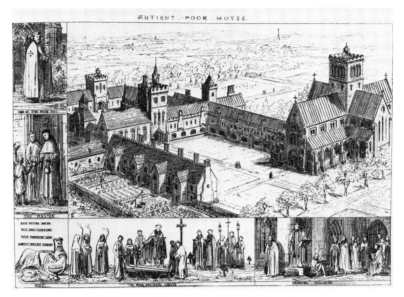

2-3. Pugin's Contrasts: Medieval Alms House
(From Pugin, *Contrasts*)

tions, and material insecurity of industrial society. "We call it a Society," he writes, "and go about professing openly the totalest separation, isolation. Our life is not a mutual helpfulness; but rather, cloaked under due laws-of-war, named 'fair competition' and so forth, it is a mutual hostility." This isolation is unreal, he argues: "Men cannot live isolated: we *are* all bound together, for mutual good or else for mutual misery, as living nerves in the same body." Despite his bondage, the Saxon thrall had "at least the certainty of supper and social lodging when he came home." In those days, "no human creature . . . went about connected with nobody; left to go his way into Bastilles or worse."[16]

It is no wonder, then, that the image from the Harley Psalter haunted the Victorians. It reminded them of a world in which rich and poor were members of one community, and where the households of the rich fed, clothed, and healed the poor at the gate. Lord Briggs writes that the Victorians "used the past for purposes of dramatic contrast to highlight what they thought were the feelings of the present. Saxons or Normans could be portrayed with long fair hair or bows and arrows, but they were endowed with Victorian motives and values."[17] I believe the Victorians used Normans and Saxons to dramatize their feelings about place change. The Norman Conquest, they suspected, was an era of place change that resembled in some obscure way the impact of industrial capitalism in their own time. In a mythical way, the Normans stood for the principle of *dominium*, which means possession and control—in the extreme form, exploitation. The Saxons represented topotherapy—the responsive dwelling, close attendance, cultivation, and care of a place. Of course, there are exceptions, and one can find Norman portraits that evoke the care and love of places, but the dual images reflect a way that Victorians expressed two different features of topistic experience.

From the perspective of *dominium*, a manor was the location of revenues and services. The lord might enjoy the fruits of his manor without ever setting foot on the place, as factory owners might drain the resources of a city but never live there. Yet the origin of the word "manor" suggests an older meaning—namely, the place where the lord dwells. According to this perspective, the manor or the dwelling of the lord established the identity of a place. The name of the manor answered the questions: "What place is this?" and "Who is responsible for this place?" Before the Norman Conquest, a manor was simply "the place." In his *Ecclesiastical History of the English People*, written in Latin, the Venerable Bede referred to it as a *locus*.

Places were identified by reference to the men who "held" them. The *Anglo-Saxon Chronicle* reads that in 1085, King William "held very deep speech with his wise men about the land, how it was held, and with what men." Then, twenty years after the Conquest, he ordered a survey of the land to determine how it was held. This investigation perceived only one dimension of the way the land was held; it was a study of *dominium*. It confined itself to cadastral realities, determining the monetary value of the land and establishing a basis for taxation and administration. The results of the survey, gathered from questions addressed to local juries, were collected in the *Domesday Book*, the earliest public record of England, which remained a "brooding presence" in subsequent centuries of administrative development. Although it listed over thirteen thousand places, the record often gave little more than the names of the manors that identified the places, along with their valuations. According to the instructions, the first question the surveyors put to the local juries was, "What is the manor called?" followed by "Who holds it?"[18]

The Saxon imagery cherished in Victorian times responded to the Norman spirit of the *Domesday Book*—the exclusive record of *dominium*—and challenged its ruthless abstractions. It suggested that there was another way of answering King William's question in the "deep speech" with his wise men: "How is the manor held?" As historian Arthur Bryant eloquently interprets the Saxon mode of holding a place:

> These people loved the soil and the tending of it and its beasts. They loved it as much as their fathers had loved fighting and the sea. They left their memorial, not like the Romans in stone or the Bronze Age men in burial-grounds, but in the imperishable shape of the earth they tilled; it is writ large across our shires, with their villages, meadows, farms and ploughlands. And in the work of their artists that has come down to us, in their carvings in wood and stone of leaves, trees and animals, we can see their deep feeling for nature. "His coat," runs the old song, "is of Saxon green," and it is of a green-clad folk in a green land that we must think of them, swinging their axes and driving their ploughs through mysterious forest and dark earth to make the land we love.[19]

While I was living in Manchester and studying the evolution of the industrial city, the Victorian fascination with Saxon places attracted my attention. I wondered what Saxon towns were really like. Besides seeking historical information, I turned to archaeological explorations of English towns that predated the Norman Conquest. From all indications, historical as well as archaeological, the typical Anglo-Saxon town was a common place, without segregated quarters occupied by the poor. Therefore, I was startled to read a report describing an "industrial slum" excavated in Thetford, a late Saxon town in East Anglia.

In the eleventh century, Thetford was a thriving town with a mint and industries producing pottery, metalwork, and wool products. It was situated at the confluence of two rivers (the Little Ouse and the Thet) that form the boundary between Norfolk and Suffolk. The Saxon town grew up on the south bank, but for some unknown reason, at the end of the eleventh century, the population relocated to the north bank to continue as a Norfolk town. The moment of relocation was also the beginning of rapid decline. Thetford had a population equal to that of Norwich—just under five thousand souls—but Norwich expanded to twenty-five times that size, while Thetford remained the same size until recently. The abandoned location on the south bank stayed free of buildings until the twentieth century; and thus Thetford provided a unique archaeological opportunity to excavate an undisturbed site of a pre-Conquest town. In the past half-century, however, modern Thetford has been spreading back on the south side of the river, reclaiming most of the original Saxon site. In 1964 a major housing scheme began to fill the area with new construction.

Archaeologists tried to stay ahead of the bulldozers, managing to extract some information before the Saxon remains disappeared forever. Between 1948 and 1952, G. M. Knocker, a retired RAF officer, excavated several sites, followed by other archaeologists including Brian Davison between 1964 and 1970.[20] Knocker died before he could publish a report, and his notes remain unpublished. A recent report organizes the details of his work and presents the archaeological evidence uncovered by him, but it does not attempt to synthesize or interpret the meaning of that evidence.[21]

Brian Davison published an interim report on the 1964 excavations, in which he referred to Knocker's discovery of an "industrial slum" in the Saxon town. Davison suggests that "the zoning of industry was a deliberate feature" in Saxon Thetford.[22] Even though he was clearly using a metaphor, setting off the words, "industrial slum," with inverted commas, the idea intrigued me. I phoned Davison, who was an inspector of ancient monuments in the Ministry of Public Buildings and Works, arranging to visit him in his office at Fortress House in London. To me, the notion of a Saxon slum was incredible, but Davison's work held exciting heuristic possibilities. I was eager to learn what he meant.

Davison and his colleagues were extremely helpful, allowing me to read the unpublished report of Knocker's work. From the evidence, Knocker inferred that in the tenth century Thetford was a long, straggling town. "Dusty with wood ash it must have been and in the summer thick with flies. Men plied their various trades and the smoke of kilns and iron furnaces could have been seen far across the open Breckland." He found remains of huts, pits, kilns, and other signs of intensive industrial activity. The vicinity was full of ash; one hut, engulfed in ash, ceased to function as a dwelling. The site seemed to be an artisan quarter, and Knocker noted that "an overall picture is given of people living in conditions of utmost squalor and discomfort and in huts far less elaborately equipped and more uncomfortable than many a prehistoric hut." The posthumous report of Knocker's work, published in

1984, observes that the archaeological evidence shows Thetford was a "flourishing manufacturing centre in the late Saxon period." The signs of intense industrial activity at two of Knocker's sites suggest that perhaps "life in this zone of the town was appallingly polluted."[23]

I asked Brian Davison what led him to use the phrase "industrial slum" when he described the area Knocker investigated. He replied that it was largely the contrast with other sections of the lost town. The sites he excavated himself were clean, well laid out, with adequate spaces between buildings, and without accumulated rubbish. Knocker's area, in contrast, was heaped up with rubbish. Davison, then, used "industrial slum" merely as a convenient term to represent a physical condition of unbounded rubbish. There was no way of knowing how those contrasting spaces of the town organized the lives of the people, and we do not even know if the artisans were poor. However, Davison's metaphor helped clarify my own thinking.

I think of the slum as a specific condition of mutual immanence, shaped by a process of exclusions, enclosures, and dissociations. This historical process transformed the typical industrial town from a common place to a system of special places. It was a topomorphic revolution because it changed the mode of dwelling together from the intimate immanence of rich and poor to separation and enclosure. At the end of the eighteenth century the process of change yielded the industrial slum in the modern sense—an environment of factories, hovels, and the workhouse.

Today it is believed without much question that it is in the nature of all great cities to contain circumscribed, squalid areas occupied exclusively by the poor (and in a few cases by those who want to live with the poor). It is taken for granted that slum districts are inevitable spatial concentrations. It is important to challenge these assumptions, because if we do not grasp what is historically true, it is hard to imagine what is historically possible. The spatial zoning of poverty is not a universal characteristic of urban life. The slum—meaning a district of the city occupied exclusively by the poor—came into the world at the end of the eighteenth century, a topomorphic product of the industrial revolution. The Victorians, with their sense of old places, probed for the roots of place change and for the meaning of cacotopes in the industrial city. Twentieth-century writers, in contrast, tend to assume that what is true of contemporary urban life is true for all cities through all time.

One example may be found in an article on slums published about a half-century ago in the *Encyclopedia of Social Sciences*—a splendid old source of information in other respects. The writer claims, "Slums are a *universal* phenomenon of communal living. Assyrian, Babylonian, Grecian and Roman towns *all* had their *districts* where the poor were housed in insubstantial buildings" (italics mine).[24] One or two examples are enough to disprove the assertion of "universality." Let us draw the examples from polar extremes of Eastern and Western Europe: Constantinople and Rome.

Constantinople was the center of the Byzantine Empire, a great cosmopolitan metropolis and a haven for immigrants. For eleven centuries it gathered all sorts and conditions of men and women. From the moment of its foundation the city dominated the empire. By the fifth century A.D., the population of the central city reached a million souls— an enormous number for the ancient world. It remained at that level— recovering slowly after the great plague of the sixth century—until its conquest by the Latin Crusaders in the thirteenth century, after which it declined to under a hundred thousand in the fifteenth century. Although rich and poor dwellings did often appear in separate clusters, there was no segregation, in this seething, turbulent metropolis, of districts distinguished by wealth. Palaces, tenements, and hovels stood close together. Windows and balconies of the poorer houses overhung the street, and the women of these households observed and shared the daily life of their neighbors.[25] The poor filled the city in great numbers. As early as the fourth century, there were fifty thousand recipients of charity in Constantinople.[26] The lives of the poor were spent in a struggle for the elementary conditions of survival, as in most societies, but such people were not isolated and restricted to special sections of the city. Relief measures did not estrange them but actually led to some degree of communal integration, however incomplete. Moreover, their single recreation, the circus, was open to them free, and they necessarily shared it with the other classes.

In ancient Rome, too, the poor did not live in homogeneous zones of poverty, as they do in cities today. From the time they emerged as a social force during the late Roman Republic, after 133 B.C., the special poignancy of their deprivation was expressed as lack of place. Losing their farms to the owners of great estates, they moved to the city, resembling in some respects the victims of the enclosure process in England some fifteen centuries later. Plutarch had Tiberius Gracchus describe their plight, in his famous speech on behalf of the dispossessed poor, in these words: "The savage beasts in Italy have their particular dens, they have their places of repose and refuge; but the men who bear arms, and expose their lives for the safety of their country, enjoy in the meantime nothing more in it but the air and light; and, having no houses or settlements of their own, are constrained to wander from place to place with their wives and children."[27] Centuries later, during the days of the Roman Empire, the distress of the poor grew more extensive and more acute, but the nature of their presence in the spaces of the city remained about the same.[28] They had no places of their own, yet they were visible everywhere. They were in the streets, on the bridges, in the shadows, on all the corners and in all the interstices of the city, searching for alms, crumbs, shelter. On the first of July, the usual day for moving, poor families wandered the streets, having been driven out and their possessions seized by the rental agents.[29]

Most of the poor, as well as the people in modest circumstances, lived in lodging houses known as *insulae* or "islands"—similar to the *synoikia* or common dwelling houses in ancient Athens. They were known as "islands" in Rome not because they were isolated from the rest of the city but because each was surrounded by a tiny strip of ground and not attached to other buildings. Only the rich or great lived in a *domus*—a dwelling occupied by one family. The proportion in the city was one *domus* to twenty-five *insulae*. An official survey made during the first half of the fourth century A.D. listed 44,171 of the latter and only 1,782 of the former.[30] The *domus* was usually no more than two stories high, but the *insula*, which usually stood on a narrow base, often loomed four stories high, with the poorest of the poor living on the top floor, occupying the space, as Juvenal wrote, where the pigeons laid their eggs. Both kinds of buildings were frequently collapsing and burning throughout the city, and it was not unusual for guests at a party to rush out into the street for safety when a suspicious rumble suggested that the house might tumble about their ears. The poorest dwellings, often constructed cheaply and hastily by dishonest speculators, were built largely of clay, plaster, and wood, and they collapsed most frequently.

Yet, although it had all the familiar features associated with the causes of segregated slums in the modern city—crowding, poor construction, characteristics of the real estate market, immigration, and so forth—Rome did not produce socially isolated, physically segregated slum neighborhoods. The more than forty thousand lodging houses mentioned above were distributed throughout all the fourteen regions of the city, with a higher density near the center.[31] As Theodor Mommsen indicates, the "splendid palaces of the rich" stood out in the midst of the "sea of wretched buildings" which housed the poor and those in modest circumstances.[32]

Indeed, quarters of the city were differentiated by wealth to some extent. An affluent person who could afford to rent rooms in an expensive *insula* might prefer the outskirts of the city to avoid the noise of vehicular traffic, which was restricted to nocturnal hours. The rich and noble built magnificent residences on the hills, especially on the slopes of the Palatine near the Forum. But even in those sections, with the probable exception of the aristocratic Palatine, one could find some dwellings of the poor.[33] Sallust wrote that during the Republic, the mansions of the nobles were as large as cities. They contained enormous gardens, for the rich noble was not content unless he had brought the countryside within the walls of his home. The Aventine, with its proximity to the Tiber and the commercial section, was a plebeian quarter housing tradesmen and workers of all sorts. Nevertheless, the differentiation of some parts of the city as quarters in which people lived high or lived low did not segregate and isolate all the residents.

In both ancient and medieval cities, the rich, the poor, and the middling settled cheek by jowl in some quarters, lived separately in others, but were thrust into one another's life space by the force of communal interdependence and sustained by the conviction that they were members of one another. The rich accepted the relentless presence of the poor, who attended, assisted, and harassed them continually as slaves, servants, clients, employees, petitioners, sycophants, suppliants, and spectators. The city in those times remained a unified urban experience for all conditions of men and women, whereas now it tends to decompose into little more than an administrative matrix for a range of differential urban experiences, alien to one another, with different moral values.

Descriptions of the great cities of the Middle Ages document the constant presence of the poor in the ambience of the rich and great. In twelfth-century London, for instance, the least respectable elements in the population were not sequestered, and they appeared in plain sight:

> The streets of London, or of any other mediaeval town, showed a
> high percentage of mutilated and diseased people. The one-armed,
> the one-legged, the blind, the half-witted, and the just plain drunk
> were numerous.

The *ribauz*, or good-for-nothings, were always on the edge of a crowd. They begged and plundered at the slightest provocation. They hung around outside the door of the banquet hall when a large feast was held. The king of England had three hundred bailiffs whose duty it was—though not all at one time—to keep these people back as food was moved from the kitchens to the hall, and to see that the guests were not disturbed. Frequently in twelfth-century romances a beautiful damsel is threatened with the awful fate of being turned over to the *ribauz*. Nothing more horrible can be imagined. These people accompanied armies on their expeditions, helping in menial tasks and plundering what was left by the knights and other fighting men. And yet they were kept under control by authority.[34]

Similarly, the great Muslim cities of the Middle Ages, such as Damascus and Aleppo, held large populations of poor people—menial workers, servants, slaves, immigrants, drifters, and so forth. Nevertheless, extreme class differences did not prevent cohesive patterns of public life. As Lapidus observed, "There was some separation of persons by community but no ghetto-like isolation of communities in the whole. . . . Certain neighborhoods were favored by the wealthy because of their salubrity, or proximity to the citadel and public affairs, and gave these districts an 'upper' class character, but no class came to dominate a district."[35] Moreover, if we turn from Europe and the Middle East to the old cities of China, we find that there as well the lives of rich and poor were "interdigitated."[36]

In the old structure of mutual immanence, both physical intimacy and social distance shaped the pattern of daily life. Hatred and repugnance added meanings to the texture of daily interactions, but these feelings did not give the rich the motive or the will to withdraw from the poor. Now the topistic structure of the modern city tends to divide the urban environnment in bounded zones of homogeneous life space. In his cultural history of European family life, Philippe Ariès writes about the great topomorphic change of the eighteenth century, observed in France as well as Britain, in which the middle class seceded from the old heterogeneous social body:

It withdrew from the vast polymorphous society to organize itself separately, in a homogeneous environment, among its families, in homes designed for privacy, in new districts kept free from lower-class contamination. . . .

The old society concentrated the maximum number of old ways of life into the minimum of space and accepted, if it did not impose, the bizarre juxtaposition of the most widely different classes. The new society, on the contrary, provided each way of life with a confined space.[37]

In the first stage of the West-European pattern, historically shaped by capitalist development, the process of change located the poor in slums within the city and the comfortable classes in the suburbs or beyond. Then, in later stages, remedial campaigns intending to clear the slums relocated the poor in high-rise estates or public-housing projects. However, the process of spatial differentiation and segregation is not restricted to capitalism. The East-European pattern shaped by bureaucratic collectivism—in systems where all housing is public and all resources administered by the government—reverses the figure, locating elites in high-rise buildings at the center and the poor in villages at the periphery.

In Eastern Europe, the process of industrialization did not follow the Western model. Urban growth was slow, and people stayed in rural villages because agricultural workers were needed there. Now, in Hungary, Yugoslavia, and other East-European societies, deteriorating villages are the topistic equivalent of the urban industrial slums in the West. By interpreting a wide range of survey data, Ivan Szelenyi, a Hungarian sociologist, shows that villages tend to lose their social independence and become urban satellites. The leaders and professional people—doctors, teachers, local government officials, and social workers—abandon the village for the inner city. As the little communities lose their population, they grow poorer as well, turning into "village slums." Poor workers move into them, because with a bit of land and a garden they can eke out an existence while they commute to a low-income job or seek employment in the city. As Szelenyi observes, "Traditionally even the smallest communities were 'total societies,' with their own social hierarchy, with their own elite, but now they are on the way to becoming 'partial societies' again in the same way as slums."[38] Therefore, in Eastern Europe as well as in the West we find a topomorphic revolution associated with industrialization—the transformation of the common place. Once the city was a place of common experience. Now it is a matrix for different places of special, homogeneous experience.

As division of labor grows more complex and more "organic" in Durkheim's sense, the special places where we dwell become more homogeneous. Economic forces make us interdependent and make us need one another's differences. The same forces, it seems, make our places more like containers of uniformity, shaping spaces where we dwell with people much like us.

In England after the industrial revolution, poverty became the *questio vexata*, the unsetting question of the Victorian town. In 1843 Carlyle wrote that the poor "put their huge inarticulate question, 'What do you mean to do with us?' in a manner audible to every reflective soul in the kingdom. . . . All England heard the question: it is the first practical form of *our* Sphinx-riddle." The riddle has been troubling cities ever since, as they make slums and clear them, erect remedial housing and allow its dilapidation, build suburbs and rebuild urban neighborhoods, exchange the populations of centers and peripheries, all in a restless pattern of avoidance and relocation. The question of what to do about the location of poverty keeps its power to unsettle places. It remains the principal riddle of the modern city.

T H R E E

Sick Places

Topistic structure means the pattern of relationships that connects or disconnects the organisms living together in a place. The nature *of* a place, therefore, depends on the qualities and distribution of nature *in* a place. Some effective presences live hidden in the soil or in the bodies of other organisms. In Europe, after the middle of the fourteenth century, the connections among four organisms supported a regular rhythm of pestilence, sustaining the chronic instability of urban life until the end of the seventeenth century, when plague epidemics ended and the era of modern cities began. This chapter explores that crucial transition from a point of view that understands a town as a location of effective presences abiding together.

Until about a century ago, "plague" was a generic term referring to the impact on populations rather than to the specific causal agent of disease. The disease, so vividly described by Thucydides, that racked Athens during the Peloponnesian War was probably typhus. In England, until recent times, people indiscriminately called any serious epidemic "the plague," "the pestilence," "sore sickness," "the infection," or, significantly, "the visitation"—suggesting that they expected the disease to come and, after it had done its worst, to depart.

Today, we make precise distinctions among the contagious diseases that scourged towns in those earlier years by identifying the microorganisms that caused them.[1] The disease known as plague or pestilence, in our precise sense, is an infection by specific bacteria, *Yersinia pestis*. In the bubonic form, fleabites inject plague bacteria into the bloodstream where they drain into lymphatic glands, which swell up in the armpit or groin—making the excruciating "buboes" that name the disease—and the skin often breaks out in dark eruptions, formerly known as "tokens" and "blains." The mortality rate from untreated bubonic infections is about 65 percent. In pneumonic plague, spread by droplets coughed into the air, the disease is virtually 100 percent fatal, but the epidemics tend to stop quickly.

No other human bacterial disease caused the frenzy that went with bubonic plague. The agony of ruptured lymphatic glands goaded victims to attack their caretakers, to plunge out of windows, or to run through the streets naked until they fell. Plague in its bubonic and pneumonic forms had the power to interrupt absolutely—to close things down until the mortality receded. A configuration of fatal infections ravaged all the great towns in ancient and medieval times—several types of malignant fever, dysentery, influenza, smallpox, and malaria, to mention some of them. In medieval and early-modern days, however, no disease matched the profound disturbance of morale associated with plague. Other infections caused less discontinuity, tending to remain chronic destructive forces that inhibited but did not stop the work and life of towns.

Pestilence remained one of the chief regulators of town life, causing industrial and commercial instability, until it declined after 1665 and then mysteriously withdrew from northern Europe. Periodically, the plague turned lively industrial towns into stinking, infected places. Sustaining a periodic rhythm of disorder, exodus, and urban isolation, plagues came and went like frightful storms or like the seasons.

The study of plague, a learned medical historian wrote, "exemplifies the unity of the cosmos," because it shows "how human fate is intimately bound up with that of a vast variety of small mammals and their ecto-parasites."[2] We might stretch that wisdom from the cosmos to the microcosmos and reflect that the history of plague also teaches the inner unity of a place.

The presence or absence of plague depended on how a place contained and connected—or disconnected—four specific organisms. The virulent infection of medieval and early-modern towns grew out of the durable intimacy of this quartet, mutually antagonistic but abiding together: bacillus, flea, rat, and human. Pestilence, the pale horseman of the Apocalypse, rode in the company of this deadly quartet. Plague, therefore, is a disease of place. A recent treatise on bacteriology observes that plague infection does not occur through direct contact with bodies of the sick, "but spreads by contiguity from place to place, so that an increasing number of small foci are established. Often the infection seems to be localized in buildings, particularly grain stores, warehouses, or shops; in these, many cases of plague are met with in persons who have no immediate relation to each other."[3]

Urban pestilence declined for reasons not precisely understood, but it withdrew from England in the seventeenth century when the proximities and spatial connections among organisms living together in towns were changing. To grasp the significance of all these changes, it is necessary to understand the intimate links between bacteria, fleas, rats, and humans. As a disease of place, bubonic plague depends on the local conditions of mutual immanence—that is, on the continuous, contiguous intimacy of organisms that share a place.

When humans occupy any piece of ground, they stand in a network of life, sharing the place with countless organisms, which ordinarily remain unacknowledged until something goes wrong. Human settlements cannot survive without the hidden presences that help to render soil, air, and water into a biosphere. An acre of land serving as field or pasture holds over a billion tiny arthropods, barely visible in the ground. A square yard of the same soil contains more than 10 trillion bacteria and other invisible organisms. No patch of ground anywhere on earth goes vacant of life. A desert wilderness, devoid of humans, may still be inhabited by visible presences such as snakes, ferrets, and prairie dogs. Burrowing rodents build underground cities, and insects share the burrows or build settlements of their own. The invisible populations occupying the same wilderness defy calculation. An apparently empty desert space may hold about ninety thousand microbes in a teaspoon of soil.[4]

Pestilence in the forest, desert, and countryside is called sylvatic plague—a disease of wild places and the open country. In this form it is older than the human species. Nature originally associated creatures without human intervention. Until the human historical work of making and breaking places changed the relationship of creatures, bacteria, fleas, and rodents lived together in stable equilibrium.

Most animals, apart from domestic rodents and humans, remain immune to *Y. pestis*. The phagocytes of most birds devour it easily, and some types of rodents enjoy a natural resistance to plague. Even a few strains of the black rat—the infamous plague carrier of medieval Europe—resist the infection. Though it has the capacity to slaughter armies and destroy cities, the plague organism is still a delicate, vulnerable microvegetable. It cannot tolerate sunshine, strong disinfectants, or the ordinary conditions outside of a nourishing bloodstream.[5] As long as it stays in the bodies of certain rodents or perhaps in the soil of their burrows, it remains harmless to humans—until it leaves the wild environment to dwell in the septic quartet.

Even though original plague was sylvatic, prehistoric people stayed free of plague epidemics before they gathered in sedentary agricultural communities and separated their dwellings from the wilderness. Everything we learn about paleolithic people from their symbols, pictures, and their perception of space suggests a pervading sense of interdependence among creatures, things, heavenly bodies, and cosmic forces—an inseparable oneness of the universe.[6] The terror of wild beasts is not paleolithic—it belongs to the agricultural era. In the Old Stone Age humans defended themselves against predators, but they did not imagine hearth and home as a separate place apart from the beasts. The primeval hut was not topistically different from other lairs or nests.

Whereas the art of agricultural civilizations represented the differences between men and beasts, paleolithic artists showed the connections. They imagined an unsegregated community of humans, beasts, and spirits, belonging together. In southern France and northern Spain, therefore, prehistoric cave pictures reveal a primeval structure of mutual immanence—a system of effective presences dwelling together in the long prehistory before the agricultural way of life.

Agriculture changed the old way of life, bringing the first topomorphic revolution, which polarized wilderness and settlement. This cleavage created the village community as a place of cultivation apart from the beasts. Men and women transformed some beasts into domestic animals. Domesticating animals literally means attaching them to a *domus*, or house. Domestication also creates the wilderness—a place for the beasts, spatially segregated from the home, the place of human settlement.

The domestic era began long ago in neolithic times, when humans began to attach nature to houses, cultivating plants and animals and making interior spaces for work and storage. The era culminated in the triumph of the house as the central place integrating human activities.

Until the end of the seventeenth century, when the structure and fabric of houses began to change, the intimate association of parasites and humans obscurely and tragically made bubonic plague the worst disease of domestic integration.

Under the predomestic arrangement, nature stocked the world with hungry carnivores as well as a generous supply of prolific rodents created (the carnivores were convinced) to feed them. Under the old conditions, the reproductive program of rodents, which breed plenty and often, promised a good life for carnivores, but human buildings changed the balance in favor of rats and mice. Human design and construction gave them a stronghold that carnivores found impregnable. Moreover, humans strove to fence out wild beasts to protect domestic animals, but the safety they won for their livestock served domestic rodents as well.

Some rodents began to live with humans in prehistoric times before the ninth millennium, when the agricultural revolution stimulated domestication and prompted humans to build settled places. These humans constructed houses for themselves and containers to save grain. While the neolithic pioneers of agricultural life gathered the livestock they wanted to bind to their houses, uninvited beasts such as rats and mice followed the grain and domesticated themselves. They occupied the places constructed by humans in order to enjoy a regular food supply, and in those places they also found shelter from natural predators. Nature rewarded the drive that linked rodent fortunes with human destiny by giving rodents a security unknown in the wilderness. Since the beginnings of domestication, rats and mice have adapted completely to an indoor life, along with similarly flexible insects including fleas, flies, spiders, lice, bedbugs, clothes-moths, and cockroaches.[7] Along with humans and animals, these parasites are effective presences abiding together, with important spatial continuities or discontinuities.

Urbanization deprives humans of their carnivorous allies against the rat. Foxes, wildcats, stoats, weasels, polecats, marten, and other predatory mammals have withdrawn from towns. Birds of prey such as owls, kestrels, and hawks are scarce, and snakes are not tolerated.[8] Domestic ease cools the cat from ratting, and in urban settings feral dogs and cats have little effect on rodent populations.[9]

In the first epoch of domestication, distance, natural barriers, and customary precautions separated human settlements from the bacteria, fleas, and rodents inhabiting locations of sylvatic plague. Then, in the centuries of domestic plague, they lived together intimately without physical separation. When barriers and distances no longer protected human settlements from plague reservoirs, the disease passed from wild, burrowing rodents to domestic rats. Humans—who were not essential to the process—got involved entirely through spatial continuities. According to M. A. C. Hinton, an expert on rodents, the scourge of plague belongs essentially to rats and their fleas. The disease penetrated the shield of domestication, which spared rodent populations from other kinds of natural regulation. In Hinton's words, plague "is nature's unfailing method of periodically reducing the rat population to reasonable proportions."[10]

The disease may smolder underground in the burrows of wild rodents, but it erupts among humans when plague bacteria infect the domestic rats that occupy a place. Humans and domestic rats do not make dependable hosts for *Y. pestis* because they die off quickly compared to the durable subterranean hosts. The bacteria stayed precariously in human places, sometimes repulsed by immune reactions, but continually lurching from carcass to living flesh, carried by fleas that were struggling to eject them. Only sufficient density—meaning an environment saturated with rats and fleas—offered plague a regular life above ground. Even then, epidemics proceeded in cycles, erupting violently and stopping abruptly. Sometimes the disease did not survive at all, but only revived after a fresh infection from out-of-town.

Today, the world's oldest reservoirs of plague, located in central Asia and central Africa, remain intractable sources of pestilence, but myths, tales, and customs on the fringes of these regions suggest that in olden times folk wisdom taught successful ways of insulating human communities from the causes of plague.[11] Traditional rules instructed nomads in the way to hunt marmots, warning them to avoid sick beasts, and in other places tradition advised settled people to move away quickly when dead rats appeared around their houses.

Even though the connection between rat epizootic and human mortality remained undisclosed until the twentieth century, a mythic awareness of the relation may be detected in some archaic but familiar stories. (The words "epizootic" and "enzootic" mean the animal equivalents of "epidemic" and "endemic.") The earliest recorded hint of bubonic plague appears in the Bible, in the story of the war with the Philistines, which happened about 1000 B.C. The nomadic Israelites suffered heavy losses in a great battle with the Philistines, people of a prosperous urban

civilization settled in five thriving commercial port cities on the Mediterranean coast. The Philistines captured the sacred Ark, but the Lord
smote their cities with pestilence: "he threw them into distress and
plagued them with tumours, and their territory swarmed with rats.
There was death and destruction all through the city."[12] Plague spread
from one city to another until the Philistines returned the Ark with a
guilt offering demanded by the Israelites. According to their instructions, the Philistines sent an indemnity, consisting of five gold models of
swollen glands, one for each city, and five gold rats. They also gave
honor to the God of Israel. As an accompaniment to the religious
gesture, the golden offering suggests a symbolic transvaluation of the
experience—the representation of epidemic evil by objects of value. At
the same time, the story clearly associates rats and human plague by
linking rodents, buboes, and urban pestilence.

The Philistine cities probably contained large deposits of grain; rats
and their fleas have followed harvests and lived in granaries since neolithic times. Until the end of the seventeenth century, urban folk in
Europe unwittingly built an environmental fabric to house the rats that
bore the fleas that carried the germs that caused the plague. The disease
exuberated in market towns, where storage of grain and cloth provided
lush nurseries for rats and fleas. In medieval and early-modern England,
the pests flourished in the houses of market towns, where grain was
stored regularly within timber-framed walls filled with wattle and daub.
Rodents penetrated this fabric easily, nesting in the tiled or thatched
roofs, often scuttling across floors covered with mats woven from
rushes. For three centuries, from the Black Death (1348) until the Great
Plague (1665), pestilence remained the great contagion of domestic
places, the rhythmic disease of human enclosures. Epidemics sprang
from infected interiors, which nourished in a common place the integrated lives of bacteria, fleas, rats, and humans.

In seaports, rats traveling in holds full of grain or fiber completed
their journey by walking across the mooring lines into dockyards, bringing the local rat population a fresh supply of infective fleas swollen with
plague bacteria. Flea larvae thrive in nests of fiber and dirt. In town and
country, the grist mills served as special nourishing places that fattened
rats on grain and bred fleas in cereal debris.

Fleas escaped attention in the early textile towns, but when plague
broke out in India early in the twentieth century, investigators observed
that cotton was even more important than grain in the spread of plague

fleas. The cotton warehouses swarmed with rats, which not only enjoyed the fiber as ideal nesting material but even adapted to a diet of raw cotton seed. Fleas bred freely in the debris and dust of cotton seed, which provided an ideal environment for eggs, larvae, pupae, and adult insects. In the old market towns, wool made a similar congenial environment for rats and fleas. Virtually every village and town in England engaged in the wool trade or made cloth. Storage of grain in the vicinity of wool made a perfect breeding ground for bubonic plague.[13] Norwich, the principal textile and market city, had a population of twenty-four thousand in the fourteenth century before the Black Death. Only seven thousand remained alive after that pestilence.[14] The sedentary life of weavers, working at home on handlooms, set them up for slaughter by plague fleas that came from the rats infesting their cottages. For example, early in the reign of Elizabeth I, plague destroyed the flourishing manufacture of woolen cloth in the Lake District by killing off the Lakeland weavers.[15]

In the old timber houses, before modern construction, rats burrowed under the soft earth floors or tunneled in the mud and wattle walls, and they nested in thatched roofs, keeping rat fleas close to the human occupants.[16] Buildings sat right on the ground with no separation from rat burrows underneath, or else covered their cellars with nothing more than wooden boards. A minority of the human population dwelt in castles and manor houses with stone walls and slate or lead roofs— buildings of two or three stories above the ground, providing material barriers to and physical distance from rat fleas. Nobility and wealth, therefore, offered some defense against plague.

Until the end of the seventeenth century, houses kept forms and fabrics inherited from the Middle Ages. In the medieval urban environment, with few barriers between animals and humans, parasites were taken for granted, and fleas circulated as naturally as grains of dust, seething among pigs, dogs, cats, and humans. A medieval grave discovered in Suffolk revealed that a Viking literally carried a bird flea in his pocket. This preserved flea was found in a leather case containing a kit of implements for kindling fire. The Viking probably slipped the flea into the pouch inadvertently when he stuffed it with twigs intended for tinder. In Ireland, another Viking excavation revealed a pit filled with material that may have once stuffed a mattress, which included a dessicated specimen of *Pulex irritans*, the human flea.[17]

The presence of the human flea was taken for granted. In Tudor and

Elizabethan times, the intimate environment remained saturated with them. A poem mentioning "the hungry fleas that frisk so fresh" in bed suggested that Elizabethans regarded blankets of fleas as a natural part of the bedding.[18] A recently discovered wardrobe from the court of Henry VIII, sealed in a forgotten recess of old Whitehall Palace for over four centuries, disclosed, preserved in the folds, many corpses of early Tudor fleas that had starved to death waiting for aristocrats to put on the clothing.[19]

In humbler places, *Pulex irritans* shuttled between pigs and people, for the human flea loved the pig as well. Abundant in houses, it also teemed in sties, where hordes of rats generated more rats in the thatched roofs, breeding fleas as well, which dropped below. The whole floor under the thatch seemed to heave with fleas, making the surface of an infested sty look like an undulating pond.[20] Moreover, swine wandered freely in towns or else were herded through the streets to a feeding place, depositing and collecting fleas on the way.

Still, rats and fleas are merely the necessary condition, and their presence is not sufficient to cause plague unless they are infected by *Y. pestis*. The human flea, *P. irritans*, is a weak transmitter or vector of plague, and it merely continues what a more powerful vector begins. European epidemics were primed by the tropical plague flea, *Xenopsylla cheopis*, which was imported from Africa and the Middle East. The difference in power to cause plague depends on the anatomical structure of the proventriculus, a tiny organ in the flea's gut. Therefore, the keystone of bubonic plague, locking the elements into sequence, is a microscopic peculiarity in one type of flea's digestive system.[21] Plague fleas have a gut that gets blocked by clots of infective bacteria. The Asiatic rat flea, *Xenopsylla cheopis*, which is prone to this condition, was identified by N. Charles Rothschild in 1901 as the principal plague flea. In an epizootic, *X. cheopis* readily abandons dying rats to feed on humans.

Nathaniel Charles Rothschild, brother of the second Baron Rothschild and father of the present Lord Rothschild, was a consultant to the Indian Plague Commission and the leading scientific authority on fleas. A reluctant banker but a keen entomologist, he made a collecting trip to Egypt in 1901 and camped on the Nile bank.[22] His daughter, Miriam, writes that he had a gift for recognizing both a "good spot" and a "good thing." Predicting that some of the fleas he collected there would be identified with the plague carriers in India, he named the deadly species *cheopis*.[23]

It seems like a small detail (so is the flea, after all), but why did Rothschild name this species of the Asiatic rat flea after Cheops—the pharaoh who built the Great Pyramid, the largest structure of the ancient world—instead of giving it a place name such as *nilotica* or *aegyptiaca*? It suggests his intuitive sense of a "good thing." Did he intend to imply ironically that *X. cheopis*, one of the tiniest creatures in the obvious world, was the architect of the plague, the immense disease of the past? I say "architect," not meaning an intentional designer, but in the sense of the first builder—the organism that linked bacilli to humans and organized the structure of pestilence.

The bank of the Nile, Gibbon wrote, was "stigmatized in every age as the original source and seminary of the plague." Ancient writers claimed that the plague of Justinian's time—probably the greatest pestilence in history—arrived in cargoes of grain shipped from Egypt. Until then, plague smoldered in underground burrows or erupted in Africa, Asia, and the Middle East, but it stayed away from Europe. Perhaps the first European outbreak of bubonic plague represents the end of the ancient era and the zero point of medieval Europe. Around 542 A.D., ships bearing grain carried plague from Alexandria to ports of the Roman Empire. Grain stands out as the principal factor in the transport of rats from one place to another, and it is reasonable to think that these cargoes may have included infected rats.

At the peak of the infection in Constantinople, ten thousand perished each day, while the disease moved on to empty many cities of the East. Chroniclers reported that pestilence spread "to the ends of the habitable world, depopulating towns, making the country into a desert, and turning human habitations into the haunts of wild beasts." Thus the plague made an era of topoclasm and place change, reducing cities to ruins and making settlements into wild places. Edward Gibbon estimated that this pandemic of the sixth century A.D., wasting the Roman Empire in the reign of Justinian, caused 100 million deaths.[24] Even if the estimate exaggerates, it is hard to dismiss the importance of the catastrophe, one of the worst calamities ever to strike humankind. Some historians identify this massive extermination as the transforming event that turned the civilization of antiquity into Europe of the Dark Ages.

Roman conquerors brought rats and fleas back to the Mediterranean from India and Egypt, but after the pandemic of Justinian's reign, plague bacteria failed to secure an ecological niche.[25] The chain of infection did not survive precarious transfers from one city to another, and the Dark

Ages—an epoch of relative isolation—extinguished the pestilence in most of Europe. Human populations settled down to a stable pattern of other infectious diseases until the twelfth century, when the Mongol empires began to change the environment between Asia and Europe. Before their decay in 1368, which was probably hastened by plague, the Mongols controlled China, Russia, and the Middle East. Inadvertently, they planted the plague in their own homeland steppe, establishing a chronic pattern of infection that still stretches across Asia. The fleas that rode in their grain supply infected the wild rodents, making the steppe a permanent reservoir of plague. In deep burrows that preserve rodents through severe winters and summers, pestilence survives the climatic extremes of Manchuria and Siberia.

Previously, only a slender thread from China to Syria—the ancient silk route—linked one oasis to another across the deserts of central Asia. The Mongols traveled farther north, expanding the territory of passage between Asia and Europe, weaving a tissue of caravansaries, camps, and headquarters. The plague spread through this wide network, reaching over Asia and eastern Europe. Each caravan stop must have contained enough stores to feed hundreds of men and beasts, thereby gathering a population of rats and fleas as well.[26]

Two centuries after the disease receded from Europe, the Victorian traveler, Charles Doughty, pictured the Arabian desert as a stronghold of plague. He described resting places where fleas vexed the bedouins as sorely as flies tormented the camels during long summer months. Ruins along his way showed that towns, hamlets, and villages inhabited the land in ancient times. Doughty passed villages shattered by plague, their unroofed walls about to fall. He noted that "the fatal plagues of Mecca return in every generation." Crowds of pilgrims carried the disease with them, and "from the Mecca pilgrimage has gone forth many a general pestilence, to the furthest of mankind."[27]

The plague began its medieval European urban career in the army of a Mongol prince who was besieging Caffa, a Crimean seaport and commercial city, in 1346. The disease embarked from that place to penetrate Europe and the Near East, spreading inland from the seaports. In 1348 it struck England, and according to contemporaneous writers, the Black Death destroyed between one-third and one-half the population. After the Great Mortality of 1348–52, plague remained in England for more than three hundred years—at first in minor waves of infection all over the country, then receding from the rural areas to settle in the great towns.

In England, a wave of pestilence often started in a coastal town when house rats bearing the fierce vector, *X. cheopis*, disembarked from an infected ship transporting grain or cloth or raw cotton and entered the ecology of the local rats. Even if tropical *cheopis* did not survive in the English climate, the blocked fleas planted deadly bacteria in the urban rat population. Then the disease would spread through the broad streams of fleas that washed through the town and gradually make its way from one urban center to the next. For more than three centuries after the Black Death, pestilence made English cities places of rhythmic instability. Experienced as a regular crisis of towns, the plague suspended ordinary routines. In London the exodus of the court and the upper classes into the countryside during the plague season was part of the routine of social life. The merchants fled as well. Trade and manufacture stopped, sometimes for half the year, and the recurrent crisis profoundly disrupted wage and price patterns.

All the traditional defenses against plague exacerbated the breakdown of continuities: evacuation, sealing up infected houses, segregation, cordons, confining suspected cases in pesthouses, prohibiting trade with infected towns, quarantine, avoiding contacts with suspected people, places, and goods, and so forth. People shunned one another and closed their doors against their own friends. Outside of London, anything coming from the metropolis caused panic. The plague generated a fear of textiles. Restrictions were placed on markets and fairs—a fatal blow to commerce. In the first three-quarters of the seventeenth century, when England was never free of plague, not a town escaped severe impoverishment from the cessation of trade.

In London, seventeenth-century England's greatest industrial city, workers toiled not in factories but in small houses and yards—many thousand workshops of all sorts spread over the city but concentrated on the banks of the Thames. People dwelt and worked in crowded houses, for all the merchants and manufacturers resided with their families, servants, apprentices, and journeymen over or near shop and countinghouse. The plague stopped work and transformed life more quickly and completely than war or famine. It damaged the tissue of social connections as well, for it made everyone suspicious. It made self-preservation every man and woman's consuming interest.[28]

Rats infested every house as a matter of course. In London, an old city composed of fragments from the past, stately mansions stood next to the most squalid quarters, where the plague flourished. Any drainage led into a cesspool. London before the Great Fire was a filthy and pictur-esque city of gabled houses with rough walls framed by exposed timbers, with each ascending story projecting out over the narrow, winding streets below. The poorest dwellings, standing back-to-back, were little more than boards tacked to shaky frames with a smear of black pitch pretending to keep out the weather.[29]

Erasmus, who lived in England early in the sixteenth century, sus-pected a connection between plague and the quality of housing. Perpet-ually anxious about the disease, he believed that English dwellings were more vulnerable to pestilence than continental houses. "We read of a city," he said, "which was freed from continual pestilence by changes made in its buildings on the advice of a philosopher. Unless I am mistaken, England may be freed in like manner." English floors made him nervous, although the exact nature of their peril eluded him. Floors of stone, clay, or loam remained open to creatures of the earth. Even the house rat, which prefers not to dig, moved easily in and out of the soft ground. The English custom of spreading hay, straw, or rushes necessi-tated special care to avoid squalor. A fresh layer of rushes mixed with herbs made a warm and fragrant carpet, but when the covering lay too long without renewal, it decayed and smelled rotten, attracting vermin. Erasmus complained that the dirt floors strewn with rushes too often covered an ancient collection of beer, grease, fragments, bones, spittle, vomit, urine, excrement of dogs and cats, "and everything that is nasty." The mess was covered with more rushes, so the floors might hold the accumulated filth of twenty years. Houses were overcrowded and poorly ventilated, and the streets were choked with garbage. The common rat swarmed in streets and houses alike.[30]

Today we know what causes plague, but we are less certain about exactly what turned the tide and why the pestilence receded from Europe in the last quarter of the seventeenth century. Until very recently the leading explanation was a theory of rat displacement. According to this explanation, one species of rat, *Rattus rattus*, was the natural host of *X. cheopis*, the plague flea, and was unintentionally carried into Europe in the fourteenth century by returning crusaders. In the eighteenth century, a great rat migration introduced a new species, *Rattus norvegi-cus*, sometimes called the sewer rat. This species, according to the theory, did not carry *X. cheopis*. More aggressive than *R. rattus*, *norvegicus* drove the incumbent species out of human habitations, thereby ending the plague. It was a plausible explanation, but is no longer consistent with what we know about these rats and their habits as well as their fleas. Yet it should not be dismissed, because the idea contains more than outmoded biology. It was connected, we shall see, to a mythology of places that imagined conflict between Whig and Tory rats. It linked feelings about place change to British political history.

The sense of plague appeared in rat mythology before people understood the biological process. The tale of the Pied Piper of Hamelin is probably even more familiar than the biblical story of the Philistine plague. Victorians learned it from the poem by Robert Browning, who probably found it in that forgotten volume, *A Restitution of Decayed Intelligence*, by Richard Verstegen, the seventeenth-century antiquary who lived in England under the name of Rowlands.[31]

The fable was inscribed on the town hall of Hamelin in the province of Hanover, but other towns such as Brandenburg have similar traditions. According to the version in Verstegen's book, in the summer of 1376 a wandering musician dressed in a coat of many colors appeared in the town and offered, for a price, to rid the place of rats, which were making a terrible nuisance. After the officials made an agreement with the magical visitor, he played through the streets on a shrill pipe, leading all the rats into the river, where they drowned. The astonished town fathers breached the contract, claiming that they agreed to the unlikely bargain because they had believed the task impossible, and offered to pay a lesser sum. The piper threatened revenge, but they told him to do his worst. Once more he danced through the streets playing his instrument, but this time he was followed by 130 children, who vanished behind him into a hillside.

On one level, the legend probably represents typical exploitation of angry town musicians by skinflint aldermen. Perhaps it also represents medieval plague in Hamelin. The loss of children in the fable was preceded by a great swarming and destruction of rats, dramatizing epidemic as the sequel of epizootic. However, even if Hamelin in the province of Hanover remained free of medieval rats after the piper had evacuated them, a new species reoccupied the town four centuries later. The English called it the Hanover rat.

The common rat of the Middle Ages, technically named *Rattus rattus* but known popularly as the house rat, ship rat, roof rat, black rat, as well

as the old English rat, did not enjoy digging but loved to climb, preferring life among the rafters when it could claim a ceiling to nest in.
Although it thrived in the holds of ships, it hated to swim, and it is easy
to imagine R. rattus following the piper to drown in a river. There is
plenty of evidence that it has lived in Europe for a long time, but
tradition claims that it entered Europe hiding in the baggage of returning crusaders. It does not actively migrate but spreads through the world
passively, stowed away in the holds and folds of cargo.

In the eighteenth century the common rat of the modern era appeared, a fierce, migratory species technically named *Rattus norvegicus*—
the Norway rat. The origin of the name is obscure, for Norway is
innocent of producing it. It was known popularly as wander rat, sewer
rat, or field rat, and it spread through Europe in great hordes, displacing
the smaller and less pugnacious incumbent. It loved to dig and to swim
but avoided intimacy with humans, preferring to live in burrows under
and near houses. Whereas the old rat had lived inside human habitations, the newcomer dug underground, constructing subterranean
shadow cities at the edges of houses. Sometimes the newcomer was
called the brown rat and the older settler the black rat, but that usage is
confusing because individuals of either species may be black, brown, or
gray.

R. norvegicus does not fraternize with *R. rattus* and, according to the
myth, extruded the latter while marching across England.[32] *R. rattus* is a
climbing animal—rarely burrowing except in the soft ground of old-
fashioned buildings—that prefers walls, ceilings, and roofs to cellars,
drains, or sewers. Spatially it stays far closer to humans than the species
that displaced it. *R. norvegicus* is a burrowing, aquatic beast, larger, more
aggressive, and a powerful fighter. It keeps apart from humans, preferring caution to intimacy. It likes sewers, drains, and cesspools; it feeds
on human wastes and lurks in basements. It digs complex cities below
ground, with winding tunnels from which it raids fields and gardens
and haunts the margins of houses. According to tradition, these rodents
arrived in England around 1728, when the context of British politics
gave them the colloquial title, "Hanover rats." Naturalist Charles Waterton wrote that his father—himself a field naturalist—maintained firmly
that the rats arrived with the House of Hanover on the same ship that
conveyed the new dynasty to England. Political sympathies invented the
idea of the Hanover rat, and the alien species inspired a new myth.

Discontented Englishmen, such as recusant Roman Catholics, Non-

jurors, Jacobites, and Tories, interpreted the invasion as an allegory
signifying the end of an era. As the first quarter of the eighteenth century
concluded, they lamented the loss of a world, seeing the Stuart dynasty
in exile, the first Jacobite rebellion a failure, Roman Catholics excluded
from power, and the Tory supremacy finished. The twin pillars of the
Hanover establishment were Protestant and Whig. None of Queen
Anne's seventeen children survived her, and the crown had passed to
George I. Two decades of Whig supremacy under Walpole encouraged a
period of stability and common sense, initiated the Augustan age of
literature, and supported great initiatives in commerce and industry. But
Tories spoke of the Hanover rats as their masters and compared their
ravages to the appetites of the Georgian kings, complaining, "this brute,
like the family which first brought it over, exists in round numbers and
demands a most plentiful supply of food."[33] Like people of the old
regime, they said, the old English rat had virtually disappeared before
the pressure of the new species. As Charles Waterton declared, "the
stranger rat has now punished us severely. . . . When I reflect on the
numbers and the appetite of the Hanoverian rat . . . I would send its
whole stock, root and branch, back again to the country whence it came,
seeing that we have gained nothing by letting it exterminate the original
English rat."[34]

The Whig theory of rats, on the other hand, considered the newcom-
ers as liberators, relieving domestic infestation by driving out the house
rat. This way of thinking eventually generated the idea that rat displacement freed England of plague. Expressing the idea in a biological idiom,
J. F. D. Shrewsbury, as late as 1970, wrote: "A profound ecological
change had occurred in the rodent population of the British Isles. . . .
Mercifully the most extensive and virulent epizootic of plague among
field-rats is of little danger to human beings in temperate climates
because, owing to its living and breeding habits, the fleas harboured by
the field-rat have few opportunities to attack human beings."[35]

Today, Whig and Tory rat fables are taken with a grain of salt. For one
thing, *R. rattus* has returned, and both species may occupy different
parts of the same building, with *rattus* living high in the upper storeys
while *norvegicus* lurks in the basement. Sometimes *norvegicus* inhabits
one house exclusively while *rattus* lives right next door. Moreover,
norvegicus no longer lives up to its reputation as a vicious cannibal, and
the two species sometimes coexist in the same laboratory cage.[36] It is
clear now that plague fleas infest both species, with a slight preference

for the larger rat.[37] Finally, despite their reputation for shyness, these rats do bite humans and cause the disease known as rat-bite fever.

Still, there is more than a grain of truth in the myths of rats and their places. Even if *norvegicus* did not drive *rattus* out of towns by mortal combat, it is reasonable to think that changes in building construction and a revolution in domestic hygiene handicapped the old house rat ecologically, encouraging the rival species lurking on the outskirts of human habitations to enter them. The displacement then turned not on a physical struggle between the two species but on the trouble of adapting to changes in human places. If these changes did not expel the house rats, they at least encouraged them to withdraw from dwellings.

Now the balance has shifted to favor the old house rat again, encouraging its return to ancient haunts in the city of London and other urban centers.[38] New structural improvements such as ferroconcrete construction, impermeable floors, and separate sewerage systems handicap *norvegicus* at the bottom of buildings, to the profit of *rattus* at the top, for the latter species swings easily on telephone wires from one building to the next.[39]

Since both species now coexist in cities, the theory of rat displacement has lost its power to explain the decline of plague in the seventeenth century. As a recent book on epidemics concluded, "Three hundred years after the Great Plague there is still no satisfactory explanation of England's freedom from major epidemics of plague."[40] Yet the mind refuses to close the door on reasons, and certain historical changes in organisms and cities keep intruding into the corridor of explanations. The idea of rat displacement gives way to a theory of bacterial displacement. Biological speculations about changes in virulence and immunity suggest that other diseases may have dislodged plague from both rats and humans. The notion that one disease may defend against a worse infection is not a new idea. During the Great Plague of London, some people believed that syphilis might prevent plague, and men sought out prostitutes to contract venereal disease intentionally.[41]

Today, a closely related bacillus classified in the same genus with *Yersinia pestis*, an organism named *Yersinia pseudotuberculosis*, causes a disease called yersiniosis. Humans may contract it from rats, mice, and other animals. The infection is not serious, with only one death occurring among 150 cases diagnosed in Britain in a decade. The disease is unknown in the Near East, the Middle East, Southeast Asia, and the African continent, except for Algeria and Morocco. The limits of yersiniosis in Europe coincide with the geographical boundaries of plague in the period from the Black Death of 1348 to the Great Plague of 1665. An infection of yersiniosis is known to produce an immunity to plague, just as cowpox protects people from smallpox. It suggests than an enzootic of yersiniosis may have driven out the plague. Some bacteriologists present evidence that the more recently discovered organism, *Y. pseudotuberculosis*, which produces yersiniosis, may have evolved from a strain of *Y. pestis*.[42]

Despite the uncertainty about biological changes, what remains certain is that the decline of plague was reinforced by a great movement of place change that disposed local organisms in a new pattern of relationships. As Erasmus had surmised, England did get liberated from plague: in his words, the "city [was] freed . . . from continual pestilence by changes made in its buildings."[43] The change was brought about not by the advice of a philosopher, as Erasmus had expected, but by a sequence of gradual modifications that culminated in a new paradigm for the built environment.

As late as 1699, households still kept remedies called "plague water" in their medicine chests, and until the turn of the century the London bills of mortality retained a column for reporting the number of deaths from plague, which continued to show reassuring zeros. By the end of the eighteenth century, people took for granted the idea that irreversible changes in the environment guaranteed the exclusion of pestilence. In London it was said that the physical renewal of the city had defeated the plague. At first, Londoners attributed their deliverance to the fire of 1666, which devastated the city but putatively burned out the plague. The urban mythology of London began to express the whole process of change as a cycle of Great Plague, Great Fire, and Great Renewal. Christopher Wren's 200-foot Doric column supporting the sculpture of a flame on top is named simply "the Monument"—as if London considered no other civic memorials important enough to call "monuments."

I believe the Monument commemorates, not the fire alone, but the victory over plague and the spirit of renewal as well. The Monument stands for London's transition from a sick place to a good place. The inscription on the Monument proclaims: "London rises again, whether with greater speed or greater magnificence is doubtful, three short years complete that which was considered the work of an age." The claim mythologizes the experience of renewal, for the actual rebuilding did stretch out as the work of an age, and for two decades ruins were prominent all over the city, with wild flowers growing profusely around the charred debris.[44] As Bell observed, "an amiable conspiracy" promoted the notion of miraculous renewal executed by supermen.

The myth of liberation by fire resists infection by evidence. Within the city, the rats undoubtedly did not wait to be incinerated in the burning houses. Even if they had perished in the fire, more rats from neighboring towns and villages would have taken their place.[45] Moreover, the fire destroyed the old city within the walls but spared the area where pestilence had raged at its worst—namely, the parishes outside the boundaries and the region known as the liberties. Nevertheless, according to local belief, the flame seared the ground deeply, sterilizing the poison in the soil. The antiquarian author, James Peller Malcolm, whose four-volume *Londinium Redivivum* celebrated the renewal, went so far as to claim that "London was burnt by Government to annihilate the Plague, which was grafted in every crevice of the hateful old houses consumed in the Fire."[46] Despite its absurdity, this delusion contains a germ of modern policy: the principle that the government might wreck the city in order to heal it.

Final departure of plague lifted the spirit of England. Writers liked to think of the event as a great turn of history, interpreting it not only as an act of Providence, but also as a human victory over death. Soon after the Great Fire, Londoners celebrated their civic triumph, saying that London had risen from the ashes as a new city. A congratulatory letter to Sir Christopher Wren, the principal architect in the reconstruction program, claimed that Londoners had erected "not only the finest but the most healthy City in the World."[47]

Fifteen years after the Great Fire, Thomas Delaune wrote, "No city in the whole world could go beyond it for beauty and magnificence . . . so that now London, for fair and stately Edifices, uniform and Regular buildings, and other publick Structures, does not only excel its former State, but (all things considered) may outvie the most Magnificent Cities of the Universe." The Great Fire had purged the city, Delaune suggested, and the citizens may have been enriched rather than impoverished by the conflagration. "Buildings are become infinitely more Beautiful, more Commodious, and more Solid . . . and whereas before they dwelt in low, dark wooden Houses, they now live in lofty, lightsome, uniform, and very stately Brick-buildings."[48]

In 1801 the learned physician, William Heberden, observed that the Great Fire, "which was at first looked upon as a scourge from Heaven, has since proved indeed a most gracious blessing. . . . Our long exemption from the plague, is not so much to be attributed to any accidental absence of its . . . causes, as to our own change of manners, our love of cleanliness, and ventilation, which have produced among us, I do not say an incapability, but a great unaptness, any longer to receive it."[49] In 1819 Heberden's observation was echoed in Parliament, where doubt was expressed that the disease could ever again return to Britain.

The fabric of London changed by parliamentary statute and by royal proclamation soon after the fire. By the stroke of a pen, it was said, Charles II transformed London from timber and mud to stone and brick—as Augustus, the first of the emperors, found Rome in brick and left it a city of marble. While the London Rebuilding Acts permitted either stone or brick as the only materials for building elevations, stone was scarce and expensive to haul, whereas large areas of inexpensive brick earth surrounded the city. Consequently, brickwork dominated the new construction, with stone reserved for civic buildings, churches, and the cathedral.[50]

The Rebuilding Acts for the first time set out regulations and uniform standards. The process of renewal gave birth to town architecture and initiated the history of street improvements. Until after the Great Fire, the London archives do not mention a single street improvement.[51] The program also established a drainage system, a better water supply, a policy of street maintenance, and a central sanitary authority. According to Heberden, the end of pestilence and the recovery from the Great Fire initiated a spirit of improvement which never ceased to exert itself after that time.

The end of pestilence also changed the industrial capacity of towns. Plague had erupted in commercial centers, spreading from one center of population to another. Because the disease isolated places for months at a time, interrupting the flow of commerce, the era of pestilence was a time of self-sufficient villages and towns with limited economic specialization. The disappearance of plague ended the discontinuities of trade, making possible a new division of labor among towns and regions. A social historian observed, "It is difficult to believe that the modern territorial division of labor could have fully developed if subject to the serious interruptions of the plague. The disappearance of plague was both directly and indirectly one cause among many of the material advance in the 18th century."[52]

Material changes made it possible to segregate humans from rats. As the structure and fabric of houses changed, people began to express new attitudes toward vermin. The new idea of the house excluded undesirable organisms. In the old dwellings, house rats and their fleas had circulated freely from floor to ceiling without interruption. The experience of a good place in our time excludes the presence of vermin. All classes of the human population expect to live, outdoors as well as indoors, in a controlled environment limited to agreeable organisms. Although rats and fleas might still choose to live naturally indoors, they are socially excluded from human dwellings and from the external environment of houses. Chemical poisons, special materials, and physical barriers keep them away. When fleas appear—usually brought in by pets—people make strenuous efforts to destroy them and often express shame in admitting that they "have" fleas. Cat fleas and dog fleas remain common but unwanted. Other species, once common—such as human fleas—are now rare, and bird fleas of the sort the Viking mentioned above carried in his pouch may occasionally cause a commotion.[53]

A recent minor crisis between 1966 and 1972 in the west of Scotland illustrates this environmental structure and also shows how it is maintained. Around some housing estates less than five years old, fleas were attacking people out-of-doors and the usual efforts that worked successfully against indoor infestations failed to stop them. Reports were appearing in newspapers and something had to be done. In Great Britain, each local authority includes an environmental health staff, which responds to complaints about fleas. In routine cases, the staff members dust and spray infested households with insecticides that easily get rid of the fleas. When fleas attacked people outside their houses and ordinary measures failed to control the nuisance, the local authority turned to specialists in the Department of Agriculture for advice.

Investigators discovered that the offenders were not cat, dog, or human fleas, but a species of bird flea that was migrating out of sparrow and starling nests to gardens and footpaths where they attacked people, usually children. They observed that the new houses and gardens had not yet established the physical barriers that usually separate bird fleas from humans. In contrast, the older buildings in the neighborhood, which never reported any trouble with fleas, stood in the midst of a nesting population of the same kinds of birds. These old nests, however, were located in well-established gardens screened by thick hedges and dense vegetation. Identifying the source of the invading bird fleas solved the problem. The local staff removed the troublesome nests, sprayed the infested areas, and made the nesting sites birdproof.[54]

In the last three centuries, changes in the structure of human space have been not only material but intangible as well. The old idea of a house is virtually unthinkable today. As a result of these changes, plague has returned to its original position as a disease of wild places and the open country. In the ancient past, it was restricted to a few wildernesses in Africa, India, and the Middle East, but in the twentieth century, plague reservoirs have increased. Chronic plague is found among wild tarbagans or marmots in Manchuria as well as susliks in Russia. The North Vietnamese suffered an epidemic of bubonic plague during the war with the United States. (The American troops, vaccinated against plague, remained virtually free of the disease.) The Vietnamese used bandicoots to dig ventilation tunnels in their underground shelter system, and these rodents were infested with plague fleas.[55] Burrowing rodents also disseminate sylvatic plague in South Africa, South America, Mexico, Canada, and throughout the western part of the United States. In 1981, the *Los Angeles Times* startled the world with a headline announcing that rats infected with plague were found near the California ranch of the president of the United States. But even though sylvatic plague continues to spread, urban plague has not revived in the Occident. In the first half of the twentieth century, at least eight minor epidemics of human plague contracted from wild rodents erupted in the United States but failed to infect the cities. In England, sporadic cases appeared around ports—in Liverpool, Suffolk, and East Anglia.

In the high altitudes of Kurdistan, within the national boundary of Iran, the plague bacillus lives in the soil of wild gerbil burrows. The deep tunnels remain an entrenched natural focus of infection, a microclimate preserving the bacteria dormant in the soil until new animals invade the burrows. While some species of the wild gerbils die of the plague, others remain resistant. Fleas go from one species to another, and plague bacteria survive in the infective fleas that live on immune gerbils. Subsequent contact with susceptible animals causes a fresh epizootic. Plague bacteria can survive in wild-rodent fleas for more than a year, and infective fleas might stay in empty rat burrows for six months. Although the same burrows or colonies probably do not remain continually infected for long periods, once sylvatic plague invades an area, it stays. In 1936, two locations of infected ground-squirrel fleas in San Mateo

County, California, were identified as the same burrows discovered to contain diseased squirrels twenty years previously.[56]

Some biologists suspect that the plague organism survives in the soil of deep caves in northeastern California as well. In these lava caves produced by volcanic activity, two species of wild rodent, the bushy-tailed wood rat and the deer mouse, live close together. Every few years great numbers of the wood rat die off in a plague epizootic, but the deer mice living in the same caves seem to resist the plague, remaining abundant without signs of increased mortality—even when their fleas are infected with plague bacteria.

The deer mouse likes to move into the abandoned den of the less fortunate wood rat, which rarely builds a new den, preferring to reha-bilitate an established site. The same dens are continually rebuilt over centuries by countless generations of wood rats. Deer mice carry infec-tive fleas into the dens. The lava caves, which are visited by tourists, may be a permanent enzootic focus of plague, with the deer mouse being the chronically infected, relatively immune, reservoir host. Plague circulates between the deer mouse and the wood rat, with the stable environment of the lava caves enabling the infective fleas to survive indefinitely in abandoned nests.[57]

In permanent reservoirs, the disease fluctuates. Some animals die off dramatically, but the infection keeps going as a stable, chronic, subacute enzootic in other rodent populations with considerable resistance to it. Sylvatic plague persists through an equilibrium of biological forces that both nourish and limit the bacteria in populations of wild rodents.[58] At this time, about two hundred animal species are naturally infected, and about twenty or thirty species—including gerbils, moles, cavies, voles, marmots, squirrels, rabbits, wild rats, cats, and mice, as well as mon-gooses—constitute the basic hosts of infective bacteria and fleas, mak-ing their habitat a natural environment of plague. Sylvatic plague does not threaten human settlements until the infected fleas spread to a liaison animal, such as the domestic rat. Then it may turn into domestic plague and urban pestilence.

However, when environmental changes at the end of the seventeenth century disturbed the old continuities, breaking the link between rats and humans, it shifted the biological balance that once had favored urban pestilence. Even minor changes in the densities and species of rats and fleas caused major effects in the capacity for epizootic disease, disrupting the chain of pestilence. The apparently inexorable disease had depended on spatial continuities. The end of the seventeenth century is another era of topomorphic revolution. Cities grew in the new form of mutual immanence, and today the structure of urban places no longer supports the plague.

For every Space larger than a Globule
of Man's blood.
Is visionary . . .

William Blake, *Milton*

F O U R

Sacred Places

Ancient Greeks believed every place had its own *keres* infesting the ground and the air. In 1903, only a few years after the discovery that a specific bacillus caused plague, Jane Harrison sorted out the shifting meanings that clustered about the term *ker*, which she considered the most untranslatable of all Greek words. "Ghost, bacillus, disease, death-angel, death-fate, fate, bogey, magician have all gone to the making of it." The two primary ideas in the cluster, she decided, were bacillus and ghost.[1]

The *ker* was the soul of a disease—the emotional experience as well as the cause. In the golden age of long ago, Hesiod said, before the *keres* were released, life on earth was free from the heavy sicknesses that *keres* brought to men.[2] Greeks pictured them as winged spirits of death, disease, and corruption and associated them with death angels, the sphinxes. They represented a sphinx as a winged hybrid with the head and breast of a woman joined to the body of a lion. This monster carried off souls to the lower world.[3]

The mythographic tradition includes a lot of different stories explaining the origin of the most famous sphinx: the *ker* that haunted Thebes.[4] In the dramatic version, the Sphinx appears at a certain moment in the story of Oedipus, but in mythology she belongs to the ground of Thebes. She begins as an immemorial destructive presence haunting the boundaries of the city. Hesiod, in his poem describing how the universe generated the gods, calls her "the Phix," and her story begins with

Hesiod.[5] The name of Mt. Phikion, which means the place of the Phix, acknowledged the location of her presence. Today that geological projection—located about six kilometers west of Thebes and about two kilometers north of the road from Delphi to Thebes—is called Mt. Phagas.[6]

When Oedipus solved the Sphinx's riddle, the hybrid monster plunged from Mt. Phikion and disintegrated, but in the next generation, Thebes fell victim to another *ker*. Oedipus, the savior-solver, replaced her as riddle and curse of Thebes, for his unintended crimes set the *ker* of plague against the city.

Sophocles dramatized Thebes, the enemy of Athens, as a city torn by conflict and bloody factionalism. Oedipus saw the city he saved from the Sphinx transformed into a bad place filled with decay, ravaged by mysterious disease, a place where nothing would grow. Sophocles gave Oedipus the worst fate he could imagine, and for Thebes he imagined plague—the worst thing that could happen to a city. Plague would reduce it to a stinking, infected cacotope. Sophocles may have alluded to a real epidemic that devastated Athens during the Peloponnesian War, but he used an imaginary plague to characterize Thebes as a sick place. In contrast, in his last play, *Oedipus at Colonus*, Sophocles imagined Athens as a good place, an ideal city, famous for piety and hospitality to strangers. He described his birthplace, Colonus, a little community on the border of Athens, as a sacred place.

Sophocles represented the qualities of Colonus by dramatizing the effective presences of the place: the goddesses in the ground, the spirit of Poseidon, the nightingale singing under wine-dark ivy, Dionysus and the nymphs haunting berry-filled enclosures, narcissus and crocus recalling Demeter and Persephone, the immortal olive tree guarded by Zeus and Athena, the wandering river Cephissus—all making a place fit for the Muses and for golden Aphrodite. Feeling the natural beauty of the place, we cannot separate sensory experience from the mythic imagination. In the plays of Sophocles, the spirits of a place actively influence human affairs. Involved with one another, human characters and these subtle energies make up a structure of mutual immanence.

For the Greeks, the balance of hidden presences determined the nature of a place. A sick place was dominated by dreadful *keres*, a sacred place was haunted by good spirits. Sacred places inspired extreme states of topistic awareness. Seneca described the numinous energy of sacred groves that contained the presence of a deity. Mysterious places in caves

4-1. Mt. Phagas, Place of the Sphinx
(Photo by author)

and forests, he wrote, pierce your soul with some inkling of holy things. Ancient people responded to the feeling and meaning of rocks, trees, and contours of the ground. They used natural features of the landscape to cultivate the experience of an independent spiritual energy acting on human feelings. They would construct altars in those places to communicate by sacrificial ritual with the presences they experienced. Sometimes they erected buildings to locate the divinity; the purpose of an ancient temple was to invite him or her to settle exactly there—to provide a house in which the god might dwell.

In the Hebrew Bible, the first sacred places are locations where God manifests himself to the patriarchs. Abraham and Isaac build altars where the Lord appears to them—notably in sanctuaries of a sacred tree (for example, the terebinths or "oaks" of Moreh and Mamre). Beginning with Jacob, stone pillars—like the sacred trees—serve as monuments that mark the presence of God. Then, after the Exodus, Moses encounters God on a mountain in the wilderness. The wonder of the burning bush attracts him to a spot where the Lord warns, "Come no closer; take the shoes off your feet; the place where you are standing is holy ground." After the hierophany on Mt. Sinai, the presence of God stays with the

4-2. Oedipus and the Sphinx
(Courtesy, Museum of Fine Arts, Boston)

Israelites, occupying a mobile tabernacle that contains the ark of the covenant. David brings the ark into Jerusalem and plans a temple to house it. Solomon completes the temple and settles the ark in the innermost sanctuary, the holy of holies, where it remains until the destruction of the temple.

The Bible mentions several sacred places, and the Jews experienced mountains as special locations of supernatural power. Nevertheless, Jerusalem remains supreme—first as Mt. Zion, then as the city of David, finally as the location of the temple. Both Mt. Sinai and Mt. Zion are pivots in the biblical imagination—Sinai as the place where God revealed the law, Zion as the center of the messianic kingdom of God. When the second temple was destroyed, some men went to Jerusalem and worshiped God on the ruins. Sanctity clings to the site, and the remaining wall of the temple draws crowds of pilgrims. However, the rabbis debated if God had forsaken his people. Did the Shechinah—the spirit of God represented as the mystic quality of light—ascend to heaven with the flames of the burning temple? They decided that the presence of God accompanied the Jews into exile.[7] The physique of the temple perished, but according to Ezekiel, God himself became their sanctuary in the countries to which they had gone (Ezek. 11:17).

Another kind of sacred place is one that leads the mind somewhere else. Perceptions and sensations in religious environments are ambiguous. Technicians of the sacred—the builders of megaliths, temples, churches, cathedrals, and other sacred places—have creatively used the ambiguities of space to move the mind. Henry Adams said the dynamism in the cathedral of Chartres, constructed by "the highest energy ever known to man" had more power to move the mind than "all the steam-engines and dynamos ever dreamed."[8] Let us explore ambiguity. The original sense of the word "ambiguous" means something that leads in more than one direction. The highest form of ambiguous language we call "poetry." An ambiguous place or object leads the mind somewhere else.

A *topos* or place is the container of experience. Figure 4-3 shows a "microtope"—a little place. This cup seems to lack any ambiguity. Because it is boring to look at, we will say it has low energy. It is the location of morning coffee or afternoon tea. The cup leads nowhere. As we gaze at this unimpressive object, the mind stays in one place, except to wonder perhaps if the cup were found in the dime store or in a thrift shop.

4-3. The Hove Cup
(From Williams, *Book of Amber*)

However, when we learn that the cup is made of amber and was discovered in Brighton, England, in 1857, along with other remains in a Bronze Age grave that may be as old as 1500 B.C., the energy changes.[9] We marvel that the shape of the humble teacup claims such remote antiquity, but the fabric of the cup evokes even more wonder than the form. Amber, to prehistoric folk, was a sacred substance. It was valued as highly as gold. The Greeks called pieces of amber "tears of the Heliades," who were the daughters of the sun god, Helios, and the sisters of unfortunate Phaëthon. In Greek myth, Helios rose in the east every morning to drive his fiery steeds, who pulled the chariot of the sun across the sky to the western horizon. When his impetuous son, Phaëthon, begged to drive the chariot for a day, Helios reluctantly consented, but Phaëthon lost control and the fiery horses ran wild, setting the Earth on fire. To save Earth, Zeus hurled a thunderbolt at Phaëthon, who fell blazing like a comet into a river. The nymphs buried him, and his sisters wept over his grave day and night until they turned into trees, and the bark of those trees, Ovid tells us, "flowed tears which, hardened into amber by the sun, dropped from the new-made branches and were received by the shining river."[10]

The power of ambiguous things to lead the mind somewhere else belongs to the roots of humanity and is probably older than *Homo sapiens sapiens.* We know now that the predecessors of our subspecies (*Homo sapiens neanderthalis*) buried the dead with flowers and that they painted bodies and things with red pigment—perhaps with some religious meaning. Long before modern humans of our subspecies—the so-called Cro-Magnons—appeared in Europe, Neanderthals were making and using symbols and images. A little piece of mammoth bone was carved into an oval shape by a Neanderthal about 45,000 B.C.—ten thousand years before the first sign of Cro-Magnon people. This little bone plaque, discovered in Hungary, was carefully carved, beveled, and painted with red ocher. When Alexander Marshack examined it under a microscope he was startled to find that the plaque was never used as a tool, for the edges were polished smooth by countless generations of handling, and all marks of scraping or carving—the signs of a tool—were absent. It was a symbolic object, probably made for ritual, and kept in use for a long time.[11]

The Greek word for amber is *electron,* the source of our word "electricity." Rubbing amber gives it a static electric charge strong enough to attract bits of feather and hair. But we have noticed that amber has another kind of energy as well—the power to lead the mind.

One has to marvel that some sacred places never lose energy. People still go to Stonehenge and to the Acropolis long after the religions that built them have disappeared. The mysterious energy of sacred places attracts pilgrims as surely as rubbed amber attracts particles. Century after century, people just go, drawn by the place and impelled there from within themselves.

On midsummer's eve in July 1976, accompanied by my wife and two of our children, I camped in the field next to Stonehenge. We watched the Druids getting ready to perform their annual ceremony. (Somewhere I have a photograph showing a sign the police put up that reads, "Druids only past this point.") We did not see much of the Druids, but the real action was happening in the improvised village where we camped. Five thousand people turned out for the occasion to watch the ceremonies, to feel the energy of Stonehenge, and to carry on rituals of their own. We wonder about the force that attracts all those people to Stonehenge, and the Department of the Environment must wonder as well. Figure 4-8

4-4. Propylaea, Gate of the Acropolis
(Photo by author)

shows a crew from the DOE with camera and tape recorder, eavesdropping on the pilgrims.

In perennially sacred places—the sanctuary of Delphi in Greece, the base of Ayre's Rock in Australia, the Acropolis, Chartres, the top of Glastonbury Tor as well as Stonehenge in England—certain forces in the invisible world of spirit establish a location in the physical world of the senses. The religious program of a sacred place engages or disengages the senses, edifies the mind, and leads the soul back to the world of spirit. A sacred place manifests a spiritual vision—the medieval cathedral, for example, is a Gothic manifesto. Any sacred place is a specific environment of phenomena that are expected to support the imagination, nourish religious experience, and convey religious truth. It organizes sight and sound, introduces light to present clarity and order, or makes things dark to suggest unseen presences and hidden power.

Mosques as well as churches have surfaces that dematerialize the walls or use other techniques to draw the believer into a meditative mood or even an altered state of consciousness. The hypnotic quality of glittering mosaics on Byzantine walls, the dialectic of light and shadow in Roman-

4-5. Parthenon
(Photo by author)

esque churches, the mystic luminosity and magic colors of great windows in Gothic buildings are all variations on a single topistic intention—to inspire an ecstasy of place change. This impulse leads the soul toward heaven, but it also changes the place, turning the building into a mystic interior that represents the heavenly Jerusalem. As Otto von Simson writes: "The church is, mystically and liturgically, an image of heaven. . . . [T]he mystical experience that murals or mosaics are to help invoke within the faithful is emphatically not of this world; the celestial vision depicted is to make us forget that we find ourselves in a building of stone and mortar, since inwardly we have entered the heavenly sanctuary."[12]

To examine two extremes, compare a Gothic cathedral with a Quaker meetinghouse. The Gothic church builds a feeling of exaltation and fascinates the eye, leading the soul to a place somewhere between heaven and earth. The meetinghouse rejects sensory excitement as carnal distraction, because the worshiper cultivates a different spiritual technique of withdrawing from the physical world, leading the mind to

4-6. Pilgrims at Stonehenge
(Photo by author)

the interior of the self to watch for the inner light and to hear the still, small voice.

We take for granted ritual and doctrine as theological subjects, but we tend to overlook the theology of building, settling, and dwelling. As expressions of religious experience, sacred places are as important as doctrine and ritual. They energize and shape religious meaning. They help to make religious experience intelligible. A sacred place is not only an environment of sensory phenomena, but a moral environment as well. The moral critique of architecture and planning divided Christendom as soon as Constantine made it possible to build churches without persecution, and it still divides religious communities today.

After a long struggle over the morality of building, the Cathedral Church of St. John the Divine in New York began an eighteen-year program in 1979 to complete the towers of the largest Gothic structure in the world. A persuasive group of churchpeople had argued that diocesan funds should instead be committed to the financial needs of the social ministry. A heated debate ensued as the Episcopal Diocese of New York considered if such a large sum—estimated then at $20 million—should be devoted to brick and mortar. The diocese resolved the

4-7. Improvised Village
(Photo by author)

dispute by declaring that the construction program would both glorify the church building and also make jobs for local unemployed workers.[13]

Earlier in 1979, parishioners of Holy Trinity Church, a fashionable Roman Catholic church in Washington, D.C., complained that one of their members was tormenting the congregation and disturbing the pastor. Mitch Snyder was protesting their church repair and restoration program by claiming that he would fast unto death unless Holy Trinity did more for the poor. Eleven men and women joined him in the fast, and several other parishioners organized a support fast. After one mass, a man shouted from the back of the church, "Mitch Snyder is dying. The poor of Washington are dying."[14]

Five years later, I still wanted to know how the conflict had turned out, so I phoned Washington and tried to reach Mitch Snyder. I was told that he had ended his fast five years ago but was not available to speak on the phone because he was presently engaged on another fast—still protesting the plight of the homeless in Washington. I also learned that he expected to be arrested in a demonstration at the White House. Let us go to the historical and theological roots of this moral question, because it is important to acknowledge that a sacred place, understood holisti-

4-8. Eavesdropping on the Pilgrims
(Photo by author)

cally, is a moral environment as well as a location of sensory and aesthetic experience.

The early Christians had to dwell among pagans in a world ruled by the Devil, but they expected it to come to an end soon. They were sojourners and not settlers. Places of worship were simple houses intended to avoid attracting attention and to escape persecution. After Constantine, churches coexisted with temples. After Theodosius, temples were closed to worship. The way of dwelling for Christians changed from sojourning to settling and to establishing Christendom in a pagan environment. The fourth century, therefore, was a time of revolution. In the year 300, pagan temples dominated and Christian churches were under attack. In 399, Christian churches were flourishing and temples were being demolished.

Constantine not only made it possible for Christians to worship

openly but also carried out a policy of church construction. The program encouraged grand designs, but from the beginning an architectural
scruple urged that material splendor should be interpreted in a special
way. In the earliest known description of a Christian church, Eusebius—
a contemporary of Athanasius and the father of ecclesiastical history—
praised the magnificent new cathedral in the old Phoenician city of Tyre
"as a marvel of beauty, utterly breathtaking, especially to those who have
eyes only for the appearance of material things. But all marvels pale
before the archetypes, the metaphysical prototypes and heavenly patterns of material things—I mean the re-establishment of the divine
spiritual edifice in our souls."[15] The particular beauty of the church
evoked the beauty of heaven. Two centuries later in Constantinople, at
the consecration of Hagia Sophia—the greatest masterpiece of Byzantine
architecture—the Emperor Justinian's court poet exclaimed that it
seemed as if the mighty arches were set in heaven.[16] The same idea
pervaded the history of church architecture, culminating in the Gothic
cathedral, often described in the Middle Ages as an image of heavenly
Jerusalem. In the twelfth century, a great time of renewal, princes,
bishops, nobles, and the rising bourgeoisie all burned with a passion
that Peter the Chanter named *libido edificandi*—the mania to construct
buildings. As W. R. Lethaby put it, the movement was an outburst of
fervor wrought in stone. This movement has been called the crusade of
cathedrals, and throughout western Europe the zeal continued for three
centuries, during which time eighty cathedrals, five hundred large
churches, and thousands of parish churches were erected.[17]

Each wave of construction inspired a moral critique challenging the
expenditure of funds on splendid buildings. In the fourth century,
desert hermits in Egypt, reacting against the building fever, called Archbishop Theophilus a "lithomaniac" and named him the Pharaoh of
Alexandria. In the twelfth century Peter the Chanter, a canon of Notre
Dame cathedral in Paris, spoke against the evil of high-rise buildings.
Constructing magnificent churches, he said, robbed the poor of resources that Christ had intended for them.

One might think that after Constantine, a Christian administration
would have helped Christians feel at home in the world. On the contrary, some were repelled by the institutions of Christendom and fled
from its compromises to seek purity in the deserted places. Athanasius
wrote, "The desert was built into a city by monks who left their own
people to enroll in the citizenship of Heaven."[18] Palladius, the Herodo-

tus of the hermits who gathered the *logoi* of the desert, told a story about John of Lycopolis, who had the gift of prophecy and whose reputation among the Egyptian monks was second only to Anthony. Before he left the world to live in the desert, John had built houses, having learned the building trade as a boy. Then, when he settled in the wilderness, he build three *tholoi*—primitive, beehive-shaped, mud huts—on the top of a mountain. The Greek text says he made three *tholoi* and, running inside, rebuilt himself.[19] In this particular case, as John walled himself up and lived as an enclosed anchorite, he was also building himself up spiritually. However, the language of Palladius suggests much more. As we rebuild the world, we rebuild ourselves.

Ironically, the refuges of the hermits became a second Holy Land, monuments of the religious imagination, sacred places of a new type; they attracted pilgrims who came to venerate living saints, to gaze at their shriveled bodies, and to be edified by them. The customary pilgrimage included the holy places in Palestine, which were not far away, but the Egyptian desert came first in the affections of the pilgrims. In the days of St. Jerome, nearly fifty thousand monks were sometimes assembled at the Easter festivals, and the Egyptian city of Oxyrhynchus devoted itself almost exclusively to the ascetic life, with twenty thousand female anchorites and cenobites as well as ten thousand monks. Toward the end of the fourth century, it was said that the monastic population in a large part of Egypt was nearly equal to the population of the cities.[20]

The ascetic principle of building and dwelling found its most eloquent champion in a former hermit, the saintly John Chrysostom, the patriarch of Constantinople. John had grown up in Antioch, abandoning a classical education to pursue the ascetic life. He lived as a hermit for six years until mortification destroyed his health and the desperate condition of his "cobweb body" forced a return to the city, where he soon entered the priesthood. He remained committed to ascetic principles, reiterated in the vast literary output that distinguishes St. John Chrysostom as the most prolific of the Greek Fathers. As the archbishop of Constantinople after 398 he attacked luxury and urged the rich to give alms. He sold the expensive furniture and treasure of the archbishop's palace and gave the proceeds to hospitals and to the poor. While still a priest in Antioch, a decade before he became patriarch of Constantinople, John had preached: "Let us . . . adorn not our houses, but our souls in preference to the house. For is it not disgraceful to clothe our walls with marble, vainly and to no end, and to neglect Christ going

about naked? . . . Do you wish to build large and splendid houses? I
forbid it not; but let it be not upon the earth. Build thyself tabernacles in
heaven, and such that thou mayest be able to receive others; tabernacles
which never fall to pieces."[21]

The cities of Antioch, Constantinople, and Alexandria took pride in
exalted places, locating religious experience by building upwards.[22] The
sacred places of the desert rejected the imposing forms of temples and
churches to settle lowly places. By regression to prehistoric dwellings—
caves and huts—the hermits located their heavenly city in the earth,
building downwards to rebuild themselves. When an anchorite made a
long journey to consult the abbot Pastor about heavenly things, he
refused to speak, explaining that he belonged to the earth. He could talk
about passions of the soul, he said, but claimed ignorance of lofty
spiritual matters.[23] The historical consequences of early monasticism
are well known, but the topistic dimension invites further exploration.
Once again, a religious movement devoted to the therapy of souls
inspired mystics pursuing salvation to find personal regeneration in a
topistic regression.

Almost a millennium before, the Greek world had experienced a
similar regression. The Greeks had settled their Olympian gods in temples, erected as dwellings for lucid, strong, willful, distinctive, immortal
personalities sculpted in comprehensible forms. In return for *therapeia*
or "tending" the civic gods (meaning worship), citizens expected the
divine persons to tend the community and its individual worshipers,
looking after vital matters such as safety, power, health, prosperity, and
every kind of material welfare. The temples, however, were not places for
the therapy of souls. The Greeks brought another set of religious concerns, including the yearning for salvation, into the places of the mysteries, where purified initiates known as *mystai* danced in labyrinths toward
presences in the dark. The *mystai* experienced topistically the journey of
the soul from state to state in their progress through caves and grottos of
the earth, passing from darkness to moments of illumination when
sacred objects appeared and were finally revealed to the senses.

The mysteries dramatized the therapy of souls in the rituals of a
prehistoric religious revival, expressed in forms derived from Crete and
Asia Minor. They also descended away from the temples on the landscape, in an historical regression, to cavities in the earth. This return in
ritual to prehistoric places suggests that the *mystai* experienced spiritual
advance through a topistic regression.

Today we call ourselves human, and we use the scientific term *Homo sapiens* to distinguish us from the other hominids that resemble us biologically. Originally, the root of *homo* was not restricted to the male gender. Both the English word "human" and the Latin word *homo* grew from the Indo-European root **ghomon* or **(dh)ghom-on-*, which means "earthling." This root issues from **dhghem-*, the Indo-European word for "earth." The earliest wisdom of our language, then, defines us as creatures of the earth.

Twenty-five thousand years before the first traces of our language, humans venerated the beasts, worshiped the Earth goddess, established sacred places in limestone caverns, and expressed their religious yearnings in pictures they scratched, painted, or modeled on the walls of caves. This tradition of imagery reaches back more than thirty thousand years—as far back as the first signs of *Homo sapiens sapiens*. Abbé Breuil, our most distinguished recorder and interpreter of cave paintings, studied prehistoric art for over fifty years, documenting more than ninety sites in France and Spain. The pictures in these caves represent beasts, humans, and monsters dwelling together, influencing one another.[24]

The pictures of beasts range from simple childlike scrawls to works of genius by artists as gifted as Michelangelo. Humans are generally masked or disguised by nonhuman features, and they look unimpressive, but the beasts are shown in the prime of their physical development. The conventional stooped posture, humility, awe, and masked face all suggest that men and women are captured in ritual moments and pictured in masked dances of communion with sacred beasts. In all of prehistoric art, no human face or figure is ever represented with the bold naturalism and consummate beauty of the bison, aurochs, and horses on the walls and ceilings of Altamira and Lascaux.

In these great caverns—the equivalents of prehistoric cathedrals— artists glorified the beasts they hunted, filling the sanctuaries with the presence of bison, deer, horses, and wild cattle. The consecration of a given spot must have augmented the sanctity of the animal image. The spirits dwelt in these places, deep in the body of the Earth Mother. Their sacred places remained inaccessible to uninitiated wanderers. Learning the way was a ritual in itself, and religious zeal probably overcame the fear of hazards. The initiates groped through twisting, slippery corridors, clinging to stalactites, descending into chasms, passing around waterfalls, climbing rock chimneys into dark chambers. Labyrinths of narrow passages above dangerous rock faces led into secret places forbidden to the profane.[25]

The oldest religious symbol we know is the labyrinth, sometimes

4-9. Bison of Altamira
(Hacker Art Books)

represented on the walls as the meander. The labyrinth meant conditional entry. Unless one knew the way, he or she would never reach the sacred center. Only the initiates might dare to try. This is a concept radically different from the design of a church, with its nave leading straight to the altar and pillars on both sides keeping the worshiper on the path.

We might think of several obvious reasons why prehistoric worshipers went to such trouble to penetrate the depths of the earth. They probably wanted to feel the grounded energies there (dowsers can tell us more about that).[26] Moreover, they probably wanted to enter the womb of the Earth goddess. But I suspect they had another reason, one that children can reveal if they are confident you will not laugh. If you ask children how they feel about going into a deep, dark cave they will probably admit that they would wonder about monsters. I suggest that our remote ancestors went into the sacred caves to think about monsters.

We still see monsters—in dreams, in fantasies, and in the cinema. In ordinary usage today, the word "monster" means something scary, huge, or grotesque. Those of us who are musicians reserve the term as a compliment for a very good player. Technically, in biology, it refers to a

4-10. Prehistoric Meanders
(National Gallery of Art. Pantheon Books. Giedion, *Eternal Present*)

grossly abnormal fetus. Comparative embryology includes a science of monsters known as teratology—derived from *teras*, a Greek word equivalent to the Latin *monstrum*. The words have different roots, but both of them mean an omen or portent—a supernatural message. In ancient and prehistoric times a monster was taken for a supernatural intervention. Seen in the wilderness or in a dream, or born to a woman, it would be interpreted as a prodigy—that is, a marvel with a message, a prophetic sign. People sought meaning in monsters.

The communal experience of abnormal births nourished the imagination of monsters. Today we are more comfortable without the presence of biological anomalies in everyday life. In earlier times, however, abnormal fetuses delivered by women as well as by animals interested the entire community. They were not rushed out of sight and restricted to the observation of medical specialists. They were a source of wonder, a topic of conversation, and a cause for alarm. Babylonian divination included a series of tablets devoted to the meaning of abnormal births, animal as well as human. These tablets listed creatures with more than one head and all sorts of other abnormalities, including eighty-nine variations on the theme, "If an ewe give birth to a lion. . . ." Undoubtedly this series recorded fantasies stimulated by the way some anomalies looked. The purpose of the tablets was to determine what the gods meant to communicate by the presence of monsters.[27]

In 1523 Luther and Melanchthon published an illustrated pamphlet on the "Monk-calf of Freiburg," interpreting the birth of a monstrous calf as an omen. This little tract may be found in volume 11 of the Weimar edition of Luther's *Werke*, and as far as I can tell, it has never been translated into English. For the most part, it is a polemic against both monasticism and the papacy. Luther said that the monstrous calf looked like a preaching monk in a cowl, and the birth of this grotesque caricature ridiculed monks and what they stood for. With this omen, God was announcing a disaster and great change in the future of Germany. All signs indicated that the world was at a turning point. God created the monk-calf to demonstrate that he had special intentions for the clergy, whose carnal doctrines had turned the Christian faith into veal. When God clothed a calf in a holy cowl, he indicated that it would soon be obvious to the world that the whole idea of monks and nuns living in monasteries and nunneries was false. They were only appearing to live holy lives. In the same vein, Luther invented another monster, the

4-11. Monk-calf of Freiburg
(From Luther, *Werke*)

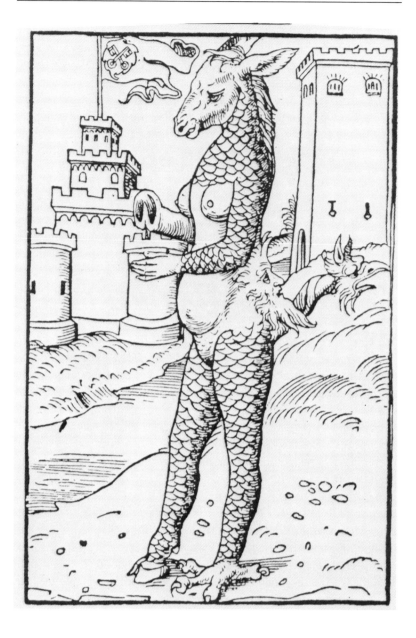

4-12. Popedonkey
(From Luther, *Werke*)

"Popedonkey," which ridiculed the pontificate. Melanchthon rendered a fascinating image of the Popedonkey (fig. 4-12).[28]

Inhuman monsters belong to the roots of humanity. Paleolithic monsters in the caves were represented as hybrids, mixing the shapes of different creatures—men and women as well as beasts. Hybrid monsters evolved and flourished, passing through paleolithic and neolithic eras to thrive in the early civilizations, occupying the imaginations of the Babylonians, Egyptians, and Greeks. The long line of monsters and demonic beings in Mesopotamia are mythic creatures of a bad place. They express the chronic anxiety and feeling of helplessness that come from living in a dangerous environment.[29]

Monsters change their nature as they change their place. In the Old Stone Age, some monsters did inspire fear and feelings of aversion, but most scenes of hybrids represented beasts and humans participating cheerfully in one another's natures. The Greeks taught us to exterminate monsters, but the prehistoric images in the caves do not, for the most part, represent monsters as the enemies of humans. They dwell comfortably with the masked humans who dance in the midst of beasts. These images reveal the primary feeling that rules prehistoric religious experience—an intense desire to participate in the life of beasts. The pictures in the caverns give us more clues to the religious motivations of prehistoric people than anything else that has come down to us.

The cave at Les Trois Frères pictures a reindeer with web feet as well as a bear with the head of a wolf and another with the tail of a bison. Le Mas D'Agil encloses a horse with the head of a duck. But the most spectacular composite beast—I am tempted to say, a creature assembled by a committee—is the "Chimera" of Lascaux. Some people name it "Unicorn," despite its two horns. It has the massive body of a rhinoceros or some bovine creature, with circles painted on its flanks, thick legs, absurdly small neck and ears, the head of a big feline, and two straight horns ending in tufts. At Les Trois Frères, in the sanctuary teeming with superimposed figures of bison, horses, ibex, and reindeer, a semihuman figure dances in the midst of the animals. He seems to be herding the beasts and playing a musical bow. He wears the head and fur of a bison with human legs showing below the edge of the pelt. About twelve feet off the floor, presiding over the beasts in the sanctuary, dances "The Sorcerer," one of the most remarkable figures in prehistoric art—a man fully dressed as an animal. Human limbs may be discerned beneath the pelt, and the head of a stag is held at a human angle, staring at us with an

4-13. Chimera of Lascaux
(Jean Vertut)

alert, intelligent expression that one never sees in representations of beasts. He is probably a shaman—a traditional sorcerer, healer, and religious leader who takes responsibility for the health and welfare of the community and is intimate with the spirits of beasts. Shamans were and still are mediators between visible and invisible powers.

Another shamanic figure, the bird-headed man, presents the "famous riddle" of Lascaux. He is placed between an angry, disemboweled bison and a rhinoceros that is trotting away. A bird fixed on top of a pole has just slipped out of the figure's grasp. The bird perched on a stick is a familiar symbol in shamanic circles. Birds are psychopomps, conductors of souls, and shamans change themselves into birds, flying to the other world to bring back "soul birds." Turning into a bird, or traveling accompanied by a bird, indicates the power of a living shaman to make ecstatic journeys to the sky and beyond. In several different cultures, the bird on a stick remains a powerful symbol of shamanic power.[30]

Shamans worked not only through power animals but also through spirit guides which they sought in trance journeys through the lower

4-14. Dancing Hybrid and Beasts
(Hacker Art Books)

world. Sometimes their guides appeared as strange forms—not stable characters from the animal kingdom. Ecstatic visions of these spirits, described by shamans, may be the original source of prehistoric monsters. The bird-headed man is a hybrid, representing two natures and binding some quality of a bird to his human nature. Therefore, he is a symbol—in Whitehead's sense—putting together in one body two different shapes of experience.

Another dual being guards the entrance to El Juyo, a fourteen-thousand-year-old sanctuary located in northern Spain that was excavated for the first time in 1955. A large stone in the cave is deliberately shaped as a face—half human and half beast. The right side looks like an adult man with a mustache and beard. The left side resembles a large carnivorous beast with an oblique eye, long snout, and a protruding fang. Black spots on the muzzle suggest the whiskers of a great cat, probably a lion or leopard. It is a face divided into halves, each with a different nature.

According to the archaeologists who excavated El Juyo, the cavern was designed by ritual specialists to make a visual impact on spectators, but the design also worked out an elaborate symbolic structure in a

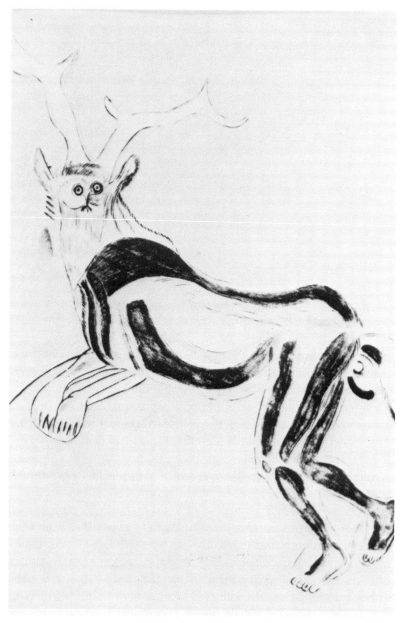

4-15. Prehistoric "Sorcerer"
(Hacker Art Books)

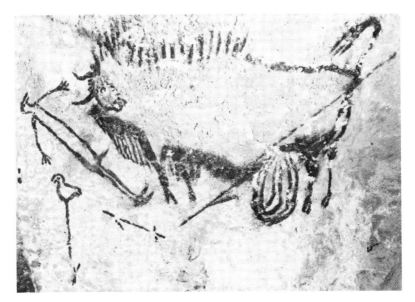

4-16. Bird-headed Shaman
(Photo Hans Hinz)

pattern of columns and rosettes that remains obscure. The hybrid stone face occupies a strategic position twenty feet from the cave entrance. It is easy to see the human side, but to observe the feline side it is necessary to move close and look at it from a certain angle with the aid of a lamp. The archaeologists suspect that the stone face has an "exoteric meaning accessible to all who entered the cave, and an occult esoteric significance known only to those who had been shown its mysteries." As a symbol, they think, the stone face may represent the dual nature of human personality, "its left side standing for the savage, unconscious, instinctive side of our nature, its right, our controlled, consciously 'human,' and social side. Then, the admirably harmonic fusion of these two natures in a single figure would be a graphic representation of their integration during the individuation process."[31]

Everything we learn about prehistoric people from their symbols, pictures, and their perception of space suggests a prevailing sense of interdependence among creatures, things, heavenly bodies, and cosmic forces—an inseparable oneness of the universe. Primeval humans yearned for contact with supernatural forces, and the invention of mon-

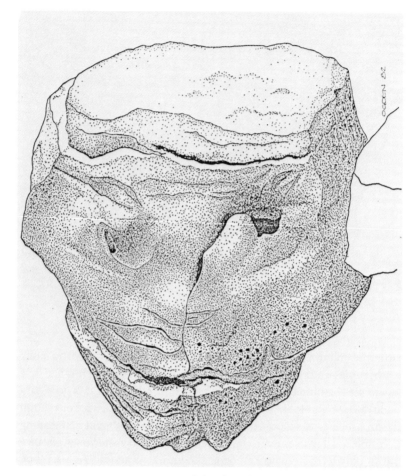

4-17. Dual-faced Sculpture
(L. G. Freeman)

sters might be a response to a desire for contact with imponderable powers. As Giedion puts it, monsters, "hybrids, composite creatures, arose in primeval times from man's longing to find a form that would make contact with those invisible powers with which his fate was intertwined."[32] Monsters, masks, and part-human hybrid creatures were symbolic forms representing the one most important process in prehistoric life. This process outrages the ideals of modern psychology because it moves in a direction opposite to the process we call individuation. Let us call it the process of reunion. The images tell us that the primary feeling of primeval life was a longing for union with the beasts.

Later civilizations represented the differences between men and beasts, but the paleolithic artists showed their connections, and they expressed an old human longing for intimacy with animal nature. Covering themselves with masks and pelts, shamans assumed hybrid characters. In the symbol of the hybrid, humans expressed their dual nature. To know yourself meant to know your animal nature. Where did you belong? You belonged with the beasts—the place of human longing. People lived in huts, which they undoubtedly defended against predators, but they did not *imagine* hearth and home as a separate place apart from the beasts. They imagined an unsegregated community of humans, beasts, and spirits, belonging together. Now we glorify our differences from the beasts and rarely acknowledge our connections with other creatures. Prehistoric people understood the differences but, in the pictures of monsters inhabiting their sacred places, affirmed the connection.

Today what can we learn from prehistory and from aboriginal people who seem to live in a prehistoric past? In our world, mechanization continues to dehumanize the conditions of living and evacuates the inner life. The vast reservoir of complacency that once encouraged the Victorians to disdain and us to patronize the paleolithic way of life has run empty. In the art and literature of the past few years there is a deep and abiding renewal of interest in humanity of the Ice Age and before. We may not be yearning to become like our prehistoric ancestors, but we may be asking the Old Stone Age to teach us how to become human.

People build or discover sacred places to experience hidden presences. In the feelings and meanings of a sacred space, and in the sacred places of all times, worshipers express a religious longing to recover a lost unity. Dynamists seek connections to invisible forces. Animists strive for relationships to spirits. And theists reach for God.

Surely a feeling can only be a source of energy
when it is itself the expression of a strong need.

Sigmund Freud,
Civilization and Its Discontents

F I V E

Ungrounded Self

About two decades before Plato settled into the garden of the Academy, another place-lover, the Athenian dramatist Sophocles, explored the energies of place in *Oedipus at Colonus*, the last play he wrote. His last drama celebrates the place of his birth, the little deme of Colonus, about a mile northwest of the Double Gate, and only a quarter of a mile from the location of Plato's garden. Until Sophocles wrote this play, Colonus was an unimpressive suburban community, a transportation depot where travelers went to get a horse or a mule to carry them to Eleusis or some other northern destination. Almost immediately the words of Sophocles made Colonus famous, transforming the little depot into one of the most meaningful places in the ancient world. The story of old Oedipus dying at Colonus remains one of the most profound myths expressing the meaning of place.

As the play opens, Oedipus asks his daughter: "Antigone, child of a blind old man, to what place have we come?" These initial words of *Oedipus at Colonus* became a frequently quoted line in antiquity—an eloquent way to ask "Where are we?" According to one amusing anecdote, a century after Sophocles died a Greek army in the field somewhere in Asia Minor, led by Demetrius, the son of Antigonus, lost its bearings and pitched camp. None of the men knew where they were. Some soldiers heckled the commanding officer by pinning a Sophoclean message on his tent. By substituting two letters, changing the name Antigone to Antigonus, they adapted the opening line of the play to read: "Child of the blind old man, Antigonus, to what place have we come?"[1]

Few people would recognize these words today, and hardly anyone remembers Colonus, which has now been absorbed, unacknowledged and rendered invisible, by the modern city of Athens. Yet almost everyone knows something about Oedipus, not because they still read Sophocles, but because Sigmund Freud discovered in the story of Oedipus a profound myth of the psyche and wrote a modern interpretation to represent the dynamics of unconscious conflict. He identified the hero as everyman and understood the earlier play, *Oedipus the King*, as a drama of self, expressing perennial truths about the human mind. The later play, *Oedipus at Colonus*, which did not interest Freud, is a drama of place. In *Oedipus the King*, the hero at great cost discovers his identity. In *Oedipus at Colonus*, he fulfills his identity by discovering his place.

Freud moved theory of the mind away from grounded experience and helped to build the couch as a vehicle abstracting patient from place. Despite his own existential recognition of the inner need that yearns for place, Freud's psychology never integrated personal identity with the sense of belonging, and the real power of places. In ancient tragedy Freud discovered a means to represent eternal human truths about intrapsychic forces. Oedipus lives in us, he claimed, and the tragedy reveals our own passions and unconscious drives. For Freud, the stages of the hero's self-discovery represented the gradual development of psychological insight.

The work of Sophocles, however, offers another meaning. Oedipus was the victim of drives, but the Athenians acknowledged these forces— working beyond consciousness—as gods. When a god drives, Antigone explained, who can escape? Yet after these forces drove Oedipus to the most terrible catastrophe an Athenian dramatist could imagine, they pulled him out of the wreckage, guided him to liberation, and settled his spirit in profound glory.

In these plays spatial references become charged with meaning. Space, place, direction, orientation, up, down, inside, outside, and so forth are magnified, illuminated, and energized. With relentless attention, the plays explore the principle categories of existential space— center, path, and boundary—evoking the power of these topistic realities. As John Gould observes, "Nowhere else in Greek tragedy does the primitively mysterious power of boundaries and thresholds, the 'extraterritoriality' of the sacred, make itself felt with the force and persuasion that Sophocles achieves in . . . *Oedipus at Colonus*."[2] Similarly, Sophocles makes us feel the power of "home" as the center of existence and the agony of its loss as well as the meaning of "the road," a dominant metaphor. The two dramas explore the expressive intelligibility of the obvious world. Taken together, *Oedipus the King* and *Oedipus at Colonus* go beyond psychological insight to grounded insight. They present the drama of place and the crisis of the placeless self. Together, they probe the riddle of alienation and explore the relation between self and its place.

In the fifth century, most people felt that mythic presences inhabited sacred places. The enlightened thinkers of the time challenged this common knowledge from a limited perspective that William Blake much later would call "single vision." Sophocles responded to this perspective dramatically—not only in the two Oedipus tragedies but also in his play *Philoctetes*. Throughout this latter play, the hero dramatizes a doctrine of primitive humanity made familiar by enlightened Athenians. As Peter Rose observes, the images associated with Philoctetes "all echo the anthropological speculations of the pre-Socratics and sophists about the circumstances of presocial human life."[3] At the end of the play, Philoctetes' perspective changes, reintegrating his experience of the environment with the world of gods and spirits. The island that served as his prison takes on a new meaning as he prepares to leave it. He refers to his cave as a house or a chamber. He calls out to the spirits of the place—springs, nymphs of fresh water, nymphs of the sea. His farewell to the island, Rose says, transforms "the formerly harsh, impersonal arena of that isolated struggle into a mythic, animate, and benign array of divine presences."[4] He establishes relations with the sacred presences, previously unperceived, that had dwelt with him in the place. In the rescue of Philoctetes, Sophocles is also rescuing the Athenian audience from single vision.

Only the Oedipus trilogy (*Oedipus the King, Antigone, Oedipus at Colonus*) and 4 other plays have survived from the more than 120 Sophocles wrote. In every one of the 7 complete dramas of Sophocles available to us, the tragic hero's predicament is expressed by his relation to place. In 5 of the 7 he is called "citiless" or a "man of no city." Oedipus, who has been called the greatest single individual in Greek tragedy, is primarily a man without a place.[5] Not until the final resolution at Colonus does Sophocles relocate Oedipus in the place where he belongs.

Philoctetes and Oedipus are placeless outcasts who arrive at topistic awareness. The final drama, *Oedipus at Colonus*, includes more than a eulogy of Colonus and Athens. It explores and reveals a way of perceiving and knowing that Sophocles feared was being lost in fifth-century Athens. On the intellectual battleground of the fifth century—a period that has been compared to the eighteenth-century Enlightenment—he defended archaic consciousness in a complex way. *Oedipus at Colonus* prepares for a mental revolution deeper than the sophistic movement and suggests a different kind of enlightenment—a profound integration of rational intellect and archaic mentality. Oedipus represents an intelligence that grows from head to foot. With subtle irony, Sophocles teaches a lesson about grounded intelligence. Rejecting the enlightened sovereignty of the eye and the head, his last play dramatizes the deeper wisdom of the ear and the feet.

Freud introduced the idea of the Oedipus complex in *The Interpretation of Dreams*, published in 1900, and thirty years later he claimed that this book contained the most valuable discoveries it was his good fortune to make.[6] According to Freud, Sophocles reworked dream material of immemorial antiquity into a play with explicit theological intention, dramatizing the vain efforts of men to avoid the will of the gods. The effect of the tragedy, however, comes not from the author's theological intention but from "the peculiar nature of the material," and the undying power of it depends on the "voice within us" recognizing ourselves in the dramatic action. "As the poet brings the guilt of Oedipus to light by his investigation, he forces us to become aware of our own inner selves, in which the same impulses are still extant, even though they are suppressed." According to Freud, the story is "nothing more or less than a wish-fulfillment—the fulfillment of the wish of our childhood," but we remain ignorant, like Oedipus, of the "desires that offend morality." Nature forces these desires upon us, "part of the permanent stock of the psychic impulses which arise in early childhood." The legends of antiquity merely confirm the universal drives of infantile mental life. The dream of sexual intercourse with one's mother and the death of one's father, he argued, was as common in the ancient world as it is today, and "the Oedipus fable is the reaction of fantasy to these two typical dreams." We become aware of our inner selves as the dramatic investigation brings to light the guilt of Oedipus, for his situation evokes our own repressed wishes. "The action of the play consists simply in the disclosure, approached step by step and artistically delayed (and comparable to the work of a psychoanalysis) that Oedipus himself is the murderer of Laius, and that he is the son of the murdered man and Jocasta."[7]

Despite Freud's explicit written views, however, which restrict the meaning of Oedipus to unconscious incestuous wishes, it is clear that the significance of Oedipus in his own life reached deeper and wider than sexual issues. Even in his last years, Freud continued to identify himself with Oedipus, and referred to his daughter as his "faithful Anna-Antigone."[8]

As we might expect, psychoanalytic biographers found the root of Freud's preoccupation with Oedipus in his early life—in the "unusual family constellation" that was "full of complications and paradoxes" and stimulated his curiosity about incest.[9] He was the oldest child of his father's second marriage, but he grew up with the two grandchildren of his father's first marriage—the son and daughter of his two older half-brothers—who were his own age. His young mother was the same age as his half-brothers and sisters-in-law. The unusual family situation, with Sigmund Freud being the same age as his own niece and nephew, resembled the anomalous condition of Oedipus, who was both the brother and the father of his own children.

Consciously, Freud never wavered from his entirely sexual interpretation of the Oedipus story. The Greek name *Oidipous* literally means "swollen foot," but Freud preferred to think of it as swollen penis, accepting a notion that the name simply means "erection" and that, originally, Oedipus may have been a prehistoric phallic demon.[10] Now that Freud's interpretation of the drama is commonplace, the sexual meaning is the manifest content of the work by Sophocles. Freud told Wilhelm Fliess that every member of the audience "was once a budding Oedipus" in fantasy, and that the impact of the play depends on the power of repressed infantile wishes.[11] That view underestimates the scope of the drama in human experience, and, as we shall see, even Freud's own identification with Oedipus is deeper and wider than he acknowledged.

The budding Freud lived his first three years in a place he loved all his life: the little town of Freiberg in Moravia, now part of Czechoslovakia. Then the family moved to Leipzig for a year before settling in Vienna, where Freud resided until the final year of his life, when he fled to London. In 1918, when the Austro-Hungarian Empire collapsed, the new Czechoslovakian Republic restored to Freiberg the ancient Czech name of Příbor—a fascinating place name with mysterious, ambiguous meanings. While it can mean "near the ruins," it also means "on the edge of the forest."[12] It is a good origin for the founder of psychoanalysis. Hilda Doolittle, an American poet who was analyzed by Freud, wrote that when she first decided to go to him in 1933, she felt that "the great forest of the unknown, the supernormal or supernatural, was all around and about us."[13] On the one hand, Freud always worked at the edge of mental wilderness, while, on the other hand, he discovered and clarified the ruins of experience.

In 1931, when Freud was seventy-five, the town of Příbor commemorated his life and work by unveiling a bronze tablet on the wall of the house in which he was born. He felt deeply honored and sent his daughter Anna to the ceremony where she read his letter to the Burgomaster, in which Freud called himself "the happy child of Freiberg . . . who received his first indelible impressions from this air, from this soil."[14] In the same decade, the Vienna city council proposed to rename the street on which Freud lived, changing it from Berggasse (which means "Hill Lane") to Sigmund Freudgasse. He called the proposal "nonsensical and not proper." For a number of reasons the idea was dropped.[15]

Freud lived, worked, and wrote in the same house at Berggasse 19 for forty-seven years.[16] Yet he never felt right in Vienna. Even though he lived in that city for seventy-eight years, he despised it. He wrote to Fliess that "Vienna is not the right place for us," for it was "extremely revolting" and living there felt depressing and miserable. He confided: "I hate Vienna with a positively personal hatred, and . . . I draw fresh strength whenever I remove my feet from the soil of the city which is my home."[17] Despite good reasons to leave—including the chronic local anti-Semitism, which he suffered long before the Nazi era—he endured Vienna until his last year. At the final moment, he was reluctant to go. Despite his conscious hatred of Vienna, Freud did not want to leave. But he fled the Nazis "to die in freedom." London welcomed him as Athens had sheltered Oedipus.

In Vienna he never belonged. The word "belong" has the same root as the verb "to long." We belong to the location of our longing—to the place that we yearn for. Freud identified himself with Freiberg, liked Berlin, loved Salzburg, and yearned for Mediterranean cities. At the age of sixty-six, he wrote to Sandor Ferenczi, "Strange secret yearnings rise in me—perhaps from my ancestral heritage—for the East and the Mediterranean and for a life of quite another kind: wishes from late childhood never to be fulfilled, which do not conform to reality as if to hint at a loosening of one's relationship to it. Instead of which—we shall meet on the soil of sober Berlin."[18]

Freud loved the ruins of Athens and declared that his visit to the Acropolis in 1903 surpassed anything he had ever seen or could imagine. The amber-colored columns there remained in his memory as the most beautiful sight of his life.[19] But an earlier experience, though less beautiful, held a deeper meaning. He identified the high point of his life as his first visit to Rome in 1901. Altogether he visited Rome seven times, and, according to Ernest Jones, Freud experienced exaltation and great happiness each time. "Its fascination never palled for a moment, and letter after letter speaks of it in the most glowing language." Jones surmises that because the experience held such vast importance, "It must therefore yield some secret of his inner life."[20]

Freud was also a keen student of ancient topography. During the years he both resisted and yearned for a visit to Rome, he read about the city, and in a letter of 1898 mentioned that he was occupying his spare time by studying the topography of Rome. About this time in his psychoanalytic work, he was turning from a mechanistic and hydraulic theoretical scheme to formulate a topographical theory of psychological forces.[21] In this new model, Freud understood the energies of the mind as an organization of layers and regions; he often used archaeological and topographic metaphors to represent the structure of the personality. I think Rome had such a profound impact on him because he felt the city as a metaphor of the psyche.

Sigmund Freud was a latent antiquarian, and he remained a lover of antiquities all his life. In his travels he collected relics of the ancient past, for the most part little statues that recalled the deepest roots of Western civilization—Egypt, Cyprus, Pompeii, Greece, and Rome. He toured ancient sites, could not stay away from museums, inspected old ruins, and gathered an impressive collection of ancient things. Sometimes he would display the latest purchase of a statuette or some other antique object on the dinner table at home, to serve as a companion through the meal or as a topic of conversation. Whenever he traveled, he usually returned with additions to the collection. During his visit to America in 1909 he showed no interest in the country, saying that all he wanted to see there was Niagara Falls. Refusing to read travel books before the trip, he studied a book on Cyprus instead and wanted to see the principal collection of Cyprian antiquities that was on exhibit in New York. In that city, the place that attracted him was the Metropolitan Museum, where he spent his time absorbed in the antiquities of Greece.[22]

Freud regarded his enthusiasm for collecting antiquities as an addiction that rivaled his tobacco habit. The objects he collected filled the two rooms of Freud's home in which he worked—the consulting room, which held the couch, and the study, which included his library. Edmund Engelman, who photographed Freud's household just before the family dismantled it and fled to London, reports his impressions:

> Antiquities filled every available spot in the [consulting] room. I was overwhelmed by the masses of figurines which overflowed every surface. To the left of the door was a large bookcase covered with tall ancient statuettes. In the corner, at the end of the wall facing these statuettes, was Freud's chair, almost hidden by the head of the couch. The couch itself was covered with an Oriental rug and pillows were piled high on it, so that it seemed a patient lying on it would almost have to sit up. The walls were covered with pictures, pieces of art, mementos, and awards. At the foot of the couch was a typical Viennese ceramic tile stove. The large double door in the adjacent wall led into Freud's study. To the left and right of the door were glass showcases filled with hundreds of antiquities. These were set up in several rows; every bit of cabinet space was filled. . . . Wherever one looked, there was a glimpse into the past. The view from Freud's chair, looking up at the elongated figures on the bookcase, was particularly dramatic.[23]

Rita Ransohoff adds that patients were always astounded by their first view of the consulting room: "It was not widely known that this room was virtually a museum of antiquities that came from Egypt, Greece, Rome, and the Near and Far East. Wherever one looked there was rich tactile evidence of Freud's ideas. The room immediately evoked a sense of the ages. The silent yet somehow eloquent figures of the past confronted the patient who came here to rediscover his own origins and buried history."[24]

Hilda Doolittle recalled, "He did not know—or did he?—that I looked at the things in his room before I looked at him; for I knew the things in his room were symbols of Eternity and contained him then, as Eternity contains him now. There were the immemorial Gods ranged in their semicircle on the Professor's table, that stood, as I have said, like the high altar in the Holy of Holies. There were those Gods, each the carved symbol of an idea or a deathless dream, that some people read: Goods."[25] When his patients departed and Freud returned to his writing, the gods were always there, "not unlike his patients, waiting to be understood."[26] One marvels that such a room—crowded with old gods, deathless dreams, images of the past, and "tactile evidence of Freud's ideas"—still allowed space for the fantasies of the patient.

Freud used the ancient objects didactically, to illustrate a point during analysis. In one famous case history, he wrote that after telling the patient about the psychological difference between the conscious and the unconscious, "I illustrated my remarks by pointing to the antiques standing about in my room. They were, in fact, I said only objects found in a tomb, and their burial had been their preservation."[27]

He instructed himself and his readers that way as well, and the references to archaeology were a permanent fixture of his thinking and writing, even after he moved away from a strictly topographic theory of the mind. He confided to Stefan Zweig, "I have read more archaeology than psychology." He worked as an emotional excavator, clearing away layers of psychic material and bringing to awareness buried memories, and he compared the mind to the Eternal City, where old ruins continue to exist along with the structures of later experience.

In Vienna, he would leave his house to take meditative walks, occasionally sharing archaeologically psychoanalytic thoughts with a colleague. Lou Andreas-Salomé recalled: "Indeed when we went out late at night for a walk (often the only time in the day he got out) we talked now and then on quite different matters and he frequently analyzed Vienna, as it were; the streets under their wintry snow reminded him of the city's remotest past. One sensed how easily such a re-creation of the past came to him and one was reminded of the antique objects in his study and that the archaeologist had created the psycho-analyst in him."[28]

Peter Gay suggests that Freud "lived far less in Vienna than in his own mind."[29] There is no doubt, however, that he both lived and belonged in the household on Berggasse—a location of comfort and well-being, filled with meaning conveyed by furniture, pictures, rugs, and statues. The collection of antiquities stayed confined to the two rooms, making all the rest of the large apartment dramatically different. All the other spaces, including the consulting room of Anna Freud, were comfortably but conventionally furnished, with none of the arresting imagery that energized Freud's work space. The household seemed to make a statement, offering the physical model for Freud's ideal of the mind—a comfortable bourgeois life proceeding quietly right next door to exciting images from the remote past.

Freud established the ground of psychoanalysis in two rooms that did not belong to Vienna, but to all the ages of humankind: a place full of new ideas, old ideas, excavated feelings, associations, case histories, cultural histories, collected images, dream symbols, revenants, gods, sacred objects, and the displaced ruins of archaic experience. The walls of the consulting room were covered with pictures, including photographs of archaeological sites such as abu Simbel in Egypt, the Sphinx, and the Roman Forum. At the foot of the couch—indeed, the foot—hung a small reproduction of a painting, *Oedipus Interrogating the Sphinx*. Peter Gay observes of the painting that it was, "of all artistic subjects the most pregnant anticipation of the psychoanalyst's organized inquisitiveness. On the narrow space of wall, archeology and psychoanalysis met and merged."[30]

The merger, however, shaped a consciousness remarkably oblivious to one dimension of archaeology—namely, the sense of place, an interest in the location and feelings about the energies of the site. In Freud's mind, the form of an excavated object—whether it was a building or a little statue—represented a symbol of personal experience or signified "the immortality of our emotions." He gave little thought to the ruin as a place. But the ancients did not imagine a god apart from the place in which he or she was experienced. Egyptian and Greek gods were represented as local manifestations of divine power. Sacred sculpture as well as architecture explored and praised the character of a god in a specific place. Temples and statues belonged together and carried a double meaning: on the one hand, the deity expressed in landscape and nature; on the other hand, the god as imagined by humans.[31] But in Freud's rooms, the displaced gods stood on his shelves as specimens of universal fantasy and as symbols of unlocated experience.

Freud is one of the giants of the twentieth century whose work has shaped the consciousness of our time. I am not diminishing his stature, or criticizing his contributions to psychology, or even quarreling with his philosophical speculations. It is possible, I believe, both to admire his work and to recover what he lost. Freud experienced topistic reality but failed to understand and therefore ignored it. Because of his influence, this specific ignorance helps us to forget the old language of places. Other schemes of psychology, because they identify reality with the experience of the individual ego, may be examined as well, but let us pursue the exact nature of Freud's topistic indifference and then retrace its direction.

Freud loved to travel, and the impressions he recorded in visits to great historical places reveal that he found them meaningful and exciting to the senses. Let us see what he wrote about them and what is missing from his thoughts about four great places: Ephesus, the Acropolis in Athens, London, and Rome.

As far as I can tell, Freud never traveled to Ephesus in the flesh, but in 1911 he visited the place in his imagination and wrote a little essay— one of the briefest things he ever published—which his physician and biographer, Max Schur, called "a daydream put to paper."[32] Freud was deeply involved in books on mythology at the time, reading extensively for his book *Totem and Taboo*. He came across a new work by a French writer on dead cities of Asia Minor, which contained a chapter on Ephesus. His reflections on this chapter stimulated the little essay, "Great Is Diana of the Ephesians," a title taken from a poem by Goethe, who of course found it in Acts 19:28—the story of the Apostle Paul in Ephesus.[33]

Ephesus, on the Turkish coast, was one of the great cities of antiquity, and its splendid temple of Artemis was one of the Seven Wonders of the ancient world. Freud noted that "with its concourse of priests, magicians, and pilgrims, and with its shops in which amulets, mementoes, and oblations were offered for sale, the commercial metropolis of Ephesus might be compared to a modern Lourdes." Several temples of the goddess were erected on the same site over the course of centuries, and the place attracted pilgrims from all over the world. Before the Greek invaders, the indigenous people there had worshiped a prehistoric mother goddess, and the Greeks absorbed features of her Asiatic cult in their Ephesian Artemis. Then the Christians erected a basilica in honor of the Blessed Virgin. "Now once again the city had its great goddess, and, apart from her name, there was little change." But although Freud observed the historical continuity of the mother goddess cult, he never asked the topistic question—the question of specific location. Why is it that exactly this place—Ephesus, or Lourdes, or Guadalupe—over countless centuries and through vicissitudes of religious form, retains its special qualities and its power to draw crowds? Why does the nature of the place remain the same despite major changes in doctrine and ritual?

What energies enable these sacred centers to survive religious revolutions and continue to attract "pilgrimages of the faithful?"

In 1904 Freud did actually visit an historic Greek sacred place—the Acropolis in Athens—and the experience moved him so strangely that he puzzled over it for three decades. In 1936 he tried to analyze the experience, saying that the phenomenon, "which I had never understood, has kept on recurring to my mind." He intended to find the mechanism at work and to trace the psychological forces operating behind the experience.

Traveling with his brother on a holiday trip, Freud experienced a feeling of alienation (*Entfremdungsgefühl*) on the Acropolis. At the moment it seemed to him that in one corner of his mind he had not believed that the Acropolis was a real place. He had the surprising thought: "So all this really *does* exist, just as we learnt at school." Freud traced the thought and the feeling of estrangement to his doubt as a schoolboy that he would actually see the Acropolis. Standing on the Acropolis in 1904, he shifted that feeling of doubt, changing it into a thought that as a schoolboy he had never believed in the reality of the Acropolis. "It is not true that in my schooldays I ever doubted the real existence of Athens. I only doubted whether I should ever see Athens." The cause of the displacement, he explained, was filial piety; there was guilt attached to the feeling of success, in having traveled such a long way, and in having gone further than his father.

In addition, I believe, Freud's idea of the Acropolis probably did not account for his actual perceptions and feelings and therefore gave a sense of unreality to the experience. He suggested, "the original factor must have been a sense of some feeling of the unbelievable and the unreal in the situation at the moment. The situation included myself, the Acropolis and my perception of it." He was prepared for Athens as a place in the mind, but he experienced the Acropolis as a place in the world. The actual feelings and perceptions, then, struck him as unreal and unbelievable. Nevertheless, he acknowledged that the phenomena of alienation "serve the purpose of defence; they aim at keeping something away from the ego, at disavowing it." In Freud's own words, "incredulity of this kind is obviously an attempt to repudiate a piece of reality." I believe that Freud was moved by the Acropolis in a way that he did not understand, and that his mind had no scheme to grasp the energies of the place.

In ancient times the Athenians would turn out seasonally for ceremo-
nial processions on the Acropolis, following a traditional route and
pausing along the way at meaningful sites to perform specific rituals.
These stops that punctuated the procession were memorial locations,
recalling to the mind of the citizens the mythology and history of the
city.[34] Joseph Rykwert shows that this experience of the ancient city as a
structure of symbols and memories enabled the citizen to integrate
himself in the urban environment, discharging his emotion in appropriate words and action. In this way, "the citizen, through a number of
bodily exercises, such as processions, seasonal festivals, sacrifices, identifies himself with his town, with its past and its founders."[35] Rykwert
notes, in a brilliant observation, that Freud considered residues of this
ancient urban pattern as a curable disease and associated them with
hysteria.

Hysterical symptoms, Freud said in his Clark University lecture of
1909, are residues of traumatic experience as well as mnemonic symbols. The monuments and memorials of cities, he observed, are also
mnemonic symbols. For example, in the streets of London, before a
large railway terminal, you will find a carved Gothic column—Charing
Cross. In the thirteenth century King Edward I followed the body of his
beloved Queen Eleanor as the funeral procession moved across England
to her burial site at Westminster, and at every place the coffin rested he
erected a Gothic cross. At another point in the city, near London Bridge,
you will find the tower known as the Monument. It was designed as a
memorial of the Great Fire of 1666. These monuments, Freud said,
being mnemonic symbols, resemble hysterical symptoms. Every hys-
teric and neurotic behaves like a Londoner who might pause in deep
melancholy before the memorial of Queen Eleanor's funeral, instead of
going about his business, or who might shed tears before the monument
that recalls the ashes of the metropolis, although it has long since risen
again in far greater brilliance. Hysterical patients suffer from reminiscences. "Not only do they remember painful experiences from the remote past, but they still cling to them emotionally." Close attention to
the city's monuments, then, suggests a sick citizenship.

Even though Freud responded emotionally to cities, his conceptual
scheme fails to grasp the ordinary realities of expressive space. Rykwert
observes, "It seems almost as if he were advocating an indifference to
one's environment." The fabric of the old pattern is gone, and what is left
of it merely gets in the way of "going about one's business in the hurry

modern working conditions demand," as Freud, the modern urban dweller, put it. According to Rykwert, "The city's monumental structure, in so far as it has an impact on its inhabitants, is seen as an analogue of a pathological condition: since the city should facilitate the circulation of goods and of persons in their pursuit of wealth, duty and ambition— and also personal gratification, Freud would certainly have wanted to add."[36] How then should healthy citizens experience Charing Cross? Should they tear down the Gothic column, forget Queen Eleanor, and get on with transportation? Similarly, should we tell the citizens of Colonus (that Athenian transportation depot) to forget all this mytho-logical rubbish of Oedipus and the Eumenides—and simply get a horse?

Finally, let us note how Freud uses the example of Rome (the most meaningful city in his own imagination) as a metaphor to illustrate the process of conservation in the mind. The first chapter of *Civilization and Its Discontents*, his most influential philosophical book, explores the origins of religion, which he associates with "oceanic feeling," the sense of being at one with the universe. This feeling survives in the mind as a relic of infantile dependence, he writes, and to show how it can exist along with mature experience, he compares the growth of the mind to "the history of the Eternal City," where all the "remains of ancient Rome are found woven into the fabric of a great metropolis which has arisen in the last few centuries since the Renaissance." Then, he suggests, "let us make the fantastic supposition that Rome were not a human dwelling-place, but a mental entity with just as long and varied a past history: that is, in which nothing once constructed has perished, and all the earlier stages of development had survived alongside the latest."[37] He lists a number of sites, naming buildings and the earlier structures they re-placed, imagining them all to exist simultaneously. He interrupts the fantasy because it leads to absurdities and because "the same space will not hold two contents," and concludes by showing the limitations of the metaphor. Visual representation cannot do justice to the peculiar char-acter of mental life.

Yet a city like Rome does hold in storage the entire contents of past experience—as the individual mind conserves its own experience in the unconscious. In Freud's metaphor, Rome is a physical reality—a set of buildings and streets. But a place is more than its physique, and the ruins of an historic city are the expressive spaces holding the experience of the past.

The men of the Renaissance discovered a new world of the mind at home as well as a new continent across the sea, but in Rome they also discovered a lost world in the ground. The fragments of antiquity stimulated the Renaissance, and the sight of Roman ruins in decay stirred the minds of scholars in the fourteenth and fifteenth centuries. The historian J. A. Symonds observed that "no small portion of the motive impulse that determined the Revival was derived from the admiration, curiosity, and awe excited by the very stones of ancient Rome."[38] The Columbus of the old world in the ground, Petrarch, first and greatest of the humanists, wandered through Rome with his friends, excited by historical memories. Unlike the hysterical patients of Freud, Petrarch and the generations of antiquaries who followed him thrived on reminiscences. One of Petrarch's letters describes their wanderings through Rome in 1337, feeling the energies of the ruins, and shows how every step brought them to something that "excited the tongue and the mind" (linguam atque animum excitaret). Like the rustic spot along the Ilissus described by Plato in the Phaedrus, Roman ruins evoked inspired utterance, and they led the soul.

Moreover, Renaissance antiquaries experienced the environment as a theater of ancestral drama, and each ruin marked the location of some legendary act. In his letter to Giovanni Colonna, Petrarch reminisced: here was Evander's palace, there the shrine of Carmentis, here the cave of Cacus, there the fig tree of Romulus, here the circus games and the rape of the Sabine women, there the swamp of the She-Goat and the spot where Romulus disappeared ... and here the temple of Jupiter, the place of all the triumphs. There Caesar triumphed, here he perished, and so forth. They would sit on the roof of the baths of Diocletian to rest, and they gazed on the prospect of memorials—all reminiscences of events out of legend or from the history of the city.[39] They knew Rome as the container of all its experience.

Almost a century later, Cyriacus of Ancona, another antiquarian explorer, searched Rome with the same excitement, going without sleep as he prowled the ruins and deciphered inscriptions on the memorials. "Mounted on a white palfrey loaned him by his cardinal patron, he scoured Rome and the Campagna, and the houses of his noble friends, for forty days, scratching, digging, sketching, copying, and ceaselessly longing" for new inscriptions to copy and translate.[40] When a dumbfounded priest wondered why he took so much trouble to rummage around like that, he replied, "I go to wake the dead." And the wakened dead had the power to reanimate the city. The antiquarian scholars knew that this vital contact with antiquity would create "a new intellectual atmosphere for Europe." About the same time as Cyriacus, Poggio Bracciolini pondered the memorials of ancient experience and learned to read the ruins like a book. He felt them stir the imagination, and according to Symonds, "it was his custom to lead strangers from point to point among the ruins, in order to enjoy the effect produced upon fresh minds by their stupendous evidence of strength and greatness in decay."[41]

Earlier in this chapter, I called Freud a "latent antiquarian," but now I am distinguishing his placeless kind of antiquarianism from the grounded tradition of the chorographic antiquaries—the perspective that goes back to the ancient world but also extends from the Renaissance in Italy to the Renaissance in England. These antiquaries perceived memories, images, and feelings in the places they explored. They grasped the energies of ruins, and the Renaissance writers understood Rome as a container of presences that included ancient images and memories. These presences enter the feelings that make a town, and they help to settle a place. Memories of settlers, therefore, should not be confused with the unsettled reminiscences of hysterics.

Freud's thinking tends to dis-locate the relics of experience. As one of his biographers advises, "Today, archeological relics seem quite appropriate as symbols of psychoanalytic procedures and its results. (What, in fact, should one do with repressed memories brought back to life and with the pictures and relics of one's past? They are kept as museum pieces—carefully put out of the way from everyday business, but near enough for contemplation and further study.)"[42] Of course, one approves therapeutic procedures that liberate neurotics from deadly memories, but the whole direction of psychoanalytic thinking—and, I might add, the direction of most psychological thinking—separates places from the energies of their memory.

Patients suffering from delusions "construct" them to include fragments of their actual experience in the past, but the pain or horror of the experience causes them to distort its true nature. Like hysterics, they are "suffering from their own recollections." The psychoanalyst also "constructs" the experience of the patient, but in a rational manner free of the distortions. The archaeologist, Freud claimed, similarly makes reconstructions from fragments of debris recovered from the ground. Finally, mankind as a whole "has developed delusions which are inaccessible to logical criticism and which contradict reality." Freud probably would have considered local myths the delusions of places. Like rational constructions, delusions "owe their power to the element of historic truth which they have built up from the repression of the forgotten and primaeval past." In all these cases, any construction is effective only "because it recovers a fragment of lost experience."[43]

Just as he de-energized the pathological recollections of his patients, Freud isolated the power of recovered fragments. He cherished his statuettes because they were old and because they represented forces at work in the mind. His notion of mind, however, is an abstraction, a systematic elaboration of Lucifer's claim in *Paradise Lost*: "The mind is its own place."

The hysterics who were Freud's model patients generated symptoms from a rigid childhood training that forbade talk about sex. Now, when virtually everyone is encouraged to talk about sex, symptoms are different, and the meaning of Oedipus at the foot of the couch recovers a deeper, wider, and older significance. Now, for complex cultural reasons, the principal issue is identity. Patients searching for an identity express the old question asked by Oedipus: "Who am I?" But the next Oedipal question, "*Where* do I belong?," does not find any ground in psychoanalytic theory, which constructs the mind as its own place.

The biographers acknowledge Freud's "veritable passion to *understand*"—the outstanding characteristic of Oedipus. In the relentless inquiry of Oedipus searching for truth about himself, Freud recognized an ancient model for psychoanalysis. Freud always thought of himself as a man driven to solve "the riddles of life," and on the wall over the foot of the analytic couch he hung the picture of Oedipus in dialogue with the Sphinx.

In high school, Freud read Greek and Latin, studied the history of ancient civilizations, and loved the classics. Later he claimed that this early vision of "an ancient culture that had vanished . . . became a never excelled comfort in the struggle of life." In his final examination he translated from Greek to German the long address of the priest to the ruler Oedipus in the prologue of *Oedipus the King*. In this speech, the priest outlines the predicament of the city, which is suffering from mysterious devastation. Freud must have known the lines by heart.[44]

On his fiftieth birthday, his followers in Vienna presented Freud with a medallion showing his own profile on one side and the figure of Oedipus answering the Sphinx on the other side, with an engraved line from Sophocles in the original Greek. These words, taken from the final chorus of *Oedipus the King*, described Oedipus as "he who knew the famous riddle and was the mightiest man." When Freud read the inscription, he turned pale and seemed very agitated, behaving, Jones writes, as a man who had seen a ghost. Freud revealed that as a young man he imagined that some day a memorial bust of himself would stand in the University of Vienna, inscribed with the identical Greek words that were engraved on the medallion.[45]

In his own imagination, Freud's identification with Oedipus went deeper and wider than the Oedipus complex. Like Oedipus, he lost his proper place as a child and lived his mature life where he never belonged. As he wrote, "I never felt really comfortable in the town. I believe now that I was never free from a longing for the beautiful woods near our home."[46] According to a psychoanalytic biographer, the move away from Freiberg (Příbor) "was a catastrophe for Freud and he spent the next forty years of his life trying to undo it." The loss created "long-lasting mourning" and "reactions that led him into his lifework."[47]

Even though Freud acknowledged the power of Freiberg in his mind, he did not ponder the effect of the place as a reality in the world. Instead he observed the work of his mind as it coped with images from the past. As his biographer wrote, "In the years from four to ten he achieved what he was later to describe as the hardest task of the mind: the renunciation of magic thinking and illusions. This renunciation left a void that he filled with legends of Greece and Rome. The golden age of civilization like the golden years of Freiberg had vanished; it could be reconstructed, however, by the findings and interpretations of history."[48] The golden years of childhood, the golden age of civilization, the legends of Greece and Rome, and the archaic sense of place all stayed in Freud's museum of antiquities along with the statues of Egyptian gods—waiting to be understood. Freud acknowledged the power of them all, but he worked to disenchant and to displace their energies. He remains one of the master strategists in the campaign to persuade modern minds that archaic thinking belongs on the shelf.

To the ancient mind, the Oedipus story evoked Thebes, Corinth, and Athens—the places identified with the tragic wanderer. Sophocles settled Oedipus in Colonus—until the power of Freud's work overcame not only Sophocles, but the traditional efforts of Theseus, the Eumenides, and Apollo as well. Freud changed the reputation of Oedipus from the grounded hero of Colonus to a universal unconscious wish generated by the structure of infantile experience. Oedipus is everywhere, and once again a wanderer.

Sophocles, in the Oedipus tragedies, explored the mythology of place as the expression of a profound need and as an effective reality as well. The wisdom in his last play responded to the Delphic maxim, "Know thyself," with the message that to know yourself you must know your place.

> *I find it hard to sum up in one word the*
> *character of Lucera—the effect it produces on*
> *the mind. . . . Yet the character is there, if one*
> *could but seize upon it, since every place has its*
> *genius.*
>
> Norman Douglas,
> *Old Calabria*

S I X

The Energies of Places

Freud believed that the great paradigmatic revolutions associated with Darwinian biology and with psychoanalysis resembled the Copernican revolution. He was not alone in choosing Copernicus as a symbol for new ventures in theory. Kant thought of himself as the Copernicus of philosophy, and Cassirer called Herder the Copernicus of history. The rage for Copernicus dominates modern ideas about theoretical innovation. Today, inspired by Thomas Kuhn, every heuristic Columbus sails under the flag of Copernicus. However, let us abandon the fashion by launching our voyage through "strange seas of thought" under the banner of Ptolemy.

A renewal of topistic consciousness demands a mental change as large and profound as the Copernican revolution, yet to guide this renewal Ptolemy may be more helpful than Copernicus. I am not suggesting we return to the idea that the sun revolves around the earth, or to any other notions drawn from Ptolemy's astronomy. Instead, I am thinking of a certain perspective revealed in the *Geographic Guide* written by Claudius Ptolemy sometime during the second century A.D. The initial chapter of this book, which figuratively shaped the earth for fifteen hundred years, opens with a distinction between geography and chorography, showing that the world and its places require two different, separate modes of representation.

According to Ptolemy, geography pictorially represented the earth as a whole, describing its nature, position, and general features. It showed the world through the perspective of unity and continuity, and this special task required mathematics. Chorography, by contrast, set off a part of the world, exhibiting it separately, representing exactly and in minute detail nearly everything contained within it. For precise description, chorography depended on correct drawings, and no one could practice chorography, in Ptolemy's words, unless he were an artist.[1]

Ptolemy felt that chorography aimed to show the quality of a place by artistic *mimesis*, representing pictorially nearly everything contained within it. Pictorial *mimesis* is selective, but we can take the method a step further if we turn to an artist who represents not nearly everything, but literally everything in a precise location. In 1969 Mark Boyle of Glasgow and London, together with his associates in a small group named the Sensual Laboratory, initiated a program called "Journey to the Surface of the Earth." At a London exhibition in the Institute of Contemporary Art, the public was invited to participate in the experiment, and each volunteer, blindfolded, threw or shot a dart at an enormous map of the world. In this way, the public selected a thousand sites randomly distributed over the surface of the earth. The idea was to make a multimedia record of all phenomena in each site, representing every datum of immediate sensory experience and thus providing a replica of each place. Most of the darts, of course, fell out of range. One landed in a remote section of Ethiopia, another plunged into the North Sea off Norway, and a third sank into the middle of the Atlantic.

Five years before the thousand sites were chosen, Mark Boyle and his friends had made a series of random studies of London, which were exhibited in that city. Pieces of London appear as giant pictures, reproducing as frozen images of reality a perfect likeness of the ground. Their plastic molds had picked up the delicate skin of each place, with bits of earth, bricks, pebbles, grit, shells, cigarette butts, vegetation, and whatever lay on the surface. Fragments of streets, yards, alleys, and cinder tracks hung on the wall as pictures. Boyle's London studies show the beauty of natural texture, revealed in one case, for example, in a section of road and pavement with cobblestones, a manhole cover, a cigarette butt held between flagstones, and a pattern that an auto tire had stamped in the wet paint of a new yellow line. Here is the surface of a place imitated exactly.[2]

Boyle's studies give us an unusual picture of located surfaces from the point of view of one artistic explorer. We must ask ourselves, however, if the record of naked perceptions, the complete account of immediate sensory experience, fully represents what may be identified as "the quality" of a place. While his pictures do evoke feeling and suggest meanings, they cannot grasp the feelings and meanings that *make* a place. We might also ask if Boyle's pictorial studies properly represent *places*.

We call locations of experience "places." Experience means perceiving, doing, thinking, and feeling. Every event happens some *where*, but we don't often locate an experience by its latitude and longitude. We say this experience happened to me in Manchester, or I felt this way in New York, or I did such and such in Boston. A place has a name and a history, which is an account of the experience located in that position.

Boyle actually calls his locations "sites" or "spots." When each dart strikes the map, it gives us simple location, deduced from the geometrical rationalization of the earth, and each position depends on what Whitehead called the process of extensive abstraction. Each location is a place only in Aristotle's special meaning of *topos*, or the sense of pure position. We identify where each dart lands by reading off its latitude and longitude, but we learn *where* it is in another sense by its relation to established places, and we say it is in the Sahara Desert, or in the middle of the Atlantic, or near Istanbul. The Sahara makes us think of trackless wastes, sandstorms, nomads, camels. The Atlantic suggests Vikings and supertankers, voyages, storms, shipping lanes. Istanbul evokes a sense of teeming urban life and the slow movement of civilizations reaching back to Constantinople and Byzantium. I am suggesting that the quality of a place depends on a human context shaped by memories and expectations, by stories of real and imagined events—that is, by the historical experience located there. Moreover, the student of topistics recognizes the way of the desert, the way of the ocean, the way of a particular city. Each place has its *nomos*, its characteristic rule of action, or customary form of making itself felt, or specific way of being in the world. That is why I call the seeker of placeways a toponomist, the name for a student of topistics.[3]

A thing has an objective reality, a person has a subjective reality, a human relationship is a social reality, and a place is its own kind, which may be called topistic reality. Geologists and painters know how to look at a rock; psychologists, philosophers, and poets have ways of knowing a mind; sociologists and dramatists examine relationships; and I suggest there is a special way for toponomists to explore places. This special perspective comprehends places through a set of conceptual categories specific to this kind of reality—without interfering with the work of geographers, sociologists, or any of the other specialized disciplines. My claim for the separate integrity of topistics finds support in many intimations—for example, in the reflections of phenomenological geographers such as Yi-Fu Tuan and Edward Relph.

Tuan says, "Place . . . is more than location and more than the spatial index of socio-economic status. It is a unique ensemble of traits that merits study in its own right."[4] And Relph observes that "any exploration of place as a phenomenon of direct experience cannot be undertaken in the terms of formal geography nor can it solely constitute part of such geography. It must, instead, be concerned with the entire range of experience through which we all know and make places."[5]

Memory and imagination, crucial elements in the quality of a place, appear only obliquely in Mark Boyle's perfect record of the surface, and they elude pictorial chorography, but they shape what is called the spirit of a place. A geographer might protest that I ask too much of chorography. After all, Ptolemy was explaining how to make maps, and cartography should not be expected to picture spirits. That kind of objection, however, exposes the problematic of topistic representation. The story of maps tells a history of progressive rationalization, proceeding according to certain rules of objectivity and subjective exclusion. We take it for granted that a map will not inform us how it feels to be in a certain place, or about the kind of experience to expect there, or to indicate perils of the soul on the way from one place to another. Yet, objectivity is the rule for a certain kind of map. It is not inherent in the nature of maps. Ancient maps differ from ours not only because they are graphically and mathematically naive, but also because they follow different rules.

In ancient China, about 600 B.C., a book known as the *Classic of the Mountains and Rivers*, which has been called the oldest traveler's guide in the world, described the Nine Cauldrons of the Hsia, metal surfaces covered with pictures that represented the nine provinces of the country:

In this way the people were instructed so that they could recognise all things and spirits both good and evil. And thus when they travelled over the rivers and marshes, and through the mountains and forests, they did not meet with any adversities. (They did not go in fear of the weird spirits and genii of mountains and waters.) Moreover, spirits such as the Chhih, the Mei and the Wang-liang did not come to meet them (were not offended at their intrusions). Thus concord reigned between men and spirits, and the people received the favour of Heaven.[6]

As Joseph Needham observes, the cauldrons belong more to magic and ritual than to geography, and they resemble ancient European maps with all their mythological figures, fabulous marvels, and fantastic creatures. Nevertheless, these representations show the spirits of places, and they preserve the memory of how people *felt* about places.

Expressive features, extruded by the progressive rationalization of cartography, gradually retreated to the margins of maps, where they remain but dimly understood.[7] Certainly the pictures stimulated fantasy, but they also served as cartographic records of imagination and memory. The so-called Gough map of fourteenth-century Britain, probably the most important medieval English map, includes a drawing between Norway and the Orkney Islands showing a wrecked ship on the rocks with a broken mast, and two rafts, one aground and the other holding a recumbent figure with long hair and clothed in a garment belted at the waist with a cord. The scene was probably intended as a warning about dangerous rocks, the Pentland Skerries, but it also may represent a story about the fatal voyage of the young Maid of Norway, Margaret, Queen of Scotland, or the shipwreck of Earl Rögnvald, Lord of Shetland.[8]

Ptolemy's brief statement about chorography never tells how to represent the spirit of a place, just as Vitruvius, in his exclusively rational treatise on architecture, never tells about the spirit of a Greek temple. Why then should we launch topistics under the banner of Ptolemy? Mainly, because we can expand the insight of Ptolemaic dualism and lift it to a higher level of generalization. Ptolemy shows us that places may be represented by two different methods, but the mathematician and the artist stand for two great perspectives. They reflect Cassirer's distinction between symbolic forms: on the one hand, a logical, geometric, scientific

worldview, the domain of precise determination and rational knowledge; on the other hand, the realm of imagery, myth, magic, religion,
and artistic imagination. Moreover, places are not only represented but
also shaped by these two different principles: geometric rationalization
on the one hand; indeterminate expressive energies on the other—the
logic of space or the spirit of place.

To differentiate certain typical features in the experience of places,
many Greek writers used two separate words—*chora* and *topos*—as
distinct verbal representations. Ptolemy's perspective, which assigns to
chorography the "quality" of places, includes the oldest significance of
the term *chora*. This word, the prefix of "chorography," meant place, and
in different contexts it also signified region, or country, or space. The
word *topos*, prefix of "topography," also meant place, but the subtle and
changing relation between *chora* and *topos* makes an important chapter
of intellectual history. *Chora* stands out as the oldest Greek word for
place, appearing in Homer and Hesiod. *Topos* emerged initially in the
work of Aeschylus, that is, not until around 470 B.C. In antiquity, a
writer could say *chorophilia* for love of place, but never *topophilia*.[9] In the
classical language, *topos* tended to suggest mere location or the objective
features of a place, and Aristotle made it into an abstract term signifying
pure position. The older word, *chora*—or sometimes *choros*—retained
subjective meanings in the classical period. It appeared in emotional
statements about places, and writers were inclined to call a sacred place
a *chora* instead of a *topos* (Plato, writing in *Phaedrus*, being a notable
exception). Sometimes the two words appeared together. For example,
in the opening of Sophocles' *Oedipus at Colonus*, Antigone and her blind
father, Oedipus, stop at a resting place, and she says, "As for this *choros* it
is clearly a holy one." He inquires where they are. She replies that she
does not know the *choros*, but asks him if she should go and find out
what *topos* it is. Later in the play, he tells Theseus that he will show him
the *choros* where Oedipus must die, but warns Theseus not to reveal the
topoi in which it lies. Here, *topos* stands for the mere location or the
container of the sacred *choros*, the grave.[10]

In Hellenistic Greek, the relation between the two words changed. In
the third century B.C., the Septuagint spread *topos* throughout its translation of the Hebrew Bible as the Greek word for a holy place. Later, the
Christians also called sacred places *topoi*, and the term *chora* carried
technical and administrative meanings. But Ptolemy carried forward the
classical tradition. *Chora* still held memories of old emotional and spiri-

tual meanings, even though Ptolemy was writing during the Greco-Roman period, in the second century A.D.

An expressive tradition in philosophy gives "Place" exalted rank in the universe. Thales, the first philosopher, is supposed to have said, "Of all things that are, the most ancient is God, for he is uncreated. The most beautiful is the cosmos, for it is God's workmanship. The greatest is place, for it holds all things." Aristotle, rejecting the confusions of the expressive tradition, restricts place to its physique. In his way of thinking, *topos* does not represent a great metaphysical principle but merely stands for the inert container of experience—more exactly the inner surface that contains a thing—and *chora* means the room or capacity of the container. He stresses the difference between the container and its contents, observing that "just as the vessel is no part of its contents, so the place is no part of that which is in it."[11]

But Plato has a great deal more to say about *chora*, the oldest Greek word for place, and he characterizes it in an entirely different way, stressing the relation between formless *chora* and the contents that give it form. *Chora* is one of the three great modes of Being in the universe. He is not content to name the receptacle of experience the natural mother of all created things, for a mother could still retain her maternal title even if she did no more than give birth. He lavishes epithets of nourishment on *chora*, naming her the wetnurse, suckler, and feeder of all things. He remains in the expressive tradition of poets and dramatists who named places like the earth or a city as the maternal nourisher of men and horses and spirits. For Plato, place is a matrix of energies, the active receptacle, in contrast to Aristotle's later idea of the neutral container. Whitehead observes that Plato's doctrine of place asserts the real connections between ultimate realities. Everything in the receptacle gives a place its qualities, and the qualities of a place cannot be abstracted from the things contained in it.[12] People and things in a place participate in one another's natures. Place is a location of mutual immanence, a unity of effective presences abiding together.

Plato tells us that to grasp the nature of place, "we must try to express and make manifest a form obscure and dim."[13] It lies outside both reason and sensation, to be apprehended by a kind of sensuous reasoning. "Some sort of bastard reasoning, which is hardly trustworthy," Plato writes, gives us the knowledge of place.[14] It is not a legitimate kind of knowledge in his view, being neither within the rules of rational thought nor even a product of sensory experience, but something else—a curious, spurious mode of grasping reality. It is a knowledge that must be "grasped," because it cannot be conceived and it cannot be perceived. Yet it is not less real than the objects of reason and perception.

Chora, which may be translated either as "place" or as "space," depending on the context, is one of the independent, eternal modes of experience—one of the three great types of Being in the universe. One type of Being refers to the eternal ideas, the changeless forms or models of things apprehended by the reason—the domain of concepts. The second type of Being includes the transient copies or exemplifications of the eternal forms, meaning perceptual phenomena, which pass from birth to decay—the domain of sensory experience. The third type of reality, *chora*, is the receptacle of sensory experience and the seat of phenomena. Whereas the eternal models exist without specific location, every instance of sensory experience must emerge in a place. Yet, despite its importance as the seat or foundation of experience, we cannot perceive the nature of *chora* or understand it rationally. In its own way, however, it is intelligible, and to grasp its nature we may turn to the peculiar mode of bastard reasoning. This mode leads the mind to archaic mythical thinking, I believe, and to the wholesome human way of grasping the expressive qualities of place. Sensuous cognitions born in the dark illuminate topistic experience.

The opposite of the reasoning Plato calls *nothos*, or "bastard," is *gnesios*, meaning "lawfully begotten" or of legitimate birth. Democritus had made a similar distinction between forms of cognition that were *gnesie*, or "legitimate," and *skotie*, or "bastard." *Skotie* was a poetic word literally meaning "darkling"—born in the dark; that is, not born in open wedlock. Democritus identified bastard cognitions as sight, hearing, smell, and so forth—the evidence of our senses. Legitimate knowledge, in contrast, came from the intellect.[15] A. E. Taylor thinks the resemblance to the formulation by Democritus is a "mere coincidence," but I doubt it.[16] I suspect that Plato is making a deliberate allusion to the distinction made by Democritus before him. The bastard mode refers to qualities the mind apprehends by sensation. For Plato, *chora* could be grasped not by sensation and not by reason but by sensuous reasoning— the curious, spurious child of reason and sensation.

Introducing *chora* as a form that is "baffling and obscure," Plato describes its essential property as "the receptacle, and as it were the nurse of all Becoming."[17] While the receptacle takes on different appearances, changed and diversified by the qualities of its contents, it never departs from its own nature as the unchanging matrix of everything that happens.[18] Then, he continues, "if we describe her as a Kind invisible and unshaped, all-receptive, and in some most perplexing and most baffling way partaking of the intelligible, we shall describe her truly."[19] The illegitimate reasoning that renders *chora* intelligible is matched by an exceptional mode of perception—dreaming with our eyes open. He writes:

> On the other hand, a third kind of Being, everlasting *chora*—which does not receive decay and furnishes a seat for all things that have birth—is itself grasped without the senses by a sort of bastard reasoning that is hard to believe. In relation to it, moreover, we not only dream with the power of sight, but we also say that by necessity everything to be at all must be somewhere in some place and occupy some space, whereas anything that is neither somewhere on earth nor in heaven is nothing.[20]

For Plato, the elements of experience—namely, the primary contents of *chora* even before creation—are *morphai, dynameis,* and *pathe*: shapes (or characters or forms), powers, and feelings. The "primeval" *morphai*— fire, air, water, and earth, the four roots of the physical world—have qualities which make the receptacle hot, cold, moist, and dry. These qualities are called powers (*dynameis*) because they act on one another and would act on the senses of an observer, if we imagine someone being there to experience them.[21] They also have associated qualities called *pathe,* or feelings; the Neoplatonic translator, Thomas Taylor, preferred to translate *pathe* as "passions." According to his version, fire produces in us that passion we call heat, and so forth.[22] The *morphai* may be understood to represent the characters or shapes of physical things. Place, or *chora,* or primeval space, then, is a unity of physique and morale, a location of shapes, powers, and feelings. Therefore, it is not only physical space but expressive space as well—a container of feelings. According to the myth of creation that Plato tells in the *Timaeus,* the powers and feelings in *chora* made the receptacle vibrate, shake, and rock wildly, until the demiurge created a cosmos by shaping the *morphai* into regular geometric forms. Nevertheless, after creation, space remains expressive—a container of feelings.

Myth is a natural expression of what may be grasped by bastard reasoning. It has been observed that archaic or primitive mythical cognition is incapable of detachment from the immediacy of perceptions and feelings. It remains an attached, expressive, and sensuous kind of think-ing.[23] In mythical thought, the place of a thing is part of a thing's being. Furthermore, as Cassirer writes, in mythical thinking "all thought and all sensory intuition and perception rest on an original foundation of feeling. Mythical space remains immersed in this feeling." Within this space, logic and intellect do not determine boundaries, zones, and directions but go back to distinctions originally made on the basis of feelings.[24]

Plato's myth describes the active work of Place in the creation of the universe. Even before the heavens, Being and Becoming and Place ex-isted on their own. Then *chora*, or Place, the nurse of Becoming, re-ceived the *morphai*, or characters of water, fire, earth, and air, and from their powers got moistened, inflamed, and so forth. Experiencing and responding to the powers as well as to the *pathe*, or feelings, that go with the characters, she began to vibrate and shake. In this passionate condi-tion, *chora* took on diverse appearances,

> but because [she] was filled with powers that were neither alike nor evenly balanced, there was no equipoise in any region . . . but [she] was everywhere swayed unevenly and shaken by these things, and by [her] motion shook them in turn. And they, being thus moved were perpetually being separated and carried in different direc-tions; just as when things are shaken and winnowed by means of winnowing-baskets and other instruments for cleaning corn, the dense and heavy things go one way, while the rare and light are carried to another place and settle there.[25]

The divine demiurge, creator of the cosmos, stabilized this agitated chaos as it designed the elementary characters, or primary bodies, in regular geometric shapes, but the primeval nature of Place is revealed as an expressive receptacle containing shapes, powers, and feelings, ac-tively responding to the passions of the universe.

Simply put, Plato defines *chora* as the location of qualities perceived by the senses, but the profundity of his definition lurks in the refusal to put it simply. Happily or unfortunately, depending on your point of view, every important phrase in the *Timaeus* works in two ways: on the one hand, elucidating a rational significance; on the other hand, illumi-nating poetic meanings. Plato's philosophy remains attached to the world of myth. While his arguments address the intellect, the images in his words evoke the nonrational features of experience.

Whitehead observes that knowledge is not some exact account of experience or its modes but a process of exploration. The movement toward clarity in Plato's exploration does not lose contact with the background of vague and unanalyzed experience from which his central notions emerge. In Whitehead's opinion, "The abiding interest of Plato's Dialogues does not lie in their enunciation of abstract doctrines. They are suffused with the implicit suggestion of the concrete unity of experience, whereby every abstract topic obtains its interest."[26]

In contrast, Aristotle moves in the direction of legitimate reasoning, restricting the experience of place to those features that lend themselves to precise determination, and he gives the terms *topos* and *chora* univocal meanings established by rational analysis. Moreover, the concept of place is less prominent in his thinking. Although he mentions place and space here and there in the *Metaphysics*, they are conspicuously excluded from the thirty principal terms defined in Book 5, and—in contrast to Plato—Place is not one of the three types of primary Being examined in Book 12. His most thorough discussion of place appears in Book 4 of the *Physics*, where it is defined as the container of bodies. The notion also appears in a nonmaterial sense in the *Rhetoric*, where *topos* means the seat of an argument, and in one of the treatises on logic, where "topic" means a focal point for discussion—that is, a commonplace or specific region of opinion.

Aristotle gives Plato credit, saying that while everyone agrees that place is something, Plato alone tried to say what it is.[27] Still, he loses no opportunity to disagree with the *Timaeus*.[28] And whereas Plato finds the old poetic and philosophical tradition about the sense of place meaningful, Aristotle rejects it, saying, "we have inherited nothing from previous thinkers, whether in the way of a statement of difficulties or of a solution."[29] Moreover, his impatience distorts Plato's position at several points, claiming that Plato identified *topos* and *chora*, that he also called space the same as matter, and that he thought the receptacle received the eternal forms directly.

For Aristotle, *topos* is something different from the things that come into being within it and go through changes. The essential feature of place is magnitude. Abstraction removes the form and the matter of a thing and leaves the dimensions of its place. He emphasizes the principle of separability, insisting that a place is no part of the thing it contains. If separation is not possible, then what cannot be separated must be part of the thing itself and not its place. The boundaries of the two coincide, for a place is like a vessel that contains a thing. He concludes by defining *topos* as the innermost motionless boundary of what it contains, and *chora* as the room or volume of the container.[30]

Like Plato, Aristotle arrives at a definition of place by abstracting away all qualities. But for him that leaves nothing but magnitude and a piece of reality without activity. At the beginning of his analysis he recognizes that place is real and thinks that the locomotion of things from place to place shows that it exerts a certain influence. He even suggests that different places have distinct potencies, but Aristotle leaves no ground for explaining any of their effects.[31] The nature of place does not lend itself to any one of the four causes that, according to Aristotle, would be needed to construct an explanation. Its nature is primarily metric, and it has no activity.

A. E. Taylor has shown that Plato's doctrine of *chora* calls attention to the nonmetrical features, such as situation, direction, and form, which precede and support the metrical notions of geometry. It is a way of thinking about space as a "network of relations between situations." In the *Timaeus*, situation and figure are primary, and *chora* is not a volume containing things, but that which organizes experience by manifesting diverse sensible properties and configurations in different regions.[32] For Plato, abstracting away all the qualities within a place leaves much more than a container. He recognizes the peculiar *activity* of place—the feature of reality that Neoplatonists would later call "energy."

Ironically, the Neoplatonists acquired the word for energy from Aristotle, for it does not appear in the work of Plato at all. The Greek word *energeia* is derived from the same stem that yields the word *ergon*, which means "work." Although it is unlikely that Aristotle invented *energeia*, it does not appear in writing before him, as far as I know.[33] He uses it extensively in his discourses on rhetoric and ethics, as well as in the books on physics and metaphysics, to signify "actuality" as opposed to "potentiality." After Aristotle, the word stretched to mean physical energy as well as subjective activity. Diodorus Siculus, a historian writing in the time of Julius Caesar and Augustus, described a battering ram that received its *energeia* in battle from a thousand men. It was also a familiar term in the Alexandrian medical tradition, and Galen used it to mean the physiological functioning of an organism as well as the pharmacological activity of drugs. Other writers mentioned all kinds of spiritual energies. The New Testament, the patristic literature, and Hellenistic philosophy are full of references to the occult effects or *energeia* of demons, angels, and divine forces. In his discussion of eternal realities, Plotinus associates activity and being, claiming that the being of a thing is the output of its particular activity or energy.[34] Neoplatonists loved the word, and in an early nineteenth-century translation, Thomas Taylor read it back into Plato, working it into the *Timaeus*. In his version of the passage in which Plato suggests how *chora* is grasped, Taylor translated, "we cannot rouse ourselves from this fallacious and dreaming energy."[35]

In the seventeenth century, as natural philosophy was settling the boundaries of objectivity, notions of subjective energy—distinct but not separate—emerged from religious disputes at the same time. The Cambridge Platonists, in their combat with materialism and atheism, talked about the "energie of the soul." Henry More wrote an interesting "Platonicall Song of the Soul" in which he distinguished between the sensual energy of the body, which stirred the soul vigorously, and the more subtle representations rising internally from within the soul itself. He defined "energy" as "the operation, efflux or activity of any being as the light of the Sunne is the energie of the Sunne, and every phantasm of the soul is the energie of the soul." The body stirred the soul in perpetual sensual energy, dimming the more subtle phantasms rising from the soul itself or occasioned by representations. Fantasy, or the indigenous imagery of the soul, as well as reason and the sensory experience of the external world all contributed to the energy of the soul, meaning every manifestation of thought and emotion. Henry More, then, suggested a complex idea of energy as a compound of elements that included reason, fantasy, impulses from the body, sensory data, and representations.[36]

In this book, I intend to restrict the meaning of subjective energy to the effect of perceptions and representations on human experience, especially the effect of words, movements, objects, and images on thoughts and feelings. "Energy" means the capacity to cause changes in interest, feeling, or action. High energy, in a subjective sense, means great attention and excitement, stimulating action; low energy is experienced as inattention, boredom, and little or no action. Something has energy if it causes changes in experience—if it makes people think, feel, or act, and if it generates representations or stimulates the imagination.

The energy of a place is not to be grasped in the same way that we understand the mechanical energy of an industrial city. The two energies belong to different orders of intelligibility. Physical energy means the capacity for interaction with features that can be measured and expressed in mathematics. In the other domain, we talk about the condition of our inner energy and vitality, about intellectual energies and psychological effects, as well as religious energy, the energy of language, of ritual, the dance, works of art, and so forth. This notion of energy is swollen with ambiguity, unlike the scientific concept of physical energy, which is lean and precise. Ambiguity, the breath of poetry, leaves a stink in the nostrils of science. It clings to the idea of human energy because it remains inherent in the relation between experience and language. As Cassirer observed, the ambiguity inherent in a word is not just a deficiency of language but is essential to its power of expression. It shows that the limits of language—like reality itself—are fluid. Certain words have hidden meanings that cannot be expressed precisely but only sensed through image and metaphor. Words, for St. Augustine, were "precious cups of meaning," but human experience flows over the rims of words.

A toponomist takes a special interest in the *genius loci*, or the spirit of the place, and in the power of human energy to shape places. In Athens the sacred procession of the Panathenaea, the major civic event of the year, worked as the organizing force establishing architectural pattern and urban form, locating buildings and determining spaces as punctuations in the flow of the ritual procession. Thus religious energy gave the city material form. In twelfth-century France, Abbot Suger wrote how the old church of St. Denis could no longer contain the ritual energy of the crowds surging inward to view the sacred relics.[37] Enlarging the church gave birth to Gothic style, and the history of Gothic architecture tells the story of master builders, technicians of the sacred, revealing the articulated energies of construction in stone, which framed splendid windows displaying the mystical energy of light. The first urbanists of America, the Indians of the Southwest, built their pueblo villages in the period from the twelfth to the fourteenth centuries, about the same time that Gothic architecture developed in Europe. Ralph Knowles, in an objective study of the Pueblo Bonito, shows how urban form emerged there as an efficient, adaptive response to the sun, which is understood by Knowles as the source of physical radiant energy. He proves that the pueblo builders shaped their architectural surfaces with great precision to catch and screen the rays of the sun, and that they understood the relationships between the form of their constructions and the dynamics of earth and sun.[38] In contrast, Vincent Scully, an architectural historian, shows how the same pueblo received its urban form from the other energy—communal ceremonies, especially the sacred energy of the dance.[39]

Plato grasped and pictured the subtle, grounded energies of place, although this side of his work is often overlooked. At the center of his great mural, "The School of Athens," Renaissance artist Raphael shows Plato and Aristotle standing side by side. Plato is pointing up to the heavens, while Aristotle gestures straight ahead. In the nineteenth century, Thomas Babington Macaulay preserved this image of Plato in an essay that replaced Aristotle with Francis Bacon as the philosopher who stayed down-to-earth. Among Victorian historians, Macaulay stands out as an apologist for the triumph of mechanical energy. He found the highest maxim of civilization in "the key of the Baconian doctrine— utility and progress," and he condemned ancient philosophy as a complete waste of intellect. Plato's philosophy began in words and ended in words, while the philosophy of Bacon began in observations and ended in mechanical progress. Macaulay wrote:

> The aim of the Platonic philosophy was to raise us far above vulgar wants. The aim of the Baconian philosophy was to supply our vulgar wants. The former aim was noble; but the latter was attainable. Plato drew a good bow; but . . . he aimed at the stars; and therefore, though there was no want of strength or skill, the shot was thrown away. . . . Bacon fixed his eye on a mark which was placed on the earth and within bow-shot, and hit it in the white.[40]

Other writers more subtle than Macaulay nevertheless shared his easy identification of Platonism as a philosophy remote from the world under our feet.

Since the Platonic doctrine for the most part exalted reason over sensory experience, readers through the ages have studied Plato's doctrine of intellect, believing that he degraded the senses to an inferior status because he thought they sometimes contaminated the activity of the mind. Most Neoplatonists wanted to escape their senses to live in the higher world of pure spirit. Nevertheless, another tradition, which I call "grounded Platonism," does not despise the experience of the senses. Several dialogues, such as *Timaeus*, *Phaedrus*, and *Menexenus*, establish foundations for a doctrine of grounded energy as well as a meaning of place. "Grounded Platonism"—clarified below in chapter 11—is not a conventional era or school of philosophy, such as "Middle Platonism" or "Neoplatonism," but a mental orientation, a framework of experience expressed by the Socratic side of Plato, and it includes his topistic ideas.

The remarkable metaphors in the *Timaeus* represent Place on the one hand as the seat of experience, and on the other hand as the nourishing matrix. They blend together in the image of a nursemaid feeding and rocking infant experience on her lap. Later in the *Timaeus*, Plato recommends that men should exercise body and soul by imitating the activity of the receptacle, the nourisher and nurse of the universe, keeping the body active, never allowing it to rest in a torpid condition, continually moving and shaking, maintaining health by moderate vibrations.[41] A. E. Taylor observes that ancient Greek nurses were notorious for the way they kept bouncing their infants up and down, rocking and dandling the babies to keep their bodies fit.[42] In the *Laws*, Plato recommends the custom as a universal rule of childcare. Infants should live day and night as if at sea, continually "rocked in the cradle of the deep," for rhythmical motion strengthens the body, relieves anxiety, and improves digestion.[43] Far from being inert containers, places actively take care of experience, filling it with energy that is busy organizing, shaking, and feeding.

For Plato, the most important feature of Place is the activity of the receptacle. Experience is a flux of shifting qualities, but *chora* is that in which qualities appear. Lacking qualities of its own, the receptacle organizes the patterns and qualities of its contents—without place, bodies could not show the qualities and configurations we perceive. This organizing activity also makes a unity out of manifold perceptions. According to Whitehead, the sole function of *chora* in Plato's doctrine of place is to impose unity on the events of Nature. To exist at all, events must occur in a place, but their being in a place makes them occur together. In Whitehead's words, "These events are together by reason of their community of locus, and they obtain their actuality by reason of emplacement within this community."[44]

Experience finds coherence through strands of unity. One strand is the unity of personal experience, which assembles personal identities so that we can locate configurations of experience, naming John Smith or Mary Brown as the locus of this or that experience. We can also talk about their feelings, thoughts, deeds, and the structure of their lives as coherent identities of experience. Another unity of experience is nature, which facilitates scientific discourse. But according to Plato, the first and greatest unity of experience is Place, the nature of which is grasped intuitively on the fringes of reason and perception. Some features of place, then, would elude patterns imposed by rationalized perspectives such as geometry, or economics, or city planning. This insight provides the philosophical ground for understanding why the rationalization of place in the modern world contributes to the disintegration of topistic unity. It also helps us to grasp what has been described as "the process leading to that division within the mind and feelings—within the human psyche as a whole" that distinguishes our modern structure of consciousness.[45] In the context of architectural history, Sigfried Giedion understood that division of consciousness as the great split between the methods of feeling and the methods of thinking.[46]

The totality of what people do, think, and feel in a specific location gives identity to a place, and through its physique and morale it shapes a reality which is unique to places—different from the reality of an object or a person. Human experience makes a place, but a place lives in its own way. Its form of experience occupies persons—the place locates experience in people. A place is a matrix of energies, generating representations and causing changes in awareness.

S E V E N

Grasping the Sense of Place

At present, the narrow range of topistic consciousness leads us to think of places as derivatives of a person's individual experience. If we say John Smith did such and such, we are locating an experience in him, and also naming John Smith as a unity of experience. But the person or the grammatical subject is not the only such unity, and if we say that something is often done in Boston, we are identifying the place as a unity of experience. To modern minds, this unity recedes into the background, for in our habit of thought, a place is no more than the mental construct of an individual. But there is another way to think of the relation between person and place, and I shall give three brief examples illustrating it.

Amos Rapoport shows that the Australian Aborigines feel that the country owns them—that they are the spiritual property of the land. It knows them, gives them life, and nourishes them. The spirit of every person in the land has lived there before in the Dreaming—that mythological, timeless time when the primordial beings lived their immortal dramas and turned into features of the landscape. "No other land, no matter how fertile, could be theirs or mean the same. Men were permanently attached to their own country and wanted to die in it."[1]

Let us consider the topistic orientation of the Pintupi, aboriginal people who live in the western desert region of central Australia. Imagine that you are standing at a place called "Yayayi," southeast of a rock hole that you want to visit, and you ask, "Where is the rock hole?" A

European would reply, so many kilometers northwest from here. But Pintupi would say the rock hole is north of Walawala and they would point the way. The extended finger, however, shows you not the way from Yayayi, where you are, but the direction of a line extended from Walawala. You will always be given directions from some other place, not from where you are. Walawala is five hundred kilometers west of Yayayi, where you are standing, and the rock hole lies north of that. They would never say go north or west of where you are or go left or right from here. Directions are always given from certain sacred places with well-known mythological associations. A person is never a center from which the direction of a place is determined.[2]

In the case of the Wintu Indians of Northern California, left and right refer exclusively to the body and never to directions on the land. As Dorothy Lee observed, "When the Wintu goes up the river, the hills are to the west, the river to the east; and a mosquito bites him on the west arm. When he returns, the hills are still to the west, but, when he scratches his mosquito bite, he scratches his east arm. The geography has remained unchanged, and the self has had to be reoriented in relation to it."[3]

The third example is linguistic. In an earlier time, people were often named as parts of a place, or, to put it another way, a name would identify a person as the derivative of a place—for example, Geoffrey of Anjou, Francis of Assisi, William of Worcester, Duns Scotus, Thomas of Aquino, Matthew Paris. Linguistically, the name does not suggest that Anjou is constructed from the experience of Geoffrey, but, on the contrary, Geoffrey is the name of an experience located in Anjou.

A place binds people together by the common emotions it elicits. Moreover, a place gathers experience and must be understood as one of the unities of experience. How do we recognize topistic integrity? How do we know a place as a whole? Plato tells us that bastard reasoning grasps the nature of *chora*. Unfortunately, the English word "grasp" does not deliver the full sense of the Greek verb *haptein*. "Grasping," in English, suggests grabbing with the hands alone, and it goes back to the Indo-European root, **ghrebh-*, which also means to dig or scratch or grub. We can imagine someone digging in the earth until he or she finds something to grab. But the Greek *haptein* suggests a wider experience of clutching and holding that does not stop with the hands but sometimes involves the entire body. More of the self is engaged in the experience of *haptein*. It means to lay hold of something—to touch, to cling, to fasten, to clasp, to link, to latch on to. It includes the grappling of wrestlers as well as the sexual embrace. It is an ample term, evoking many different ways of contact, involvement, and participation.

This old meaning is being revived in the doctrine of haptic perception, which is new to the English language. In architecture, which is fundamentally the technique of building places, it is recognized as "the way the whole body senses and feels the environment." An intriguing book by Kent Bloomer and Charles Moore challenges the tyranny of visual perception in architectural design, arguing that the feeling of buildings and our sense of dwelling in them are the roots of architectural experience. The authors explain, "To sense haptically is to experience objects in the environment by actually touching them (by climbing a mountain rather than staring at it)." The term "haptic" is not yet a registered English word, for you will not find it in a dictionary. It is a sense of touch that means not just contact with the fingers or the skin but an entire perceptual system conveying sensations of pressure, temperature, pain, and the sense of movement within the body as well as the feelings of the body moving through space. "No other sense engages in feeling and doing simultaneously. This action/reaction characteristic of haptic perception separates it from all other forms of sensing which, in comparison, come to seem rather abstract." Our primordial haptic experiences, "our feelings of rhythm, of hard and soft edges, of huge and tiny elements, of openings and closures, and a myriad of landmarks and directions . . . taken together form the core of our human identity." The sense of dwelling in a house and the ways our bodies get to know the nooks and turns and surfaces of a place depend on haptic feelings.[4]

James Gibson, a psychologist working in the field of environmental perception, first developed the concept of haptic perception. Reversing the trend of research that has traditionally isolated the senses and made inventories of separate sensations, he describes the senses as active perceptual systems seeking and organizing information about the environment. He calls the haptic sense "the perceptual system by which animals and men are *literally* in touch with the environment." The body feels the articulations of shapes and surfaces in the world by means of its own inner articulations. Neural receptors in the joints turn them into sense organs, registering geometric relations to the ground and to the force of gravity by the relative positions of the bones. The system links bones and extremities to the environment, as we literally feel the world in our bones. With this elaborate perceptual apparatus, by haptic and dynamic touching, we lay hold of the environment, detecting size and shape, surface and texture, substance and consistency, and relative temperature; with the same apparatus we perform exploratory manipulations. Gibson observes:

> It is only half the truth to realize that animals feel the layout of the earth and its furniture. They also *seek* contact with things—at least some kinds of things and some kinds of contacts, for certain solids are beneficial and others are noxious. The infant clings to the mother and one adult clings to another in need. The earth itself has been compared to a mother in this respect. The metaphors of the search for contact hold true not only for the terrestrial, the sexual, and the social realm, but also for the cognitive and the intellectual. One can be "in touch" with other people, or with world affairs, or with reality.
>
> Active exploratory touch permits both the grasping of an object and a grasp of its meaning.[5]

Furthermore, human relationships are filled with the perceptions and meanings of haptic experience. A whole genre of popular homiletic literature written in the past two decades of haptic revival admonishes us about the joys and responsibilities of touching and feeling. Even without the sensory inputs of hearing and vision, the haptic system "provides an adequate means of social interaction and communication." Gibson documents the richness of haptic perception, which often escapes conscious attention, especially "the pattern and flow of geometrical information from the joints, which yield perceptions of body pose and the shapes of touching surfaces but not a collection of sensations from each joint."[6] This powerful and elaborate perceptual system is not located in a clearly definable anatomical group with an exact inventory of nerves and sensations. Gathering information from receptors distributed all over the body, the haptic sense organizes a unity of function from anatomical diversity.

Haptic perception reminds us that the whole self may grasp reality without seeing, hearing, or thinking. It also calls attention to a primitive way of knowing that resembles mythical thought, in contrast to the analytical stages of seeing, thinking, and acting—a unified structure of feeling and doing.

Although architects and environmental psychologists are rediscovering the ways that haptic perception grasps the qualities of places, Plato's bastard reasoning is not such a sensory experience but rather is a kind of haptic *reasoning* that grasps the nature of place. Plato also joins two other contradictory modes of experience. He writes that in relation to that peculiar sensuous reasoning, which is neither sensory nor reasonable, we dream with our eyes open. Commentators have interpreted the phrase to mean that we take to be true what we experience by the senses, not understanding that we are sensing only copies of the eternal forms—just as a dreamer believes the contents of his dream to be real. The dreamy illusion, they suggest, leads us to believe that the eternal forms in themselves, which have no material location, cannot be real. This interpretation of the phrase is sound, as far as it goes, but I think we must draw some illegitimate inferences from Plato's language. In relation to *chora*, he writes, we dream with the capacity of vision. This dream vision, he suggests, gives us the nature of place.

A wide-awake dream vision that grasps the nature of place describes the mode of consciousness the Australian Aborigines call "the Dreaming." It is the core of their social and religious life and has been described as one of the most remarkable and sophisticated religious and philosophical systems ever known.[7] For the Aborigines, familiar shapes of the land literally give form to intuitive feelings about life's deeper mysteries, and their structure of consciousness linking forms, myths, and rites grasps an ontological reality that eludes our legitimate thoughts. As W. E. H. Stanner, a profound interpreter of aboriginal life, has observed, "understanding can founder before it begins if the method of inquiry is controlled by a rational logic which suppresses consideration of an ontological reality that—as is clearly the case among the Aborigines—*has begun to excite feeling.*"[8]

The Dreaming is a creation myth, full of stories delivered in song and ritual for incalculable generations, but the tradition is connected psychically to ordinary nocturnal dream life. The time of the Dreaming is everywhen, but through it every place in the present lives in the sacred past. Long, long ago, the Dreaming sings, the land existed—like Plato's primeval *chora*—without form and without living things, until the primordial beings, the spirit ancestors, who also existed in a dormant state, woke up and rose from the earth. They made great journeys throughout the empty country and left a record of exciting adventures. They hunted and camped, chased and fled, played tricks, cooperated, fought battles, made love, and filled the land with their activity or energy. Their actions filled the landscape with plants, animals, waterholes, rivers, and finally human beings.[9] Every physical feature, then, is a record of some primordial dramatic action: every rock, hill, headland, lagoon, and island is an event. Every spot in the desert holds mythological significance for someone.

Eventually, the ancestors vanished, but some left behind, as they disappeared, physical forms in the shape of rocks, carved surfaces, painted figures, and notable features of the terrain. The forms of the landscape, therefore, are the miraculous relics of ancestral beings. Meaningless objects do not exist. Everything in the phenomenal world has a dramatic meaning, preserved in an indivisible tradition. The Dreaming is a cosmology as well as a road map, a story of genesis serving as a guide to the world underfoot. It is an indivisible, seamless unity of religion, geography, and local history.

Aboriginal myths describe formations of the land as climactic outcomes of dramas played out in the Dreaming. As Stanner wrote:

> The places of climax were known and named, and each one contained proof—a shape, or form, or pattern—of a great event. Even when not well understood, the presence of such evidence was taken to be a sign betokening old intent and present significance. The forces expressed in the dramas were thought to be immanent in all such places and to be dynamically available for men to use. The whole environment, though charged with numinous import, was still a ground of confidence since it had been continuously occupied by their own people.[10]

The Dreaming makes the desert, which Europeans experience as a dreary, trackless waste, an environment filled with exciting, meaningful physical features, populated with invisible spirits, and crisscrossed with the meandering tracks of ancestral beings. Where Europeans find a dead landscape, the Aborigines live in a theater of energy. They are never bored in their desert. David Lewis, an anthropologist who investigated their uncanny orientation in space and place, records their deep feeling of rapport with the arid land. Lewis writes:

> Even so, I failed fully to understand the deep satisfaction elicited in my Aboriginal friends by monotonous driving from dawn to dusk day after day, across a landscape that was vivified in sacred myth. Every terrestrial feature, plant or track of an animal, was meticulously noted and aroused very lively discussion. Highly coloured

subsequent accounts of the features of the country traversed, such
as the height of the sandhills, the colour of the rocks, the profu-
sion of honey flowers, were given to envious friends back at the
settlement.[11]

For the Aborigines any journey in the desert must resemble the excitement of devout pilgrims visiting the holy places in Jerusalem.

Some aboriginal people who move to the city cannot wait for holidays
when they may return to the desert. Those who become steelworkers
and businessmen retain a deep emotional relationship with the bush
country, together with their remarkable bushcraft. They continue to
enjoy an encyclopedic knowledge of desert resources as well as a mas-
tery of the terrain. Aborigines are never lost in the desert. Always
knowing exactly where they are, they know the directions of significant
places as well. From sacred myths expressed in song, they know the land
by heart. From traditional designs carved on the ground and on ritual
instruments, as well as from the songs, people learn maps of the tribal,
family, and personal places to which they belong. Topographical features
are represented in the Dreaming as a record of who did what in each
place and who are the immanent spirits dwelling invisibly in that place
now.[12] Richard Gould observes that the landmarks of the desert

> are nothing less than the bodies of the totemic beings, or items
> connected with them, transformed during the dreamtime into indi-
> vidual waterholes, trees, sandhills, ridges, and other physiographic
> features, as well as into rock alignments and sacred rockpiles, but
> still spiritually alive and influencing the present. The emotional
> sentiments of kinship are extended by the Aborigines to these
> sacred landmarks. Thus the sight of virtually every landmark, no
> matter how insignificant it may seem to the foreign visitor passing
> through the desert, brings deep emotional satisfaction to the Ab-
> origine. No wonder Aborigines are able to find their way through
> this apparently featureless country, since their memories are con-
> stantly reinforced by spiritual ties with even the smallest rock
> outcrop.[13]

For the Aborigines, physical nature is a domain of located experience.
Moreover, the dramatic history of the ancestral spirits—the great mythic
persons of the Dreaming—is also the grand design for nature, society,
and place, all contained within a spiritual-physical unity. The Aborigines

cannot separate their way of feeling from their way of thinking about places. The Dreaming, like Plato's open-eyed dream vision of *chora*, grasps the nature of place holistically as a unified location of forms, powers, and feelings. The gulf separating the Aborigines' complete topistic integration from our divided way of life may be illustrated by a fantasy. Imagine that you are lost, walking in a city, and you go up to a stranger to ask for directions. Imagine that he or she responds by pulling a Bible out of his or her pocket to find your location and to give you directions. The event is so absurd that it belongs in a dream. But for the Aborigines, the Dreaming is the equivalent of sacred scripture as well as a road map.

Let us return to our obvious world to ask if any features of aboriginal awareness or expression survive in our experience. A good place to begin is the landscape, for the Aborigines take a keen interest in prominent material shapes, such as expressive rock formations, which they interpret as the physical remains of mythical ancestors who lived and breathed as humans do during the Dreamtime. The heroic, gigantic acts performed by the ancestors created the landscape.

In my neighborhood, a rock called "pudding stone," with a massive, deeply textured feeling, makes the most interesting expressive masonry. It was quarried not far from where I live, from a deposit known as "Roxbury conglomerate." Richard Upjohn, a Gothic revival architect, designed St. Paul's, the local church in my neighborhood, around 1850, erecting a picturesque landmark from the stone.[14] The pudding stone endured a recent fire, and the restored church gives the sense of a building here to stay. The sensitive, imaginative use of pudding stone makes it not only a distinguished Gothic church, but also a pivot of settled energy. It stands as an interesting place—good to see, good to feel, and good to think.

From an objective perspective, the formation of pudding stone is explained this way:

> Mechanical weathering usually produces angular rock fragments that, if transported only a short distance from their source, preserve their angularity. If these angular fragments become cemented together the resulting rock is called a *breccia* (pronounced bret'sha).
>
> Most breccias result from catastrophic processes such as landslides, cave collapse or volcanic eruption. Far more commonly, the fragments are transported long distances by streams, waves or

moving ice before they reach their final resting place. In this process they become smooth and rounded as they rub against one
another and against the bedrock over which they move. An accu-
mulation of such rounded boulders, cobbles and pebbles after
cementation is called conglomerate, or, quaintly, pudding stone.[15]

But there is another way to think about pudding stone and the
Roxbury conglomerate, an expressive way that we call "poetic." Oliver
Wendell Holmes sang of pudding stone in a silly poem, "The Dorchester
Giant," the tale of a giant in time of old who shut up his family in a
mammoth pen and "bought them a pudding stuffed with plums, / As big
as the State-House dome." The giant's family, enraged at being kept in
the pen, threw their pudding all over the landscape:

> O! they are in a terrible rout,
> Screaming, and throwing their pudding about,
>   Acting as they were mad.
>
> They flung it over to Roxbury hills,
>   They flung it over the plain,
> And all over Milton and Dorchester too
> Great lumps of pudding the giants threw;
>   They tumbled as thick as rain.
>
> Giant and mammoth have passed away,
>   For ages have floated by;
> The suet is hard as a marrow bone,
> And every plum is turned to a stone,
>   But there the puddings lie. . . .[16]

The way the Aborigines think about landscape, then, may remain
constant in human nature—as Giedion put it, a quality that resurfaces
sunken knowledge.[17] In the modern world, that quality is latent but not
lost, for it remained available to Oliver Wendell Holmes, a civilized,
serious, nineteenth-century Bostonian, even though he and we set it
aside as a bit of child's play not relevant to our important issues. With
the same kind of imagination, many people have walked in the country
and spied a mountain crag that resembles a human head—or have even
gone out to see for themselves a special peak in the White Mountains of
New Hampshire that the local folk call "the Old Man of the Mountain."
Architectural historian Vincent Scully observes that landscape fea-

tures are "sometimes seen as the recognizable images of organic creatures, man, animal, or god." Sir Arthur Evans, digging in Crete, noted
that the profile of Mt. Jouctas from a certain angle suggested a man's face
turned up to the sky, and mentioned that the local population called it
"the head of Zeus." Scully wonders: "When neolithic men . . . first
moved down into Greece as shepherds and farmers, did they already
sense patterns in the landscape which could cause them to build in
certain places and in certain ways for purposes of psychic rather than
simply of physical security?"[18]

Sometimes the Greeks imagined their ground was made by the act of a
God. For example, when the brothers of the Titans—twenty-four tall
and terrible giants born of Mother Earth—revolted against the dominion of Olympus, the gods routed them in a great battle. In the pursuit,
Athena crushed one with a great boulder which became the island of
Sicily. Poseidon hurled a slice excised from the island of Cos (later the
place of Hippocrates) to bury another giant under the Isle of Nisyros.[19]
The earth-shaking, world-making row between gods and giants recalls
events of the Dreaming, not to speak of the pudding stone distributed by
the Dorchester Giant.

Different kinds of people, then, including aboriginal Australians, ancient Greeks, and modern Bostonians, have enjoyed this playful, imaginative way of thinking about landscape. The Greeks often connected
features of landscape or architecture with the mythical adventures of
gods and human or half-human ancestral heroes such as Orestes and
Oedipus, Heracles and Theseus.

The world of the Australian Aborigines is one of the last surviving
examples of perfect topistic unity, but we should pause to consider why
the mythical consciousness of the most primitive people on earth,
whose way of life resembles prehistoric, paleolithic cultures, has any
relevance for an investigation of modern cities. Why do some thinkers in
the vanguard of inquiry about the modern urban world, such as Sigfried
Giedion, Lewis Mumford, and Amos Rapoport, keep going back to the
roots of humanity in the Old Stone Age? Perhaps they know that exploring archaic forms of experience may help us to grasp where we are and
how we stand. The roots of renewal may be nourished by a "restitution
of decayed intelligence."

From the work of developmental psychologists, Cassirer concludes
that the purely expressive character of experience takes precedence over
the capacity to sort out things as discrete entities with determinate

substances and specific attributes. "The understanding of expression is essentially earlier than the knowledge of things." The sense that a place is friendly or unfriendly is an extremely primitive quality of experience—more primitive, Cassirer shows, than the perception of color or form. Mythical thinking conveys this quality: "[I]n the mythical world there is no logical representation or significative meaning, but . . . pure expressive meaning still enjoys almost unrestricted sway." Imagery dominates mythical thought—"It is the *image* which opens up the true essentiality and makes it knowable." The soul or spirit of a place, therefore, may be perceived as the quality of its expressive space, and the spirit of a place means an independent expressive energy that evokes feelings and representations. Moreover, "for mythical thinking the relation between what a thing 'is' and the place in which it is situated is never purely external and accidental; the place is itself a part of the thing's being."[20]

Furthermore, Cassirer writes, "Primitive space is a space of action; and the action is centered around immediate practical needs and interests. So far as we can speak of a primitive 'conception' of space, this conception is not of a purely theoretical character. It is still fraught with concrete personal or social feeling with emotional elements." Perceived and felt qualities remain together in an undifferentiated unity. Cassirer underestimates the importance of representing expressive space. He views it only as a rudimentary stage on the way to the scientific concept of space. As he puts it, "geometrical space takes the place of mythical and magical space. It was a false and erroneous form of symbolic thought that first paved the way to a new and true symbolism, the symbolism of modern science."[21] In his view of the relation between myth and science, Cassirer remained "blinded by condescension."[22]

The criteria that establish rational space are sometimes used to condemn mythic space as false and erroneous, but to the mythic structure of consciousness, rational space is insensate and emptied of meaning.[23] Modern "space" is universal and abstract, whereas a "place" is concrete and particular. People do not experience abstract space; they experience places. A place is seen, heard, smelled, imagined, loved, hated, feared, revered, enjoyed, or avoided. Abstract space is infinite; in modern thinking it means a framework of possibilities. A place is immediate, concrete, particular, bounded, finite, unique. Abstract space is repetitive and uniform. Abstraction moves away from the fullness of experience. Abstract space against concrete place contrasts abstract representation with the pulse of life feeling. The rationalization of space breaks the unity of located experience. Nevertheless, we need abstraction to distinguish the qualities of experience, and the idea of human life without abstractions is absurd. The issue is not to avoid abstractions, but to find what Whitehead called "a right adjustment of the process of abstraction."[24] A renewal of connection to the totality of experience may end the drift of an abstraction toward irrelevance.

Moral categories, moods, and conditions of morale help to define the qualities of places. A place is good or bad, blessed or damned, happy or unhappy, lively or depressed, exciting or dull. The concept of expressive space means the subjective dimension of located experience. Expressive reality refers to what people feel and think and imagine, just as perceptual reality signifies things they perceive, and cognitive reality, things they understand. A place is a concrete milieu and an expressive universe within specific social and physical boundaries, with a location in physical space and time and an identity. "Expressive" means laden with emotional and symbolic features of experience. Both nostalgia and exotic longings represent opposite extremes of imaginary experience. Homesickness presents the yearning for a specific, familiar but lost expressive space. The exotic evokes a feeling about strange and wonderful places we do not know.

Expressive space is not only found but also made. Henry Adams wrote eloquently about experience captured in stone, and he showed how the eleventh century built an emotion into the church of Mont-Saint-Michel. Ruskin defined architecture as the emotional power of arranging and decorating buildings: "Architecture is the art which so disposes and adorns the edifices raised by man for whatsoever uses, that the sight of them contributes to his mental health, power, and pleasure."[25]

Ruskin's definition begs enlargement, for the experience of bad construction and the sight of destruction may contribute to unwanted emotional conditions as well. Moreover, rationally planned space, exclusively intent on providing a machine for living, may nourish unintended feelings, notably boredom, malaise, and violence.

Architecture is one element in a larger process I call "pathetecture." William Lethaby called architecture "building touched with emotion."[26] Pathetecture means constructing emotion by building. It is the process of making expressive space by material means—locating experience by

distributing objects and representations. The process works by organizing or disorganizing materials through construction, dilapidation, and
excavation.

Construction means enclosing space or building houses. Dilapidation
literally means throwing down stones. We recognize unintended, natural dilapidation as the consequence of gravity and decay. Other kinds of
dilapidation make ruins by deliberate acts—for example, as military
forces raze places. In modern cities, the forces of intentional, private,
illegitimate dilapidation are called "vandalism." Legitimate, corporate
dilapidation—communal demolition to make transitional ruins—is
called clearance and renewal. Demolition, even though it destroys
houses, remains a work of pathetecture, for it constructs ruins, which
are expressive spaces. The third type of pathetecture, excavation, includes archaeology, which augments the significance of ruins by the
recovery of expressive surfaces. Wilderness, house, and ruin are three
fundamental topistic ideas that identify categories of expressive space.

The obvious world, therefore, is a world of pathetecture, and I keep
thinking of a fragment from the pre-Socratic philosopher Xenophanes,
which reads *dókos depi pasi tetuktai*, meaning that "appearance"—in the
sense of the world we "suppose"—"is built on everything."[27] The translation remains vacuous unless it leads us to the wisdom in the original
language. Why did Xenophanes use *dókos* instead of more familiar
words such as *dokē* and *dokēsis* to mean appearance, vision, fancy, or
opinion—the several possible meanings of *dókos*? Because the noun
dókos (with the accent on the first syllable) evokes *dokós* (with the accent
on the last syllable), the term for the principal bearing beam of a house.
And *tetuktai*, a form of the verb "to build," evoking the sense of crafts-
manship in building houses and ships, is a term in the ancient vocabu-
lary of industrial construction. The language of the saying of Xenophanes, that appearance is constructed on everything, suggests that the
obvious world is built up by the process that constructs the forms of the
city.

Because architecture is but a stage in the larger process of pathetecture, the built environment should not be narrowly construed as the
child of architecture. The architect is only the first builder in a series of
forces building, unbuilding, and rebuilding structures as well as decorating and redecorating surfaces. The kind of relationship—cooperative
or antagonistic—between the people who make and preserve obvious
surfaces and the rest of the people who share the place determines the

expressive quality of a building. An absence of the types of decoration and demolition we call "vandalism" implies an agreement to let the first builder have the last word.

Moral and emotional qualities give places their most familiar characterizations. "A good place to work." "A nice place to live." Let us imagine anyone living in a place he or she does not like because it is full of bad experiences. The elegance of the "space" or its rational appeal will hardly determine whether a person stays there or moves away. The action in the place, the general feeling of what it means to live there, and the sense of how good or bad it is will probably be decisive. The "soul" of a place is the pure, expressive meaning of a location, a concrete image that represents its quality of expressive space.

*What a powerful thing one's love for a place
can be!*

Aristophanes, *Wasps*
(trans. A. H. Sommerstein)

E I G H T

Expressive Space

In *Phaedrus*, Plato dramatizes the power of places to move the soul. Love and rhetoric are the manifest topics of the *Phaedrus*, but the dialogue also explores different kinds of expressive energy, and I believe that the principal subject unifying this complex inquiry is what Plato calls "psychagogy"—the power to lead the soul.

The dramatic action in the dialogue shows that the expressive energy of a place can match the force of rhetoric as well as the power of romantic love. Socrates discusses different kinds of love, including carnal passion as well as the love of words—and of course, philosophy, the love of wisdom. The context dramatizes still another love not explicitly named in the dialogue. Nevertheless, the Greeks did have a word for it: *philochoria*, the love of place.

As the dialogue opens, Socrates asks Phaedrus where he is coming from and where he is going. They go for a walk just outside the city to a sacred place on the River Ilissus, where they stay awhile, experiencing the beauty of the place, engaged in conversation about love and rhetoric, the nature of the soul, and philosophy. Finally Socrates offers a prayer to the spirits of the place and concludes the dialogue with a word that means "Let us go"—a simple, quiet ending that distills in a single word the framework of the dialogue: the existential meaning of going, and the movement of the soul from one place to another.

Talking about the difference between city and country, Socrates and Phaedrus walk from one to the other and back again. Socrates claims he prefers the energy of the city, protesting that country places and trees make no impression on him. The entire dialogue proves the opposite; here in this rustic location, the men in the marketplace have nothing to tell him, but the trees as well as the forces represented as divinities of the place teach him a great deal.[1]

The two men sit down under a plane tree. From the images and little statues, Socrates identifies the spot as a sacred place of some nymphs and of the river god, Achelous. Under the tall plane tree, a species resembling the sycamore, Socrates turns the conversation to the qualities of this lovely *katagoge*, or resting place. The tree is shady and fragrant, with the cool stream flowing under it, and a chorus of locusts fills the summer breeze with music. Socrates observes the sensory qualities of the *topos* and their expressive effect on the soul. The term Socrates uses, *katagoge*, means a resting place, but it also means anything that leads down. It matches *psychagogia*, the subject of the dialogue. The *katagoge*, leading down to the earth, exercises the power of a sacred place to lead the soul.

Yet Socrates describes the qualities of the place with a certain irony, causing Phaedrus to marvel that he seems like a person who is *atopos* or out of place, a stranger rather than a native. Socrates admits he never goes outside the walls of the city because the trees and the countryside teach him nothing, while the people in the city teach him a great deal. Still, he declares, Phaedrus has found a way to lead him out. Just as people lead hungry animals by holding food in front of them, Phaedrus can lead Socrates, the lover of discourse, by holding a book in front of him.

Before he begins his speech, Socrates covers his head in mock embarrassment and appeals to the Muses for inspiration. Then, waxing eloquent, he interrupts his speech to notice that he seems divinely inspired. He is almost singing a dithyramb, his voice recalling the tone of a Bacchic chant, suggesting that he is possessed by religious frenzy. He is in a state of enthusiasm, which literally means filled by god. Socrates attributes his inspiration not to the Muses but to the work of a divine presence within the *topos*.[2] Then, at the end of the speech, he observes that his delivery has reached a new stage of exaltation, and he pretends to fear an attack of nympholepsy—that is, demonic possession by the nymphs of the place. This is the condition I called "topolepsy" in chapter 1.

Socrates includes love as one species of divine madness, along with three other types: prophetic divination, ritual healing, and poetic creativity. The dramatic action in the dialogue hints at a fifth but unnamed type of divine mania caused by the power of place—implied in the madness of topolepsy or nympholepsy, which was experienced as a serious affliction in archaic times before Plato.[3] I might add other derangements caused by places, such as nostalgia, which was treated in medical circles as a prominent neurophysiological syndrome in the seventeenth and eighteenth centuries.[4] Toward the end of the dialogue, Socrates reviews the typology. Love is a madness, but there are two kinds of madness—one arising from human illness and the other from a divine liberation from customary ways of living. The four types of divine madness are ascribed to the agency of four gods: prophecy by Apollo, ritual madness by Dionysus, poetic inspiration by the Muses, and the insanity of love by Aphrodite and Eros.[5] The implied fifth kind, presumably, would be inspired by the indigenous spirits of a place and by gods of the earth such as Pan, Achelous the river god, and the nymphs.

To clarify the nature of love and to distinguish it from carnal appetite, Socrates examines the nature of the soul. Indestructible and immortal, the soul is a composite unit like a pair of winged horses and a charioteer. Souls are the curators of the universe, and they travel over heaven taking care of all things that have no souls. In vivid mythical terms, Socrates describes the heavenly procession of souls. Some lose their wings and fall, to occupy earthly bodies until, after the allotted millennia of living according to justice, they again grow wings and fly back to heaven. Meanwhile, their exalted experiences on earth, such as love, recollect the vision of beauty and other realities previously beheld in heaven.

Socrates describes heaven as a *topos*, and the *topos* above the vault of heaven as the ultimately good expressive space. Zeus, the greatest psychagogue, regularly leads the celestial procession of souls, including the gods, across the vault of heaven where they enjoy in feasts and banquets a diet of pure mental activity. The *topos* above heaven is the location of pure Being, to be ingested by reason alone, the pilot of the soul. Here the gods and other elevated souls find their nourishment and happiness, while the souls who fall to earth must feed on an inferior diet of appearance. The *topos* at the summit of heaven is described as a meadow that nourishes the best part of the soul with its own true pasturage.[6]

After exploring love and the nature of the soul, the discourse turns to dialectic, rhetoric, and philosophy, with continual reference to their psychagogic energy—their power to lead the soul. Throughout, Socrates keeps calling attention to the eloquence of the place, reporting that he feels the excitement of invisible spirits. His language remains ironic, but the irony does not mean that he is not telling the truth. It suggests that the experience is real but also signals a playful attitude to the mythical imagery in which the experience is expressed. He calls attention to the locusts, imagined as local spies who report back to the Muses, but attributes his own inspired eloquence not to the Muses but to the nymphs of the place.[7] The dialogue ends with his prayer, "O beloved Pan and all the gods here. . . ." The concluding thought, therefore, addresses Pan, who represents chthonic eloquence, as well as the entopic gods, the immanent deities—the divine forces who represent the energy of the place.[8]

Socrates characterizes the place, exploring its qualities not only by what he says but also by the change in the way he talks about it. His language shifts to show a change of perspective, from the glib observation of a pleasant place to the profound experience of a sacred place. Just as he makes successive speeches about love, ascending from shallow infatuation to profound erotic experience, he offers two different interpretations of the place. At first, referring to it as a pleasant spot, he speaks with patent irony and in a sophisticated, affected style, praising the charms of the site. Commentaries suggest that his remark is a parody of some contemporaneous, urbane way of talking about a country place. Socrates discards this way of speaking immediately and eventually shifts to an idiom more appropriate to the qualities of a sacred place.

In the first speech, Socrates merely reports the effect of the place on his senses: the trees spread shade and smell fragrant; the water feels cool; the grass is thick and comfortable; and the locusts sound like music.[9] The second interpretation expresses the effect of the place on the soul. Phaedrus never mentions the qualities of the place and takes it all for granted, expressing amazement that Socrates behaves as a stranger in the countryside, although they are only a short stroll away from the city gate. Nevertheless, even though he arrives as a stranger, Socrates serves as a guide to the place because he gives an account of its meaning.

The main issue, we should remember, is psychagogy and the energies that lead the soul. The dialogue plays with the meaning of guidance. As Phaedrus conducts Socrates over the ground, leading him out of the city to the sacred place in the country, Socrates guides Phaedrus to wisdom by philosophical discourse. Socrates compliments Phaedrus on being an excellent guide, or "xenagogue"—the kind of guide who shows strangers around. Phaedrus replies that Socrates speaks like a man out of place, resembling indeed a stranger being led around by a guide. But although he pretends to be led by Phaedrus on the surface, Socrates serves in a deeper sense as a guide to the place, directing thought and shaping experience. The Socratic side of Plato, it is clear, reaches beyond the city walls, but stays close to the earth.

In *Phaedrus*, place resembles a lover; in *Timaeus*, *chora* serves as a nurse. The latter image, showing that experience is nourished by place, leads us to recognize that we internalize the environment not only materially but also emotionally and symbolically. Resembling the way nurse serves child, place distributes the qualities of experience. The Aborigines find their physical food in the desert, but the same environment also feeds them a diet of forms, feelings, and symbols. We absorb what Plato calls the *pathemata*, meaning the qualities and feelings of places. In other words, our matrix serves food for the spirit—an expressive diet. I call the expressive diet of a place the topistic diet.

We experience the qualities of places through sensations; we see, smell, hear, touch, and walk around a place. In this series, the only one of the traditional five senses we exclude as irrelevant is the sensation of taste. Nevertheless, a gastronomic metaphor illuminates topistic experience. The energy of a place is fed by intangible provisions—that is, by the ration of symbols, meanings, feelings, and sentiments found or built there. In some parts of India the festival of the goddess Laxshmi dramatizes topistic nourishment. The people, Brahmin and Untouchable alike, ceremonially paint their houses at this time, calling the ritual "feeding" the buildings.[10]

Originally, the Greek word *diaita*, meaning diet, did not signify material food alone. It meant a characteristic way of living—a mode of life, with special reference to food and dress, maintenance, board and lodging. The Latin equivalent of the Greek *diaita* is *cultus victusque*, which means both culture and the necessities of life. A "diet" in its original sense, then, suggests the specific manner in which life-styles are rationed or divided up.[11]

In the ancient and medieval worlds, the town was a common place in which all the people shared the same diet of symbols expressed in the forms of buildings, monuments, and natural features of the landscape. Sacred processions turned into communal banquets of the spirit, ritual perambulations in which the entire population meditatively digested the meanings and feelings built into the town. Lewis Mumford writes:

> To starve the eye, the ear, the skin, the nose is just as much to court death as to withhold food from the stomach. Though diet was often meager in the Middle Ages, though many comforts for the body were lacking even for those who did not impose penitential abstentions upon themselves, the most destitute or the most ascetic could not wholly close his eyes to beauty. The town itself was an ever-present work of art, and the very clothes of its citizens on festival days were like a flower garden in bloom. Today one can still capture some of that feeling by following the evening procession on Saint John's day in Florence, from Santa Maria Novella to the Piazza della Signoria.[12]

In *Antigone*, the drama by Sophocles, the chorus praises the wonderful powers of man. He has taught himself many things: navigation, agriculture, hunting, animal husbandry, language, architecture, medical skill, and so forth. In this series of accomplishments, Sophocles includes—just before architecture—"the feelings that make the town."[13] The use of materials to build such feelings is pathetecture. Each year, in the Panathenaic Festival, the people absorbed the feelings of the town in the course of a ritual procession that articulated the sources of energy rhythmically evoking interest, excitement, and wonder.

The content of the topistic diet makes the form and symbolism of buildings important. It reveals another dimension of the medieval conflicts over ecclesiastical architecture, dramatized in the moment when Gothic style emerged by the confrontation between the ascetic convictions of St. Bernard of Clairvaux and the gourmet spiritual appetite of Suger, the Abbot of St. Denis.

In the ideal medieval town, rich and poor shared a common expressive diet, just as the religious ideal expected the rich man to share his "broken meats"—that is, his leftover food—with the poor at his gate. But in the modern town, we expect separate neighborhoods to distribute a range of expressive diets according to class. At the extremes, the rich enjoy pretty houses in nice suburbs while the poor endure squalid ruins in the slum or occupy dreary high-rise containers intended as remedial housing. To put it in the style of the *Timaeus*, a cacotope is a rough nurse serving poisonous things to make unhappy experience. For the most part, the poor live in cacotopes where noxious objects collect to serve up a regular menu of bad experiences. The surfaces of these places are expected to show images and symbols consistent with the poverty of the interiors. In modern cities, the places of rich and poor are distinguished by their expressive diets.

Topistic feelings make their way to the surface and achieve graphic expression there. The surface of a place gathers symbols and through them achieves a unity of expression. Surfaces of a city are covered with marks, stains, images, symbols, and messages that give something to think about. A large number of designs and inscriptions deliberately claim attention, seeking to give direction, to shape thought, or to inspire sentiments. These claims are not all equally important. Everyone who knows how to live in a city learns to distinguish and evaluate the meanings smeared, inscribed, modeled, and carved on the surfaces. Urban sensibility is molded within the framework that sorts out notices, warnings, orders, suggestions, requests, as well as mementos, from a wide range of official, commercial, communal, political, popular, and personal sources.

Besides practical messages of all sorts, the surfaces carry records of subjective experience, including representations of place. Because the most ready surfaces are found on walls, floors, roofs, or pavements, the laws of property control their availability for representing experience. No surface gets marked or shaped legitimately without title or permission. In this way, through their exclusive rights of presenting surfaces, the government or the property owners claim the legitimate monopoly of representing the collective experience of the city. Similarly, they execute the power to shape its subjective space.

Mere ownership of a surface is not sufficient. The owners will often erect a statue, commission a painting, show a scene, or put up a sign that satisfies rules of propriety as well as laws of property. This expensive procedure requires private revenue or public funds. To put it another way, there is no representation without taxation. Nevertheless, everyone knows that legitimate authority does not guarantee effective control. Surfaces gather graffiti, images, and other illegitimate, clandestine representations. Graffiti must be understood not only as the public calligraphy of the lowly, but also as monuments of the poor.

The word "monument" comes from a Latin verb that means "to remind." Monuments are representations of any form intended to remind people of something or someone. In the range of graffiti, one always finds political reminders: "Remember Kent State!" "Remember

Attica!" "Remember Red Lion Square!" But for the most part, graffiti inscribe personal memorials—hundreds of thousands of names are monuments of specific identity. By spraying names in paint, the graffiti artists seek to achieve what every monument maker wants: imperishability. Their representations, familiar in every city, make up the little tradition of urban aesthetics. The rich and powerful, who also erect their names and tell their stories, have preferred to do it in stone and bronze, the medium of the great tradition.

Simple monuments merely register an identity or stimulate the memory. During World War II, countless servicemen immortalized the name of a mysterious person whose only known characteristic was a passion for monuments. An impressive portion of the world's surface was inscribed with the memorable words, "Kilroy was here." No one ever identified Kilroy, but he inspired the little tradition's ironic version of the great tradition's monuments to the Unknown Soldier.

The imagination of the great tradition strives to express visions of the good life through the representation of paradigmatic figures, making them look sublime and picturesque. The little tradition, which sometimes conveys goodness and beauty, also offers a glimpse of the bad life, expressed in a vulgar idiom by ugly forms. Conventional sensibility will not acknowledge that ugliness is an aesthetic category as well as beauty, and that all representations—sublime and vulgar, beautiful and ugly— may be grasped by principles of art.

Those who manage the poor spaces of the city would prefer to keep them neutral, invisible, and unexpressive, rejecting the calligraphy and iconography on the surface. In public housing, the poor are expected to dwell in an environment of administered surfaces. The artists of the *vulgus*, by covering the surface with monuments of the experience within and making an emotional impact that forces outsiders to turn away, claim the power to represent their own subjective space. They modify their topistic diet by painting the walls with marks, stains, names, and symbols. Sometime around the end of the 1960s, the graffiti artists of New York began a campaign that changed the diet of the city. The smooth, profitable surface turned into a location of trouble. A band of expressive guerrillas surfaced to share their diet with the rest of the city. It is an illegitimate, vernacular movement of pathetecture—constructing feelings that make a town—and consistent with one of the perennial intentions of Western architecture: the dematerialization of the wall.

8-1. *Painted Fence*
(Photo by author)

In 1974, Norman Mailer eloquently described the outbreak of graffiti on the surfaces of New York, recognizing it as a reaction to technocratic architecture and an effort to change the expressive space of the city. He suggested that if the movement continued, "this entire city of bland architectural high-rise horrors would have been covered with paint." But the people who hate the sight of colossal polychrome calligraphy would prefer a diet of dull monotony for public surfaces. The graffiti movement, according to Mailer, suggests a rebellion of slum populations chilled by the bleakness of modern design. Yet the impulse was broken, and Mailer asked, "was it that one could never understand graffiti until there was a clue to the opposite passion to look upon monotony and call it health?" Profoundly depressing to some people, the graffiti hurt their moods. Mailer observed that reports came in saying "The life would go out of everybody when they saw the [subway] cars defaced."

The graffiti made other people feel that the surface was out of control, confirming that the city was a dangerous place.[14] The marks, stains, and scrawls—as well as some masterpieces of vernacular calligraphy—appeared as a topistic invasion, a campaign for illegitimate control of the

8-2. Detail from Painted Fence
(Photo by author)

surface of experience. Engaged in surface warfare, outlaws and officials struggled to claim the veneer of the city. The war was an extension of an emotional politics of spaces—the struggle to maintain or to change expressive space. People like to control their own diet of symbols or at least turn it over to agencies that will design an expressive desert or patrol neutral surfaces that make no extravagant claims on psychic energy.

In my own fieldwork in 1970, I observed a crisis of topistic diet. In the midst of ethnographic research in the Boston public housing project, I was charmed by a lively panorama that some of the children in the community had painted on a wooden fence around the Roman Catholic church and convent, which stands just across the street from the housing project. In bright and lovely colors, the children of the neighborhood—encouraged by the nuns, authorized by the pastor, supplied with plenty of paint by the local APAC (a federal antipoverty agency), and inspired by Boston's first SUMMERTHING (an arts and recreation program)—had produced an extensive mural that stretched across the fence for almost an entire block. It showed celestial objects, happy faces,

8-3. Fence Repainted
(Photo by author)

children enjoying themselves, a whale, lots of amiable fauna and flora, a spaceman, and an abundance of exuberant forms, but some of the symbols evoked political meanings. One saw the sign for peace or disarmament as well as the words, "Peace and Hope," and a Star of David. Some of the local people were proud of the fence and enjoyed showing it off to visitors. Others expressed discomfort over it.

In October of that year, I brought some students who wanted to do fieldwork on an introductory tour of the housing projects and their environment. Intending to point out the fence, I drove around the block several times absentmindedly, looking for it in vain. It took a while for it to dawn on me that the beautiful fence was gone. On closer inspection, it appeared that all the pretty pictures were covered over by a coat of green paint that was still wet.

We went into the convent and talked to the nun who had organized the summer program. She was surprised at the news and said she did not even know that the fence had been painted over. I suggested that perhaps some hostile people in the neighborhood had wiped it out, but she offered that if the paint were green—the same color as the other

8-4. Detail from Repainted Fence
(Photo by author)

wooden structures—then the pastor himself had probably given the order. Why had he done so after expressing personal delight with the children's paintings the previous summer? Had he changed his mind? Had he yielded to specific forces in the community who found the paintings offensive? Did he fear or anticipate criticism from a specific group? It was not crucial that he did or did not give the order to paint the fence. The important issue, it seemed to me, was that a collective effort producing symbolic expressions on a highly visible surface in the community had been censored.

The mystery of the painted fence intrigued me and opened a line of inquiry. The original imagery and subsequent censorship together dramatized conflicting forces with different attitudes about how the community should be experienced and expressed. Interviews and conversations eventually revealed that many people did not want to absorb the images on the fence as a regular diet. Moreover, they felt that the mural did not faithfully represent the emotions of the neighborhood—the true sense of place. Still, I must add that for its entire life of five months, the mural had remained undisturbed by irrelevant marks or stains. But soon after the fence was painted over in monotonous, institutional green, the surface gathered new symbols. Now deprived of images, the fence said in words: "Bloody Murder . . . Bloody Murder . . . Love . . . Peace and War."

Both the subway graffiti in New York and the images on the wooden fence in Boston influenced the mood of their places. The people who wanted them removed feared that the marks, stains, and images had the power to establish a dominant atmosphere. Both places brought to the surface hidden features of human experience. The painted surfaces of the New York subway support a nocturnal world of demonic energy in which hidden presences violate boundaries to express their rage in ceaseless scrawls. The painted fence for a brief moment supported a solar world of cheerful feelings. In both places, the signs on the walls were experienced as unwanted omens.

N I N E

Ominous Space

Writing on the wall—when inscribed by an unknown hand—conveys a warning of impending doom. It remains one of the most vivid and durable idea-images in the Western tradition, haunting the corridors of topistic imagination from one century to the next. The ominous meaning originates in the Hebrew Bible, where the fifth chapter of the Book of Daniel represents dramatically the collapse of the Babylonian empire. The obscure message on the wall takes us back to the Chaldean world, by which I mean Assyro-Babylonian experience, and even before that to the Sumerians, who built the first civilization in recorded history.

According to the story, Belshazzar—represented as the son of Nebuchadnezzar and the last Babylonian king before the Persian conquest—gave a great feast for a thousand nobles and the women of his palace, at which they drank wine from the sacred vessels looted from the temple in Jerusalem. In the midst of this revelry and sacrilege, the king saw the weird fingers of a human hand, illuminated by the lamp, writing four legible but inscrutable Aramaic words on the plaster of the wall. Terrified by the apparition, he called for diviners, exorcists, and astrologers to interpret the ominous writing. None of the wise men of Babylon was able to make sense of it, but Daniel, famous for great spiritual powers, was fetched from the community of Jewish captives and deciphered the words. Weighed and numbered, the kingdom did not measure up, and God was signing it over to the Persians. Impressed by the interpretation, the king raised Daniel to exalted rank. That very night, however, Belshazzar was slain, and the Persians took the kingdom.

The story of Daniel ridicules the helpless servants of gods who are confronted by the prophet inspired by God. In the ancient world, Chaldean divination claimed to have all the answers, and biblical writers enjoyed deflating this pretension by pitting a Jewish sage against a Babylonian magician. In that world, however, ominous space or a surface bearing omens did not always convey bad news. The Babylonians read all kinds of meaning in the perceptions of everyday life, from cracks and bulges on walls to stars in the sky. They read the phenomena of the universe not simply as appearances but as signs communicating messages from invisible forces. Omens gave warnings, but they also reassured anxious mortals that the environment was regulated by spirits who cared. Through the interpretation of omens, trained observers grasped the surface of experience with a system of divination. Regarding the perceptions they recorded as expressions of divine intention, they saved the expressive energy of phenomena.

Among the myriad schemes of Chaldean divination, finger reading or dactylomancy is obsolete, although fortune-tellers continue to practice palm reading, or cheiromancy, which remains a form of personal divination. Dactylomancy included a range of phenomena perceived on or by fingers, from images discerned on a prepared, polished thumbnail to any spiritual message that might be indicated by a finger on the hand or in the mind.

A king and his wise men would expect to see the grand vicissitudes of royal destiny written in the skies, traced in the signals of planets, meteors, comets, and eclipses, interpreted by formulas that we now loosely call "astrology." Instead, in the Book of Daniel, they saw the fall of the dynasty written on a wall—a conventional location for the humblest kind of divination. Such divinations were interpreted in the series of tablets we now classify as the *shumma ālu*, named after the first words on one tablet. The Babylonians knew this collection of omens by the initial line, "If a city is located on a hill. . . ."

For millennia the image of a city on a hill has suggested, in different ways, the expressive intelligibility of urban life. In 1630 John Winthrop, aboard the *Arabella*, told the "great company of religious people" about to reach the shore of New England that they would be "as a Citty upon a

Hill," meaning that the entire Christian world would be observing their conduct. His image refers to the Sermon on the Mount, which declares that "a city that is set on a hill cannot be hid," and the biblical text follows this saying with the observation that people do not light a candle to hide it under a bushel but to illuminate the house (Matt. 5:14–15). Moreover, one of the parables in another book of the New Testament teaches that secrets are meant to be revealed, following the same saying about the candle by the words, "there is nothing hid, which shall not be manifested" (Mark 4:21–22).

The Babylonian "city on a hill" texts illuminated hidden messages in the little phenomena of everyday life. Babylonian wise men, trained as professional observers—the theorists of Chaldea—scrutinized and preserved all the manifestations of daily life in a great, complex scheme of interpretation, designed to reveal what was obscure and to render the environment intelligible. From the appearances in the skies to the trivia of a peasant household, they read, decoded, and recorded the phenomena in universal catalogs of signs. Meaningless perceptions were unthinkable. They experienced the visible surface of the world as a tablet on which gods and other invisible spirits wrote their intentions or issued commands.

The Babylonians experienced the obvious world as a tissue of expressive signs. Their diviners, working as see-ers and cryptographers, saved the phenomena in thousands of reference books that decoded the signs—the omen texts written on clay. Some procedures, classified as "queries," deliberately asked the gods to communicate answers to specific questions in oil, smoke, or the liver of a sheep. But quite apart from mantic rituals soliciting divine instruction by certain procedures—such as pouring oil in a bowl of water (lecanomancy) or burning incense (libanomancy) to observe the movement and figuration of the oil or the smoke—divination by simple observation organized an encyclopedic discipline for interpreting unsolicited, spontaneous signs. It sought omens in all the observable phenomena of the world—celestial and terrestrial, inanimate and animate, animal and human, physiological and psychological—including dreams.[1] The diviners extracted significance from every imaginable perception that attracted unusual attention. To put it another way, they read the expressive energy of urgent perceptions, recording interpretations that made them intelligible.

Of course, our imaginations still play with figuration, discovering shapes in clouds and on different surfaces. When we were children, my sister and I used to inspect the chocolate pudding our mother often served for dessert, discerning and interpreting pictures on the coagulated surface, and we may have invented the only kind of divination not anticipated by the Babylonians. Those diviners, more than sixteen hundred years before our era, were the first scholars known to history, and the ancient world considered the omen texts and treatises written in the Akkadian language as major intellectual achievements. With a few important exceptions—such as the Jews, who rejected its idolatrous and magical thinking on religious grounds—almost everyone admired "Chaldean science," meaning astral studies, which in turn had to be understood in the larger context of its scheme of divination. The codification of omens—a system of observations and predictions—matched the importance of Hammurabi's Code, which was compiled about the same time and remains the earliest written code of law in the historical record.

The scholars organized the omens in comprehensive treatises, and the most famous as well as the most abundant of these studies make up a kind of omen encyclopedia, with an inventory of the risks and conditions of daily life in the midst of home, family, work, social networks, the city, and the environment. In this category, something like ten thousand omens occupy more than one hundred tablets, identified by the initial Akkadian words, *shumma ālu*, and known to us in English as the series, "If a city is located on a hill."[2]

> If a city is located on a hill: the inhabitants of this city will not prosper.

> If a city is located on low ground: the inhabitants of this city will prosper.

> If in a city there are many deaf people: this city will prosper.

> If in a city there are many blind people: there will be sorrow in the city.

> If pigs gnash their teeth: that town will be scattered.

> If fish are numerous in a river: quiet dwelling for the land.

> If a white dog pisses on a man: hard times will seize that man.

> If a red dog pisses on a man: that man will have happiness.

If black ants are seen on the foundations of a new house . . . that house will get built and the owner will live to grow old.

If yellow ants are seen . . . the foundations will collapse and the house will not get built.

If white ants are seen . . . the house will be destroyed.

If red ants are seen . . . the owner will die before his time.

If a snake keeps thrashing about in a man's house: that house will be thrown down or destroyed.

If a scorpion lurks in a man's bed: that man will have riches.

If a falcon eats a bird on the roof of a man's house and puts it down: someone in that house will die.[3]

Ranging over the phenomena of everyday life, the omens in this series observed cities, houses and the events within them, animals of all kinds, insects, fires, and so forth. Nothing escaped observation and prediction, for every phenomenon recorded served as a sign and a message from invisible spiritual forces. The observers remained alert to the behavior of insects, ants, snakes, scorpions, lizards, and domesticated animals, especially dogs. Inside houses, they paid special attention to the condition of walls. Cracks on the wall were especially significant, as were fungi, buckling, and crumbling plaster. The position of a fungus, figuration of cracks, and pattern of crumbling plaster were read as divine handwriting on the walls.[4]

These homely signs spelled out the private fate of the little man, who anxiously inspected his intimate environment to predict health or illness, family fortunes, success or failure in business, and every thought of his future. Because this kind of divination remained open to the humblest peasant, it occupied the lowest status; highest esteem was reserved for the mantic wisdom of the *bārû*, a word meaning "observer" which is usually translated as "diviner." The most exalted signs—interpreted by the *bārû* in the way judges interpret the law, by studying the records of previous decisions and making new ones by analogy and by reference to the older cases—determined the fate of kings, commanders, and the whole public domain.

Enjoying privileged education, the scholarly community studying *bārûtu*, the lore of divination, worked as official observers—or inspectors of the universe—who were required to take an oath of loyalty to the king, and the government depended on their reports for every important decision. Only a rare king would fail to consult a *bārû*, or perhaps several diviners, at every turn and demand: "What does that sign mean?" and "What should we do now?" Kings ruled the state according to divine instructions.[5] Indispensable to public affairs, the *bārû* explored the skies to find royal destiny written in the stars, observed the behavior of noble birds—such as the eagle, falcon, and raven—to learn the outcome of military campaigns, and searched for policy in the livers of sheep.[6] Therefore, the irony in Dan. 5 adds an extra sting of humiliation when the divine hand writes the fall of Babylon not in the sky but on a wall.

Although the ancient Jews rejected the magic and theology of their Babylonian inheritance, condemning the practice of divination, they never abandoned their awareness of signs, and they interpreted remarkable events on earth and in the sky as "signs and wonders" revealing the intentions of God. As the apostle Paul said, "the Jews require a sign, and the Greeks seek after wisdom" (1 Cor. 1:22). The prophet Jeremiah cautioned the Israelites to shun the ways of heathen nations and not to *fear* signs in the heavens (Jer. 10:2). He did not deny the presence of celestial signs, but he defined an orthodox emotional response, warning his people to avoid feelings of awe and dismay when they observed signs. They were commanded not to worship the stars (2 Kings 23:5) but not forbidden to make the sky intelligible.

Modern translations of the Bible have disenchanted the skies, eliminating the sacromagical, archaic sense of signs. The original Hebrew words in the story of Creation say that on the fourth day, God said: "Let luminaries be in the expanse of the heavens . . . and let them be for signs and for seasons and for days and years" (Gen. 1:14). All the old translations, including the Greek Septuagint, the Latin Vulgate, and the English King James Bible translate the passage to mean that the lights in the sky were to serve as *signs* as well as for seasons and for units of temporal measurement. But the language may be interpreted to read another way, and both the New English Bible and the Jerusalem Bible say that God created the lights in the sky as signs to indicate festivals, seasons, days, and so forth; that is, to serve exclusively the rational or utilitarian function of making up a calendar or marking time. The difference suggests that modern translators do not believe in "signs," whereas the old versions convey a sense of the ancient world, where Jews as well as Chaldeans experienced the phenomena of divination.

Mesopotamian people called stars "the writing of the heavens," which spelled out divine messages in the same way that spiritual forces expressed their feelings and intentions through signs on a wall or in the intestines of a sheep. A seventh-century king of Assyria compared the constellations in the sky to the writing of his own name. The same goddess who expressed the spirit of growing reeds held the stylus as well—the reed instrument for inscribing on clay tablets—presiding over both the art of writing and the science of the stars, which included all the disciplines we now call astronomy, astrology, and astromythology.[7] Eventually the epithet "Chaldean" came to mean a star sage, and for a thousand years—until Athens replaced Babylon as the school of the civilized mind—the mystique of Chaldean wisdom dominated intellectual life.[8]

Thoughtful attention to the appearances in the sky, as well as systematic records of the observables, probably go back to the origin of humanity. Everyone knows about the practical uses of the stars. Mariners probably navigated by them long before the Phoenicians. Farmers watched the constellations for the proper time of sowing and reaping. Shepherds watched them to mark the cycle of night, anticipating by their positions in the sky the subtle approach of dawn. In the same way, they marked the cycle of seasons; in Greece, when Arcturus, guardian of the Great Bear, appeared on the eastern horizon at dawn, the shepherds prepared to shift their flocks from summer pasture to winter fold, taking pleasure in knowing that down in the plain, villagers responded to the same astral signal by gathering the new wine, moving the grapes from vines to tubs.[9] Along with the practical uses of celestial observation, however, archaic people also explored the sky for "theory."

The ancient roots of several words in our language suggest that watching the sky became the model for informed, theoretical observation. For example, "contemplation" derives from *templum*, the imaginary celestial-terrestrial grid projected by a Roman augur as he observed the direction of lightning or the flight of birds. Similarly, to "consider"— meaning to study something carefully—derives from *sidus*, the Latin word for "star" or a constellation of stars, and in that language *considerare*, originally a technical term in the Roman practice of divination, meant "to observe the stars carefully."

The Greeks imagined nine Muses ruling over story and song, including Urania, the Muse of astronomy, who inspired the mythic lore of the skies. We might expect Muses of poetry and history, but a Muse of

astronomy seems odd until we learn that paleoastronomy included what
people said or sang about the stars. The domain of archaic astronomy
embraced *astro-nomoi* (the ways of the stars) as well as *astro-logoi* (stories
about the stars), but it held more than the sum of what we now call
"astronomy" and "astrology" because it included a mythology of the sky.

The paleoastronomers saved the observations in their own way by
preserving a dimension of perception irrelevant to scientific astronomy,
namely, the eloquence of the stars—the expressive energy of astral
phenomena. They read the stars superstitiously, making sense of the
patterns by mythical thinking, whereas modern astronomers observe
them rationally, seeking intelligibility in mathematical expression.

As the rational outlook drove out celestial mythology, it also lost an
intimate connection with the sky. A scientist reflects:

> Here we find ourselves more baffled: we cannot properly compre-
> hend the pattern of the stars. Our astronomers are working hard to
> find rules of brain action that shall make us able to do so, but in
> spite of their considerable discoveries I feel sure that they would
> agree that they have not yet found the really significant clue. In this
> respect we are all like the people born blind, who on receiving their
> sight see only a revolving mass of lights. It is not to belittle the
> conclusions of astronomers to say that when we look at the heavens
> we are as babies—we have no means of understanding the signifi-
> cance of what we see.[10]

Mythic imagination gave archaic people a means of grasping the
significance of what they saw. In their frame of mind, the sky was a
meaningful place where mortals did not dwell yet felt at home. Today, we
identify intelligibility with rationality, which means thinking according
to certain rules, but archaic people knew and understood the sky in the
same way they knew a place on earth—through feelings, imagination,
and through mythology, or anecdotes about the gods. Their sense of sky
was an expressive, dramaturgic intelligibility, conveyed by an association
of impulses, emotions, dramatic encounters, and stories—an intelligibility with its center in the life of feeling. The Greeks, for example, said
they saw the tender, feminine Pleiades dive into the sea to escape the
rude strength of the hunter Orion.

Ancient civilizations preserved stories of the heavens that interpreted
the meaning of celestial bodies and explained their movements in the
language of myth. On the surface of the sky they mapped a net of

intangible, invisible qualities: fear, flight, strength, courage, wisdom, humor, piety, envy, rage, domination. They experienced the sky as expressive space, full of drama, meaning, and feeling. Mythology brought the sky near and made it intimate, and people learned celestial topography as the Australian Aborigines knew the desert through the songs of the Dreaming. Jerome Lettvin suggests that myths helped the ancients to map and memorize the relations of stars. The ambiguities and broad interpretations of mythic thinking

> only adds to the richness and, if you wish, the memorability of the ideas. For myths are more memorable the more things one can map on them. And there is for me a great poetic quality in a language whereby the relations of animals to each other, people to each other, the heavens to the earth, the gods to humankind, can all be worded in about the same way, until finally, by a single set of sentences, I can remember all of the universes as if they were maps of one another.[11]

The language of myths—memorable, dramatic, emotional, full of imagination, designed to enchant the mind as well as the stars—preserved a way of talking, singing, and thinking that expressively connected the sky, the earth, and human life. Stories as well as omens animated the sky.

Celestial animism may be as old as humanity. Prehistoric artists discerned animal forms in the cracks and lumps of cavern walls, and it is not unreasonable to suppose that prehistoric observers may have also pictured animals in the sky. The Babylonians passed on the zodiac, which in Greek literally means the "girdle of beasts," or "circle of living things," but it is doubtful that they invented it. Historians like to associate the zodiac and the constellations with the needs of agriculture in the neolithic period, but even before that era, paleolithic hunters may have observed beasts in the sky. Archaeological evidence suggests that at the time *Homo sapiens sapiens* first appears in the fossil record, people were not only watching the sky, but also leaving systematic records of the observables. Cro-Magnon observers about thirty thousand years ago carved a small bone tool with twenty-nine sets of marks arranged in a serpentine pattern that may be a lunar notation system. The pattern corresponds to the changing phases of the moon, with full moons recorded on the left, half moons in the middle, and crescents on the right. About the same time, an artist sculpted the Vogelherd horse, a small, remarkably sophisticated image carved from the ivory tusk of a

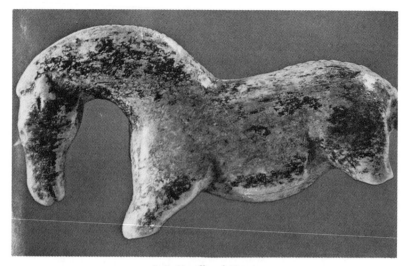

9-1. *Vogelherd Horse*
(Alexander Marshack)

mammoth, and the earliest known example of animal sculpture.[12] From what we surmise about prehistoric imagination, we might guess that animal images and celestial observation joined together in the forms of constellations. Pictures of celestial beasts and the stories they inspire have a way of making hunters as well as shepherds feel at home in the sky.

Everything we can interpret from the remains of early civilizations suggests the continuity of prehistoric ideas about the emotional, dramaturgic unity of the world. In addition these ideas represented the interrelated lives of deities, humans, and beasts. Giedion believes that this conviction of interdependence and unity pervaded the whole of prehistoric experience from its language of symbols to its sense of space.[13]

The old Babylonian or Chaldean system identified certain stars as representations of the major gods, picked out a group of them as the "councillor gods," and named the planets—for example, the ones we call Mercury and Venus—after the most powerful gods, such as Marduk and Ishtar. They also called the planets "the Interpreters," because their irregular but intelligible movements supposedly communicated the will of the gods. The diviner-astronomers studied the tracks of all the heavenly bodies as celestial writing on a great map that contained all the routes of destiny, thus initiating the study of astrology. Their determination to know exact positions and destinations of celestial presences drove Babylonian scholars to invent a mathematics for observation, thus initiating the science of astronomy. Yet, in the history of thought, astrology as well as astronomy moved in a direction that objectified celestial phenomena, and now both of them work out their observations in computer programs. Both astrology and astronomy abandoned the old Babylonian experience of the sky as expressive space.

With vivid imagery, paleoastronomy represented cosmos and human self in an organic whole. Today we acknowledge that relation again, with less eloquence, as new scientific research hints at cosmic forces that link the metabolisms of stars and humans. Moreover, in unexpected ways the philosophical assumptions of physics and biology have drifted away from the ideas of Galileo, Descartes, and Newton. We also know that all observations of natural phenomena contain traces of ourselves. The profound change of mind in the past few decades, restless for a synthesis of objective and subjective experience, advises a new regard for the old rubbish of divination, which expressed in mythic idiom the deep sense that humans are implicated in the processes they examine.[14]

Our "common sense" assumes that eyes, ears, and other organs of perception register the world independently, without direct help from the rest of our experience. When we see an object with a certain form, color, and texture, the mind automatically registers "tree." If we pause to think about the "critical tradition" in philosophy and psychology, we may recall that the thought, "tree," is what Kant called an "intuition" that the mind associates with specific data received by the eye. However, the intuition—or whatever name you prefer to give the mental representation—is not a "natural" psychological event but the complex product of social and civilizational processes. From infancy we are trained not only in *what* but also in *how* to see. We learn to build the world and the things in it by organizing selected fragments of experience. The sense organs arouse sensations, but the mind selects, sorts, combines, and builds them into the name-bearing, identifiable objects we know as *things*. Therefore, the obvious world is indeed a *scheme of things*.

The familiar world depends on what we contribute to the data received by our sense organs. As Owen Barfield writes, we perceive things with the great part of our whole human being. Hearing a certain sound, I may say, for example, that I hear a thrush singing. All I hear with my ears is the sound the bird makes, but to "'hear a thrush singing,' I am hearing, not with my ears alone, but with all sorts of other things like mental habits, memory, imagination, feeling and . . . will." The mind of the perceiver, trained in a particular society and civilization, *represents* what is perceived.[15]

People who are born blind and then gain their sight after optical surgery as adults report a long and painful process of learning to see. At first they experience a spinning confusion of lights and colors. Then they struggle to learn how to identify objects visually in different conditions of appearance. It may take years for them to learn the rules of seeing, and to experience space with objects in it. As a biologist who studies the brain concludes, "These most interesting observations on the difficulties of people born blind show that we have to learn from others how to see."[16]

In perception, we learn not only how to connect selected parts of sensory input, but also how to include or disconnect feelings and parts of our inner life. Sanity, in our civilization, depends on rules for distinguishing automatically and without awareness the "thing" we perceive from the way we feel about the perception. We distrust the mental competence of people who regularly fuse perceptions with their anxieties, free associations, dreams, and unconscious processes. Yet pure perceptions, uncontaminated by expressive material, are not "natural," but the refined products of our own civilization's school of "common sense." The Babylonians ordered their percepts in a different way, cultivating expressive elements of the perceptual process that we tend to segregate or to exclude. The structure of consciousness is a fabric of associations and dissociations.

Our "common sense" urges us to dissociate expressive feeling from the raw data of perceptions. The mental scheme we acknowledge as the "real world" adapts the raw data to forms of rational explanation. Nevertheless, while the theoretical requirements of constructing nature as an objective order with lawlike regularities make us set aside or abstract the expressive qualities of phenomena, they cannot do away with expressive presences. Our perceptions are inherently expressive, and the core of every phenomenon holds a kernel of expressive energy. Perception remains alive and vibrant—not a dead record of things—because phenomena live and vibrate. The energy of phenomena moves people to feel, think, act, and imagine. The world of experience trembles with excitement.

Pure expression, according to Cassirer, is the root of experience. The qualities of being attractive or menacing, familiar or uncanny, reassuring or alarming, do not come from thinking that closely follows the event, but from the immediate vibrations of the phenomenon—it is a part of the essential fact of perception. In the mythical frame of experience, the imagination gathers the *expressions* of phenomena in a magical web of connected meanings that make no sense to our rational intellect. In this archaic frame of mind, the universe breathes intentionality in phenomena, manifesting omens and warnings in the whole of reality. As Cassirer puts it, "A whispering or rustling in the woods, a shadow darting over the ground, a light flickering on the water: all these are demonic in their nature and origin. . . . All intuitive reality is surrounded by a breath of magic, bathed in a magical mist. . . . Everything is connected with everything else by invisible threads. . . . Precisely because this perpetual pointing and warning forms the element in which the mythical consciousness lives, it requires no special explanation."[17]

Historically and biologically, Cassirer writes, expressive intelligibility precedes the intellectual knowledge of things. Prehistoric, primitive, and infantile perceptions contain expressive meaning in the sensuous matter of immediate impressions. For example, the sense of a perception being friendly or hostile, helpful or dangerous, is an impression more original or rudimentary than its being sensed as a blue spot.[18] The intuition of good and evil, then, attends the very beginning of perception. An omen therefore magnifies this quality of perception, and divination attends the kind of sensibility that makes it the keystone of experience. In this mode of experience, the person observes a phenomenon, and before the mind "knows" what the thing "is," the observation demands: "What is in store for me? Hurt? Help? Danger? Good fortune? What will happen to me next, as a result of this thing?" The mind leaps, not to find an explanation, but to respond.

In the Babylonian scheme of things, phenomena contained meaning as a principal ingredient, because they were expressions of hidden forces that wanted to be understood. Today, we inspect phenomena in order to dominate nature—we are the master, nature the slave. The ancient Mesopotamians thought of themselves as slaves of gods. Therefore, they treated the invisible forces as slaves dealt with masters: obeying commands, trying to fathom feelings and intentions to keep one step ahead, to ward off wrath, to cajole and manipulate—in short, to survive. Gods needed people and cities, and they communicated through signs out of their personal concern for humans.

An omen recorded the sign in the "if clause" (protasis). The "then clause," or consequence (apodosis), reported the meaning of the sign. For example, to repeat an omen from the *shumma ālu*: "If fish are numerous in a river: then the land will dwell in quiet." The meaning of the sign was extracted from the encyclopedia of omens, or found by analogy, or intuited directly by the observer. Through his extensive training, the *bārû* probably had mastered a technique of mantic reverie, in which he meditated on the virtual spaces of constellations or the entrails of sheep, discovering their secret design by choosing an interpretation from a flow of preconscious associations. Since we do not share the ancient Babylonian frame of mind, it is difficult to trace the mental processes in the ominous texts. They speak nonsense to us. The lost science of omens, which coordinated human life with natural phenomena and made sense of the Babylonian world, ignores logic, violates our rules of thought, and flaunts our laws of causality.

We are at a loss, moreover, because we lack an emotional history of the words in the ominous texts. Words gather signification from their emotional uses in the past, and this history gets transferred symbolically in later uses.[19] Omens are symbols in the sense Whitehead stipulated: "The human mind is functioning symbolically when some components of its experience elicit consciousness, beliefs, emotions, and usages, respecting other components of its experience."[20]

Sometimes the meaning of an omen seems to emerge from free association and the resemblance of images. Why do numerous fish portend quiet dwelling for the land? A scholar in ancient Semitic languages, H. W. F. Saggs, proposes: "The shoals of fish obviously suggest contented crowds in the city streets." Dream omens reveal a similar pattern of sign interpretation. If, in a dream, someone receives a gift of perfumed oil, it portends sweet words and pleasantness. If he dreams that someone gives him a seal-cylinder (which is like a signet ring, bearing his name and projecting his personality), then he will become well known—literally, "have a name"—and have children who will carry on his name. If he dreams someone deprives him of such a seal, then his child will die. Sometimes, a play on words makes the connection between "if" and "then." For example, if a man dreams he eats a raven (*arbu*), then income (*irbu*) will come in. Certain words, moreover, carry favorable or unfavorable overtones of meaning, which determine the prediction through preconscious associations.

An Assyrian manual of omen interpretation teaches some standard associations of ideas: if length is the predominant characteristic of a sign, it suggests attainment; thickness means strength; bending downwards suggests acquisition; brightness means joy. In the ominous world, humans stood in a twilight region between external things of nature and the inner life of their own nature.[21] Signs and predictions crossed categories, and in some cases groups of omens expanded by analogy. Sometimes the predictions appeared as stock phrases, and stereotyped "then" clauses (apodoses) kept occurring throughout all the omen literature. In those cases, the stock predictions, in all probability, simply signified good or bad consequences. They appear in the shreds of Babylonian thinking that survive in our familiar superstitions today: if a black cat crosses your path, then you will have bad luck; if you walk under a ladder, you will have bad luck; if you break a mirror, you will have seven years of bad luck. None of these apodoses specifies the exact kind of bad luck.

To be on the safe side in Babylonia, it was better to come up with bad omens, for a good prediction that failed to materialize threw blame on the diviner, but if an evil omen never came true, the person who expected bad luck would be relieved and happy to forget the whole matter.[22] Moreover, the Babylonians did not expect inexorable disaster always to follow bad omens, for they also relied on an inexhaustible supply of apotropaic rituals to ward off predicted doom. While omens saved the phenomena, rituals preserved their hopes.

Nevertheless, the Mesopotamian world remained full of profound disquiet. Babylonians lived in constant anxiety, waiting for catastrophe. Their collective imagination represented the destructive energies of Mesopotamian existence as a large population of evil spirits, perpetually scheming to trap humans in disease, famine, natural disaster, or magical calamities. This nursery of fright generated our lineage of phantasms, for the satanic families of demons and witches in medieval Europe had lived their infancy in the Babylonian imagination.

As Henri Frankfort observed, the Babylonians felt they lived in a turbulent, unpredictable universe. The perpetual dread of their nocturnal, ominous existence, anxiously watching the dark sky for signs, contrasted dramatically with the bright, cheerful life of Egypt, which was contemporaneous with Mesopotamian civilization. Except for dream omens, Egypt lived without ominous divination. The two civilizations were indeed as different as night and day. The two opposite moods were expressed in ritual occasions, and Frankfort noted "the lack of anxiety, the unqualified joy, which distinguish the Egyptian festivals from their Mesopotamian counterparts." Similarly, their cosmogonic myths reflected the difference as well: "Thus while creation was assumed in Mesopotamia to be the outcome of a fierce struggle and existence remained in an unstable balance without certainty of duration, the world was believed in Egypt to have arisen in the undimmed brightness of the first sunrise and to remain for all time such as it had then been created."[23]

Modern readers, brought up on clinical metaphors, might hasten to label Babylonian life as a paranoid condition or as a massive anxiety neurosis. However, if we trace the characteristic feelings of apprehension, we do not find the chronic anxiety of Babylonia located in a psychological crisis of the individual. It does not emerge from typical intrapsychic conflicts or from the pattern of infant socialization. It belongs to the Mesopotamian city. It is a feeling of the place—a sense of the dangerous ground between Tigris and Euphrates.

The steady Nile, rising and withdrawing in dependable periods and regularly depositing the ground of Egypt, nourished the dwellers with a feeling of security. But the Tigris and Euphrates rivers grudged their alluvial gift, unpredictably snatching it away. Early nomads in the region, adapting to the irregular flood and fall of the rivers, kept leaving shattered villages to build in new places. Then the first civilized humans determined to stay and built cities that were not only physical strongholds but also nervous containers of settled apprehension. They risked the peril of dwelling between the violent rivers, working to inhabit a solid place and holding their ground through drought and marsh fire as well as storm and flood. To keep a city on this shifting ground required drainage, irrigation, and steady watercourses. But climatic forces discouraged confidence in human works. Spring tides in the Persian Gulf, monstrous gales, landslides in distant mountains, excessive snow in Armenia, or too much rain in the south would frequently send the rivers over their banks to smash fragile houses within the great walls of the city. The Babylonians survived precariously, building an ominous world in a dangerous place. Their system of divination made the destructive energies intelligible.

Divination is dominated by sacromagical imagination, or, in the case of Babylonia, anxious imagination. Still, Babylonian divination integrated human experience in a comprehensive environmental universe that preserved and connected every feature of human experience. It embraced phenomena in the widest sense—not merely what appeared to the senses, but whatever appeared to the mind and the imagination, including dreams and feelings as well as perceptions. As an Assyriologist puts it:

> Thus all phenomena subject to contemplation, animate and inanimate things, abstract notions, concepts, institutions, language and grammar, and the phenomenon of man as well as the gods, were apprehended by the same cognitive approach; they could be known and understood in their apparent features and characteristics. Ultimate understanding of the universe would, in theory, require nothing but the painstaking accumulation of as much detail as possible about literally everything: no phenomenon was too trivial to record.[24]

The system, therefore, did not exclude the kernel of expressive energy at the core of every experience.

Our complacent freedom from superstition obscures the elegance and wisdom in this scheme of experience. We reject it entirely because the Babylonians represented their own expressive energies as divine presences with independent existences—that is, as gods—and we know better. But superstition, Plutarch said, kept fear awake and reason asleep. Perhaps if we return to the dustbin of history without fear and with reason fully awake, we may rescue something of value from the "rubbish" of archaic intelligence. For all its absurdity, superstitious thinking was nonetheless an effort to express experience holistically.

Babylonian society was riddled with superstition, but one kind of superstitious riddling made claims to wisdom that eluded rational thinking. Archaic people pondered signs, omens, oracles, dark sayings, enigmas, and riddles. The Greek word "enigma," which we translate as "riddle," means a dark saying. The English word "riddle" comes from the same root as "order," and this root *ar- means "to fit together." A riddle ponders the structure of experience and grasps the way different features of experience fit together. Riddles are dark ways of expressing the profound ambiguities of experience. For a restitution of decayed intelligence, it will be necessary to save the riddles.

The riddling Sphinx forced us to look at
what was at our feet.

Sophocles,
Oedipus the King

T E N

Riddles and Problems

Today, what we call "problem" is a method of experience. When the city is experienced exclusively as a problem, when people live their entire lives as problems, and when places are reduced to geometric mechanisms, then the remainder of experience turns into rubbish. Even when they are "solved," problems may be formulated at the expense of discarding the expressive dimension of experience. Every mode of intelligibility selects and excludes features of experience, but the way of the problem sets hard boundaries of relevance. It sorts out only a few features of experience—or, to use a modern term, it chooses parameters—and shuts out the rest.

Plato invented the "problem," and the emergence of a mathematical way of "saving" appearances in the sky remains a turning point in the expressive intelligibility of the obvious world. In this chapter, we explore Plato's problem as a paradigm of experience and as the first step toward ungrounded Platonism. In tracing this mode of experience, I am not rejecting either problems in themselves or rationality, for problem solving is necessary to any sane and humane scheme of things. My intention is not to eliminate thinking about problems, but to make room for riddles.

The drama, *Oedipus the King*, begins with an urban predicament. The city of Thebes is dying from a mysterious pollution, and the people implore Oedipus, their ruler, to find some way to save them. They recall that he rescued the city once before by solving the riddle of the Sphinx, at which time they rewarded their savior and liberator by making him sovereign. The Sphinx was a mythical monster brooding over Thebes until Oedipus solved her riddle: "What is the name of the only creature on earth with one voice that goes on four feet in the morning, on two at noon, and on three in the evening? Of all things that creep on the earth and move in the air and sea, this one alone changes its form, and when it goes on most feet, then its speed is feeblest." Oedipus answered, "Man," and the Sphinx hurled itself to destruction.[1]

The full complexity of this riddle is often overlooked. The answer identifies man as the creature that changes its ways: crawling in infancy, walking upright in its prime, and tottering with a cane in old age. But the riddle also locates man expressively, relating each stage of his life dramatically to earth and sky, to his position on the ground as well as to the position of the sun in the sky. In the morning of his life, when the sun is rising, he crawls on the ground on all fours; at noon, with the sun directly overhead, he stands unassisted; in the evening, when the sun declines, he leans on the earth, propped up by a staff. The riddle expresses the holistic mystery of the astrobiological principle—that in some inscrutable way, the universe fits together the rhythmical phenomena of body, earth, and sky. Because the Sphinx disintegrated when the answer was declared, the myth suggests that the spirit of disease vanishes when man re-collects his proper relation to earth and sky. The microcosmic riddle represents the structure of the universe. It fits together diverse features of experience.

We still rely on simple riddles to amuse children: "What goes up white but comes down yellow?" The answer is "an egg," and this bit of wit merely calls attention to the polychrome fate of eggs, which stay white in one direction but turn yellow in the other. However, by personifying the egg with a name, we darken the riddle. "Humpty Dumpty sat on a wall . . ." tells us that human life resembles an egg, for when it is shattered, no power on earth can put it back together again.

Like the Humpty Dumpty verse, the earliest riddles were probably not questions but metaphorical statements or symbols (in Whitehead's sense), using words to put together phenomena from different categories of experience. Riddles served as table games in the ancient world and during the Middle Ages, but in the earliest stage the riddle was an effort by primitive people to solve the mysteries of life through the discovery of remote analogies.[2] Babylonian riddles specialized in associating different kinds of objects or ideas. The riddle always included a metaphor.

Characteristically, however, the language of a riddle stays close to grounded experience. It does not express an attitude of intellectual detachment, but on the contrary preserves feelings, passions, and existential choices. The riddle often served as a deadly wager that determined personal survival or even the fate of a kingdom. Princes challenged one another with riddles to claim superior mental power, which was as important to a political leader as physical prowess.[3] According to the Bible, the Queen of Sheba made a long journey to test the wisdom of Solomon with a series of riddles.

The most famous riddle in the Bible, formulated in the story of Samson, draws together the mysteries of earth and sky (Judg. 14–16). Before the Israelites organized a kingdom under Saul, David, and Solomon, they were governed by a succession of charismatic chiefs, known in the biblical tradition as the Judges, whose leadership depended on divine gifts of judicial wisdom, prophecy, military sagacity, or—in the case of Samson—supernatural physical strength. Like Viking berserkers, Samson would go into a destructive frenzy and slaughter entire regiments of enemies. The career of Samson remained unwritten folklore for a long time and seems to contain little of an edifying nature. Scripture turns it into an ironic paradigm of reckless, impulsive conduct—the opposite of wisdom. On the surface it seems that the biblical writer gave the folktale religious meaning by describing Samson as an ascetic consecrated from birth to the service of God and by representing his berserk trances as moments of ecstatic possession by the spirit of the Lord, who used Samson to stir up the initial conflict with the Philistines. Under the surface, however, an older cosmological wisdom with traces of the folk cycle animates the scriptural message with vivid imagery. The story resists superficial interpretation, and commentators have kept returning to this enigmatic tale of a preposterous strong man. The episodes of Samson's life suggest a cryptic message behind their fantastic imagery. Thoughtful readers find mythic references to celestial phenomena, and traces of these same references in Babylonian, Phoenician, Greek, Roman, and Arabic astromythology suggest their preservation in Hebrew lore as well.

First of all, Samson's name means "solar" or "sunling," implying a sun god or devotion to the sun. His people, the tribe of Dan, descended from a sect of Babylonians who worshiped the sun. The entire story of Samson, especially the riddle, is filled with earthy images, but their meaning keeps drawing attention to the sky—not only to the sun but to the stars and planets as well.

In his first exploit, Samson—on his way to court a Philistine woman —killed a young lion that attacked him, tearing it apart with his bare hands. After a time, he found a swarm of bees settled in the carcass, and he scooped out the honey. Then at his wedding feast he challenged the company of thirty young Philistines who attended the banquet with a riddle based on his experience with the lion. If they guessed it, he promised them each a suit of fine clothing, but if they failed they were to pay him thirty suits of fine clothing. The riddle declared:

> Out of the eater came something to eat,
> Out of the strong came something sweet.

It is an elegant, symmetric paradox—for the Hebrew word for "strong" could also mean "bitter"—but impossible to guess, for no one (not even his parents) knew about the lion. The young Philistines threatened to burn the bride as well as her father's house if she did not wheedle the answer out of Samson, and she nagged until he revealed the secret. On the last day of the wedding feast, when the sun went down and Samson was about to enter the bridal chamber, the men of the town responded to his challenge with a rhetorical question couched in the language of riddles:

> What is sweeter than honey?
> What is stronger than a lion?

The meaning of this couplet turns on a pun exploiting an ancient Hebrew word (*ary*) which had two meanings: either "lion" or "honey."[4]

Samson replied with a metaphor still in the riddling idiom: "If you had not ploughed with my heifer, you would not have found out my riddle." The spirit of the Lord seized him and Samson went down to Ashkelon, a Philistine city, and killed thirty men there, taking their clothes to pay the men of the wedding feast. In his rage, he returned to his father's house, abandoning his bride, who was then given in marriage to the best man. But he could not escape his passion for the woman, and during the harvest he returned to her. Learning of her marriage, he avenged his loss by catching three hundred foxes, binding them tail to tail with torches fastened to every pair of tails, and turning them loose to burn down the Philistine fields.

All the images in the story stay close to the earth, but symbolic interpretations read them as representations of celestial myths. The hero, Samson, represents solar energy—the effect of the sun on human experience—as well as the human struggle against the destructive power of summer heat. According to H. Steinthal, who argued for a solar interpretation of the Samson myth, "the lion was accepted by the Semitic nations as a symbol of the summer heat." The Assyrians and Lydians worshiped a sun god named Sandon who was pictured as a lion killer. In Greek mythology, Heracles started his heroic labors by killing a lion with his hands. The fox also represented summer heat, and in the ancient Mediterranean world, a fierce mildew, caused by the action of solar heat on dew-drenched crops and called "red fox" by the Romans, blazed like a fire through the grain fields.[5]

Samson's florid sexual energy also suggests the solar power to make the earth fruitful. Moreover, his hair represents the unrestricted summer growth of vegetation until the harvest, when the growth is cut and the power of the sun declines. After Delilah (the third woman in his story) betrays him and the Philistines shave his head and blind him, he loses his strength until the hair starts to grow back—as nature revives with the new growth of spring.

The legend associated Samson's strength with his hair. The Bible assimilated this heathen idea by presenting Samson as a Nazarite, meaning an ascetic living according to a strict rule, including a taboo against cutting the hair. Phoenician and Greek images of the sun god (Helios) showed a strong young man with flowing locks, the rays of the sun appearing to radiate from his head. Similar associations involved other celestial bodies, and the Arabs, observing rays emanating from Sirius, named it the hairy star. In the dog days, when hairy Sirius prevails and the sun is in the zodiacal house known as the Lion, Orion—the mighty killer of beasts, who, like Samson, was blind—dominates the sky. According to Giorgio de Santillana, in the Far East a story similar to the Samson myth represents not the sun but Orion, the mighty hunter. Still, in the Near East, he also suggests the planet Mars: "Who could Samson have been? Clearly a god, and a planetary Power, for such were the gods of old. As Brave-Swift-Impetuous Male, as the Nazarite Strong One, he has all the countersigns that belong to Mars and to none other."[6] Indeed, when we consider Samson's vulnerability to sexual traps, the three erotic misadventures in his story may stand for celestial occasions when Mars gave way to Venus.

In the previous chapter, we observed how the ancients perceived "a complex web of encounters, drama, mating and conflict" in the positions and relations of heavenly bodies. They could grasp the riddle of the cosmos by observing the appearances in the sky and by telling the adventures of the planets.[7]

Samson told his riddle at the wedding feast and, in Greece as well as in ancient Israel, riddles seasoned the table conversation of banquets. The legends of the Seven Sages imagined them telling rounds of riddles as they dined together. Plato mentioned the riddles, customarily told at banquets, which played with double meanings.[8] The Greeks called them "enigmas" or dark sayings. However, the Septuagint—the Greek translation of the Hebrew Bible written in Alexandria about two centuries after Plato—selected another word for Samson's riddle, calling it a "problem." In this Greek version, Samson told the young Philistines: "I am going to problematize you a problem [*problēma*]." It is a poor choice of terms and a puzzle. Why did the translator avoid the obvious word, "enigma"?

In any case, "problems" as well as "riddles" were tossed around at Greek banquets. Burnet writes that problems "originate in the Greek custom of asking riddles at banquets. . . . That accounts in turn for investigation taking the form of a quest for solutions of certain problems or difficulties." The work of Aristotle contains a collection of such problems, and an important passage in a commentary by Simplicius shows that the method of research by "propounding a problem" and thinking up a "solution" originated in Plato's Academy.[9] Plato initiated the problem as a way of thinking. The method of the problem guided the mind to a line of analytical thinking detached from feeling and mythic imagination and confined to certain sensory data abstracted from the whole context of experience. The invention of the problem—a way of thinking that segregates dimensions of experience—is a turning point in the history of expressive intelligibility.

Riddles, which played with double meanings, Plato dismissed as trivial, but he believed the solution of problems in geometry and astronomy to be the highest form of inquiry and a mental activity that "purified" the soul.[10] He considered the ways of the planets as the main interest of astronomy, and he wanted to deal with them as a problem because they did not follow the regular course of the stars. The "plan-

ets"—from a Greek word for wanderers, tramps, and vagabonds—
showed irregular movements that he found intellectually unaccountable
and morally offensive, unlike all the other stars. His problem of settling
the wanderers, which laid the intellectual foundations of modern science, yielded a method of experience as well. Not restricted to science,
this method of experience also formulated the first rational segregation
of expressive and mechanical energies.

According to Simplicius, Plato asked the astronomers to find a geometric explanation for planetary motion. An historian of science says
that Plato set before the astronomers

> the methodological problem which under the name of the Platonic
> axiom was to dominate theoretical astronomy for twenty centuries:
> to detect in the confused irregularity of the motions of the planets
> the ideal mathematical system of uniform circular motions which
> represents the true facts of the processes in a mathematical sky and
> thus saves the empirical phenomena exhibited by the planets from
> the verdict of unreality that seems to be invited by their irregular-
> ity; although that which the eye perceives is appearance, thought
> may at least apprehend the reality underlying this appearance.[11]

Thus, Plato posed the basic question for all astronomy, and Eudoxus
came up with the first serious answer.[12] Plato and his student or associate, Eudoxus of Cnidus—who was a philosopher, physician, astronomer, mathematician, and the intellectual father of Euclid—worked out a
way of thinking about the planets detached from feelings, myths, and
religious associations. Geometry offered eternal truths not subject to the
uncertainties of sensory experience, and Eudoxus carried out Plato's
recommendation in the *Republic* that the astronomer ought to take the
appearances in the sky as a geometrician works with his figures: not as
visible lines known in a surface but as sensory clues to the discovery of
intelligible, mathematical truth.[13] However, before they engaged the
mind as a problem, the planets had engaged the imagination as a riddle.

Early Greek literature, including the poems of Homer and Hesiod,
did not recognize the planets at all, and the Greeks learned about them
(probably in the fifth century) from the Babylonians, who identified
planets as representatives of the gods. The Babylonians, we observed in
the previous chapter, called planets the Interpreters, who communicated divine messages to humans, and they considered the peculiar

courses of the planets not as behavior below the dignity of gods, as Plato thought, but as sublime, mysterious writing to be deciphered.

The Babylonians worked out an arithmetical system of plotting and tracking the mysterious trails against the stable background of constellations, keeping emotional contact with the appearances. As they watched a presence such as Ishtar (renamed Aphrodite by the Greeks and Venus by the Romans), recognized as both the morning and evening star, their system for observations implicitly kept inquiring: Where exactly is she located right now? Where is she going? What is she up to? What does she want us to do? Her successive appearances were not taken as meandering errors or deviations from regularity, but as special occasions full of meaning.

The Babylonians discovered astronomy, a follower of Plato once boasted, but the Greeks improved it.[14] The distinctive feature of Greek astronomy represented celestial motions by a geometric model, and the idea that the fixed stars revolved in rigid spheres "remained the fundamental postulate of all astronomy up to Copernicus."[15] The Greek "improvement" of the Babylonian discovery also dissociated the experience of celestial phenomena from their old symbolic and emotional meanings, thus initiating the mode of ungrounded, intellectual experience. Yet the rule to save the appearances by geometric construction originated in Plato's sense of the "question." His trouble with the planets derived from an old, inherited, grounded experience—from the existential meaning of traveling from place to place. Later in this chapter, we shall explore the idea of *hodos*, or the Greek sense of the right way to go.

Plato wanted to *rescue* the planetary appearances. Historians often say that in Plato's famous problem, he asked the astronomers "*sōzein tai phainomena*," a phrase translated by them as "to save the appearances," which they interpret as an instruction to come up with a hypothesis that would "account" for the observations.[16] This way of thinking about the problem remains on the intellectual level of seeking a rational explanation, but Plato urged much more than an "account." The problem expressed a spiritual mission, a feeling about the planets, and a moral agenda. It included not merely the search for an explanation but also an existential response. According to Simplicius, Plato did not say "*sōzein*," which means "to save" the appearances or to "rescue" them. Simplicius wrote that Plato used a form of the verb *diasōzein*, which is an even stronger word. It means to preserve through a danger or to rescue from a serious predicament.[17] What was this serious danger from which Plato wanted to rescue the planetary appearances? It was not merely incredulity, as some commentators propose, but scandal and impiety. Observations that suggested the planets wandered about in the sky led humans to tell lies about the "great gods" and encouraged blasphemy.[18]

As far as we know, the death of Socrates was the most important event in Plato's life. After it he withdrew from Athenian politics and saved the memory of his teacher by making Socrates the principal voice in the Dialogues. Early in his career, Socrates had studied astronomy and cosmology with great excitement, but by the time Plato knew him, he had abandoned this interest and, according to Xenophon, turned against astronomy, criticizing research that investigated the movements of planets, comets, and so forth, for he could not see what useful purpose it served. He deprecated the curiosity that sought to know how divine forces engineered the phenomena of the skies, and he considered it madness to spend mental energy meddling in secrets of the divine machinery. He felt that the gods were not pleased with human efforts to discover what they had not chosen to reveal. At his trial, Socrates insisted that he believed that the sun and the moon were gods, as the rest of humankind believed.[19]

One might expect that the judgment condemning Socrates would have outraged Plato so thoroughly as to make him reject the whole idea of criminal laws regulating piety. Yet in the *Laws*, written at the end of his life, he proposed heavy sanctions for offenses against religion, recommending the death penalty for serious cases of impiety.[20] While he believed Socrates to have been falsely charged with criminal impiety, he nevertheless wanted the government to police the expression of religion.

Plato remained agnostic about the traditional gods imagined by the epic poets to dwell in human form on Mt. Olympus. For the most part, humans imagined gods they could not see or rightly conceive. They might have had some vague intuitions of invisible spirits, but the imagination gave them figure, modeling shapes out of vague impressions as a plastic artist worked in clay. But the visible, celestial gods—the stars and planets—reached human experience through reason and perception in a way of knowing that was much more certain than the artistic imagination.[21] Plato shared the Socratic conviction that celestial presences were gods, but he differed from Socrates when it came to investigating their mechanism.

In the *Republic*, Plato made astronomy the servant of geometry, so that celestial appearances provided material for intellectual abstraction. In the *Laws*, however, he made astronomy the handmaid of religion. Correct knowledge of the gods in heaven enabled citizens to carry out sacrificial ritual, to pray in pious language, and to avoid telling lies about the gods. The lack of astronomical language led to ignorance about the gods, which in turn led to blasphemy.

Plato called all the unwandering stars living beings, divine and eternal, abiding forever as settled presences, revolving in the same locations.[22] We observe them circling from east to west, moving uniformly in the same direction as the sun and moon. But the five visible planets travel from west to east in an irregular course observed against the background of the zodiac, rising a little farther east each day, sometimes not changing position at all for a while, and even reversing direction altogether to go from east to west in intermittent retrograde movements.[23] The Babylonians accepted the irregularity, expecting the gods to move in mysterious ways, and scrutinized each step for an omen. But the irregularity unsettled the Greeks, and they interpreted it to mean vagrancy. Plato objected to the traditional Greek notion of wandering stars, feeling keenly that calling them vagabonds or tramps insulted the gods. Moreover, vagrancy, straying, wandering, or errancy implied deviation from the true course of being. The Greek verb associated with the word "planet" is like the Latin verb *errare*: it means to rove as well as to go wrong. In both Greek and Latin, to make an error means to stray from the truth. At the heart of Greek planetary feeling stayed a profound, unconscious topistic experience—a powerful, grounded conviction about the right way to go. From this existential experience of travel on earth, the Greeks derived their sense of planets.

The doctrine of "route" dominates the philosophy of Parmenides—a pre-Socratic who influenced Plato profoundly—and stands out as the principal theme in epic poetry as well. As an underlying metaphysical assumption, the right *way* is as important to Hellenic experience as the *tao* is to Chinese. However, the *tao* remains close to the contours of natural landscape and avoids rationalization, preferring wiggly paths or the irregular course of water. In contrast, the Greek sense of *hodos* or "route" expects rationalization. Our term "method," which means a *way* of proceeding but implies rational conduct, comes from the Greek words *meta* plus *hodos*.

At the core of Hellenic expectation, all persons—especially paradigmatic figures such as heroes or kings—belong in their proper places. If they break out and live *atopos* or out of place, they move beyond the boundaries of personal identity to be where and what they are not. We would say that they experience alienation or self-estrangement.[24] This assumption did not inhibit people from going places, for the Greeks traveled a great deal, but it worked to regulate the meaning of movement. To go the right way, one made a journey to a proper destination, and after the journey out, sought a return (*nostos*) or homecoming. The traveler followed instructions, looked for tidings of the route, and depended on escorts, guides, and hosts to help him on his way. Advancing along the route, he was said to "accomplish" the journey, which was usually understood as a round-trip back to his proper place. The opposite of going the right way was to wander or to go astray.[25]

Before Plato, the Pythagoreans were the first to reject the idea that the planets, which they regarded as divine and eternal beings, moved in wandering, disorderly ways, and sought geometric explanations for the appearances, preferring a hypothesis of circular, uniform motion as the correct way of the gods. For the Greeks, geometry was the morality of motion.

Centuries after Plato, a Hellenistic astronomer named Geminus, explaining the old Pythagorean viewpoint, came up with illustrations from grounded experience to discredit the idea that planets wandered. Even on earth, he observed, dignified gentlemen did not wander. Therefore, if irregularity of this sort was incompatible with the conduct of dignified mortals, how could we expect it of the gods? Benjamin Farrington, a Marxist historian, identifies the Pythagorean sentiment as a social prejudice against the lower classes who were forced by unemployment into unsettled lives. The prejudice hardened, he suggests, in Plato's time, when the aristocrats were casting about for a solution to the social problem of unemployed outcasts. The presence of vagabonds and wandering beggars reached such a crisis that Isocrates, a contemporary of Plato, warned that they might become as great a danger as the Persian barbarians.[26] Plato's disdain for irregularity extended to the rich as well as the poor, and he included in the class of wanderers the Sophists, who roamed from city to city with no settled home of their own.[27]

Like the Pythagoreans before him, Plato expected the planets to move in perfect circular routes, the only course appropriate for the movement of divine beings. To acknowledge the visual appearances of planets moving irregularly, like undignified beggars, contradicted and scandalized the principles of his astral religion. In *Timaeus* he saved them from blasphemy by calling their swerving, wandering appearances a "choric dance." An adequate description of the complicated maneuvers in this celestial dance required visible demonstration by a three-dimensional model of the solar system.[28] The Academy probably owned such a planetary model, with spheres representing sun, moon, and the planets revolving around the earth—a kind known in modern astronomy as an armillary sphere or an orrery. This physical sphere, while it demonstrated the routes of the planets, also revealed the mechanism supporting the appearances.

In the *Laws*, his last written work, Plato said that in his later years he at last found an improved way of understanding the planets. A recent astronomical discovery, he wrote, proved to his satisfaction the hidden regularity of planetary motion. This discovery replaced the physical three-dimensional model with an intellectual geometric model. It is reasonable to identify this ultimate discovery with the solution Eudoxus proposed to Plato's problem. Plato wanted to rescue the appearances not only from blasphemy, but from atheism and superstition as well. To atheists, the planets were lifeless chunks of rock without souls. To superstitious people, deprived of the rational faculty, the complicated evolutions of the planetary dance inspired panic or appeared as omens telling of things to come. The geometric model restored planetary divinity and took away the fear.

The forms of visibility change historically, as does the whole structure of perception, in which the visible dwells with the invisible.[29] To make perceptions intelligible, the mind often links them to an idea-image (such as a myth) or to an abstraction (such as a geometric figure). Grasping the visible geometrically describes it in a mathematical language that gives it a discursive existence, but this language does not exhaust the whole energy of the perceived. The original powers of the perceived in the whole structure of experience prevent the selected mode of expression from determining the perception in any final way.

Plato chose to save the visible perceptions of the stars by dissociating them from the remainder of celestial experience, thereby excluding from the boundaries of the problem feelings, myths, and collective expectations. This exclusion and dissociation make sense to the rational side of the mind. They do not satisfy the expressive side, which is full of sentiment, poetry, and mystery. As Walt Whitman represented this other side:

When I heard the learn'd astronomer;
When the proofs, the figures, were ranged in
    columns before me;
When I was shown the charts and the diagrams,
    to add, divide, and measure them . . .
How soon, unaccountable, I became tired and sick;
Till rising and gliding out, I wander'd off by myself,
In the mystical moist night-air, and from time to time,
Look'd up in perfect silence at the stars.[30]

Or, to express this side of celestial experience in the idiom of the
Nineteenth Psalm: "The heavens declare the glory of God; and the
firmament sheweth his handiwork."

Geometry in motion suggests the design of a machine, and we may
experience the obvious world—the structure of appearances on earth—
as an ungrounded system of solutions. We may think of the chair (as did
Le Corbusier) as a machine for sitting, the house as a machine for
dwelling. We may also think of the city as a machine for circulating
business, the highway as a machine for travel—in the same mode we
consider the sky a machine for space traffic. As we construct experience,
we also construct our world. Plato's advice to suppose a geometric sky
eventually reached the earth as well. To adapt the words of Xenophanes,
we build the world we suppose. John Milton sensed the connection in
his reference to the astronomers: "Hereafter, when they come to model
heav'n / And calculate the stars, how they will wield / The mighty frame,
how build, unbuild, contrive / To save appearances . . ."[31] By construction we ratify the features of experience that we take for granted and
accept.

Plato stirred up admiration for mathematics, according to the ancient
writers, and directors of the Academy who succeeded him were math-
ematicians. The tradition culminated in the work of Euclid, who perpet-
uated Platonic geometry in Alexandria.[32] An interesting but unreliable
story relates that when Ptolemy I, the king of Egypt, asked him for
lessons, Euclid replied, "There is no royal road to geometry." Nevertheless, since then, royal roads are built *through* geometry.

It is said that Plato inscribed over the portal of the Academy the
warning, "You cannot enter here unless you know geometry." But that
does not mean that Plato and his friends lived their common life there as
a "problem," or that they ignored the expressive energy of the place. No

part of Athens contained more meaning and feeling than the Academy, to be grasped holistically, on the fringe of reason and perception. Despite the zeal for geometric astronomy, the Academy preserved a hidden doctrine of grounded Platonism. This doctrine emerged again during the Renaissance in the antiquarian tradition, passing on to the chorographic movement in early-modern England. While the scientific astronomers were still saying, "Save the appearances," the antiquary Thomas Fuller urged a grounded imperative, which would be understood through an older method of experience: "Rescue the observables!"

A fine life I should lead if I went away at my age, wandering from city to city, and always being driven out.

Plato, *Apology*

E L E V E N

The Ground of Platonism

Virtually every Greek city celebrated festivals with torch races, using them to honor not only the moon goddess, Artemis-Bendis, but also the fire gods, Prometheus, Hephaestus, and Pan. No other form of celebration matched their popularity in Athens, which enhanced the splendor of the Panathenaea and seven other festivals with them.[1] The ritual symbolized spiritual purification by transmitting the sacred flame from one altar to another, and it also represented the birth of civilization by dramatizing the gift of fire by Prometheus. The torch never ceased to kindle metaphors in the Greek imagination, and the symbolism of the flame passed on from hand to hand in one kind of torch race evoked familiar meanings. Writers used the image of the passing torch to express the sense of human continuity. Plato, for example, wrote that when parents brought up children, they were handing over "the torch of life from one generation to another."[2] Active participation in the ritual or watching the torchbearers run or gallop with the flame refreshed the image and kept it from degenerating into a cliché.

The torch race stood out as the city's most popular ritual, and three different torch races began at the altars of Prometheus and Hephaestus in the precinct of the Academy. Therefore, the Athenians knew the Academy as a location with special ritual significance as well as a place of exceptional beauty. Located on the way to sacred Eleusis, this region, once lovely and wooded, pictured by John Milton as "the olive grove of Academe . . . where the Attic bird trills her thick-warbl'd notes the

summer long," remained one of the most important expressive places in
the environment of ancient Athens for a thousand years.

Plato, having failed to turn Dionysius, the tyrant of Syracuse, into a
philosopher king, returned to Athens and founded a school in the
garden of the Academy around 388 B.C. According to tradition, Plato's
school held its ground there for over nine hundred years, until 529 A.D.
While Athens schooled humanity, the Academy remained the school of
Athens. City and school survived four great assaults. The Roman dicta-
tor Sulla invaded in 86 B.C., cutting down the trees of the Academy to
make engines of war. The Athenians endured three more topoclasms
after the attack by Sulla: the city was sacked by the Heruli, an army of
northern barbarians, in 267 A.D.; menaced by Alaric leading a Gothic
force in 396; and finally devastated in 579 by a Slavic raid, which left the
city in ruins.[3]

In 529 the Roman Emperor Justinian, in a campaign against pagan
religious culture, banned non-Christian teachers, causing the seven
philosophers teaching in the Academy—the last seven sages of ancient
Greece, including Damascius and Simplicius—to carry the written and
unwritten Platonic teaching from Athens to the court of the Persian king,
reputed for his interest in philosophy. Thus the school of Plato began
and ended with political disappointment and the doomed search for a
philosopher king.

In Persia the ascetic Neoplatonists found the monarch ignorant and
pretentious; they despised the religious practices of his subjects and felt
outraged by promiscuous sexual customs. Condemning the placeways
of this Asiatic kingdom, they yearned for their own civilization, preferring to cross the border and die on Greco-Roman ground rather than to
remain in Persia with the highest honors. Their tact is impressive in the
face of these feelings of revulsion, for the king continued to like them
and wanted them to stay. Respecting their wishes, however, he granted
their release and even wrote into a treaty with Justinian a guarantee that
permitted them to live as pagans in Greco-Roman Christendom without
persecution.

Simplicius lived out his remaining years in Athens, no longer teaching
but still writing philosophy, engaged in a project to reconcile the works
of Plato and Aristotle, and turning out several thousand pages of tedious
commentaries. Gibbon said that he lived in peace and obscurity, but
Alan Cameron shows that his return may have stimulated a twilight
revival of pagan philosophy in Christian Athens. The Academy probably

continued to function in some guise—no longer as a school, but as a kind of institute for advanced study—and its fellows enjoyed both leisure for research and freedom from governmental molestation. Perhaps even the devastation of Athens by the Slavic raid of 579 did not rid the city of philosophy. Theodore of Tarsus, a monk distinguished for his learning who became the first Archbishop of Canterbury in 669, had been educated in philosophy at Athens.[4]

In the previous chapter, we explored the Platonic rule, "Save the appearances," an unforgettable phrase in the commentaries of Simplicius that was destined to escape oblivion and become the principal rule of scientific astronomy. A terrestrial counterpart of this maxim—an implicit rule of grounded Platonism, preserving an entirely different structure of experience—also remained alive. It survived underground in the pattern of thinking I identify as Plato's hidden doctrine of place. According to this hidden teaching, *chora*—the first and greatest unity of experience—is grasped intuitively, emotionally, and holistically on the fringes of reason and perception. This doctrine emerged again during the Renaissance after the rebirth of Platonic academies and is partially expressed in a maxim of the antiquarian movement: "Rescue the observables." When we ask what is meant by "observables," how they differ from "appearances," and exactly how they may be "rescued," the early-modern antiquarian movement provides further guidance: in "the restitution of decayed intelligence." Both ideas, I shall argue, are rooted in the historical experience of grounded Platonism.

Philip Slater notes that "Greece is exciting precisely because it included such disparate elements: reason, superstition, humanity, brutality, imagination, pedantry, originality, conservatism, and so on."[5] With typical Greek complexity, the Academy, when it lost its ground in the sixth century A.D., left the world a double inheritance with two different kinds of intelligibility: on the one hand, the rationalized perspective of astronomy based on a geometric model, a rudiment of modern science; on the other hand, the expressive intelligibility of grounded Platonism—a source of topistics—which nourished the Renaissance tradition of antiquarian chorography. In astronomy, "Save the appearances" became a command to the intellect, a detached, conceptual effort to design hypotheses that would explain observations. In contrast, the warning to "Rescue the observables," expressed by Thomas Fuller in the seventeenth century, urged the antiquary to make his *theoria* save from decay the expressive meanings of the obvious world.

In Plato's time, the religious imagination animated places for the Athenians, as it still does for the Australian Aborigines, rendering the ground meaningful through stories of ancestors larger than life. The Athenians experienced the landscape as a theater of myth, making the urban environment a tissue of drama that linked place to place. They repeated the local myths, not as substitutes for historical facts, but to keep places open to the imagination—to experience places through the dimension of mind that makes, hears, enjoys, and needs mythology. Then and now, to deny the imagination is to diminish the experience of a place.

Topistic myths are local treasures of imagination. Rarely do they work as delusions to falsify past experience. John Burnet insists, "It is certain that not only Plato but all intelligent Greeks regarded mythology as purely fanciful." In the Platonic dialogues, myths turned up when Socrates had something to say that could not be expressed in any other way.[6] In *Phaedrus*, Socrates passed no judgment on the official mythology, but went on to express his own myth of the place. Pausanias repeated what people said about a place even when he did not believe it. At Colonus, for example, he wrote that this is "where they say Oedipus entered Attica. This is not what Homer wrote, but they say it." His attitude toward the legends of places recalls the declaration of Herodotus: "I am obliged to tell what people say but not by any means obliged to believe it."[7] Then and now, most people know how to sort out imaginary tales from accurate reports of events.

The Academy—an Eden of the rational mind—began as the grave of a mythical hero. Recent excavations confirm that the area was first settled in the Neolithic period, about the same time as the inner city of Athens. The legend of the place names it after Hekademos, the first settler or founding hero, later known as Academus. In 1966 the electric company, while digging a trench, turned up the boundary stone dated around 500 B.C., which reads "Boundary of the Hekademeia," removing any doubt about the original name.[8] The region included the hill of Colonus made immortal by the drama of Sophocles, *Oedipus at Colonus*, which is only about a quarter of a mile away from the Academy. Like many places all over Athens, each site—Academy as well as Colonus—acquired its earliest identity, meaning, and feeling from prehistoric tradition through the legend of a mythical person. His bones in the soil grounded the spirit of the hero as lord of the place and guardian of mortals who dwelt there. The civilized Greeks, therefore, experienced places holistically—

11-1. Site of Boundary Stone, Plato's Academy
(Photo by author)

through the imagination as well as the senses and the intellect—in a way that resembled the topistic experience of Australian Aborigines.

Around 510 B.C., the Greeks made Theseus a national hero, and the Athenians, developing a civic ancestry for themselves, gave him a central place in their urban mythology. Athenian mythographers claimed him for Athens as Virgil later claimed Aeneas for Rome. They identified Theseus as the mythical father of Athens, who established the city as the capital of Attica by persuading the towns and villages around the Acropolis to give up their sovereignty for a union of peoples.

A fifth-century legend of the Academy links Theseus to Hekademos. Writers of the classical period idealized Theseus in words and pictures as a perfect king, shaping him to represent all the virtues of Athens, but earlier versions of the myth paint a less rosy picture; they portray him as embarrassing the Athenians with his violent career of rapes and seductions. When he was fifty years old, according to the version recorded by Hellanicus and Plutarch, he carried off the beautiful Helen of Sparta, who was still a child, as she was dancing in the temple of Artemis. Her brothers, Castor and Pollux, the Heavenly Twins, pursued them, but

11-2. Site of Plato's Academy Today
(Photo by author)

Theseus hid her away under the care of his mother until she was old enough to marry him, leaving them to join his comrade Perithous in another adventure—an unsuccessful raid to steal Persephone from the Underworld for his friend.[9] While Theseus remained trapped in Hades, the Spartan army, led by Helen's brothers, marched on Athens, but Hekademos saved the city from a miniature anticipation of the Trojan and Peloponnesian wars by revealing her location to the invaders. Content to recover Helen, the Spartans spared Athens and returned home. As a result of this myth, the place of Hekademos enjoyed immunity in historic times, for during the Peloponnesian War, when the enemy ravaged Attica every year, the Spartans out of reverence for the hero never touched the Academy.

The ancient Athenians did not segregate topography from history, as we are inclined to do. The early history of the ground of the Academy fetched memories from the age of tyrants, "who beautified the city," Thucydides tells us. Two generations later, Cimon made the place into a lovely park, which remained—until the urbanization of the present century—a garden of delight.[10] According to Plutarch, Cimon found the

11-3. Colonus Today
(Photo by author)

Academy a bare and dusty spot and converted it into a watered grove with shady walks and trim avenues. In the gymnasium there, Aristophanes said, young men raced under the sacred olive trees, happy in the springtime when the plane tree whispered to the elm. The gymnasium dated back to archaic times. A gymnasium held not only open courts for running and leaping but also alcoves and colonnaded walks for philosophical discussion, and a lecture hall as well as a building to contain a library. The opening of Plato's *Lysis* has Socrates walking from the Academy to discuss philosophy by the new wrestling ground in the Lyceum.

After his travels, Plato settled in the Academy around 388 B.C., teaching at first in the gymnasium there and then in the garden of his own house nearby. This school in the garden established the meaning of the region located less than a mile northwest of the Double Gate, the principal entrance to the city of Athens. The importance of Hekademos faded as the place became known as *Plato's* Academy, absorbing the park, the gymnasium, and the old shrines. Near the school, Plato founded a shrine dedicated to the Muses—often called the first "museum"—which was augmented by his successor, Speusippus, who erected statues of the Graces. When Plato died, he was buried near the place he loved, between the Academy and Colonus.[11] His statue remained to represent the living presence of the master. For nine centuries, the school celebrated his birthday and, of course, studied his work. It was the first university, a settled community of inquiry engaged in study and discourse, shaping the ideas of Western philosophy, mathematics, and science.

The place was damp and may have earned its reputation as an unhealthy site by breeding malarial mosquitoes. According to legend, Plato rejected medical advice to move to a higher elevation.[12] An exclusively rational choice would have avoided the spot, and enlightened thinkers knew better than to settle there. Aristotle would have picked a healthier location, according to the maxims of Hippocrates followed in the sections of Aristotle's *Politics* that deal with town planning. Hippocrates, an older contemporary of Plato and the founder of scientific medicine, wrote an influential treatise on the environment called "Air, Water, and Places," which offered principles of hygiene directing the proper selection of sites, orienting streets and buildings to make the best of sun, wind, and water, and warning against settling on marshy ground.

Plato, however, turned into a place-lover and refused to leave the Academy, even when his doctor claimed it was too damp for his health and advised him to move to the Lyceum. The early directors in the "golden chain" of successors to Plato also remained attached to the place. Xenocrates, who followed Speusippus as head of the school, left the Academy only one day in the year to see the new tragedies performed in the festival of Dionysus. His successor, Polemo, lived in the garden, and his disciples constructed little huts close at hand, where they dwelt by the shrine of the Muses and the lecture hall.

Civilized Romans, traveling for *theoria*, stayed in Athens to study philosophy and rhetoric. In 88 B.C. Cicero made himself the devoted student of Philo of Larissa, then the director of the Academy. Horace stayed there in 45 B.C.—the next generation—"searching after truth in the groves of Academus." The groves must have grown back quickly, for in the interval between Cicero's and Horace's visits, indeed only two years after Cicero studied there, Sulla's invasion completely deforested the Academy, not even sparing the sacred olive trees.

Plato made philosophy a *therapeia* of the soul, and soon after his death in 327 B.C., his followers worked up a mystique that elevated him as a savior god—a healer and savior of souls.[13] The entire population of the district attended his body to the tomb. One of the epitaphs called Asclepius the healer of the body and Plato the healer of the soul. Asclepius was a mythical figure, the founding hero of medicine, whose father was the god Apollo. Hippocrates, a hereditary priest of Asclepius, once said that a philosophical physician resembled a god. Since Plato was a therapeutic philosopher, he resembled a god as well. Another epitaph proclaimed: "Apollo sent mortals Asclepius and Plato—the one to save the body, the other to save the soul."[14] Plato's epitaphs express a strong sense of his immortality. Speusippus, the nephew who succeeded him as director of the Academy, propagated a legend of Plato's miraculous birth, begat by Apollo. Speusippus wanted to elevate his uncle to the rank of their philosophical predecessor Pythagoras, who was rumored to be the son of a god.

If we think of expressive energies as the souls of things, then indeed the Socratic side of Plato remains a savior of souls. He valued mythical thinking and showed how to grasp the soul of things. In philosophical history, however, the Pythagorean or mathematical side of Plato is remembered as the savior of appearances, because his teaching turned into the rule for the astronomers to "save the appearances." Rational astronomy applied mathematics to discover the *logos* of celestial bodies, rendering their appearances intelligible, whereas paleoastronomy, inspired by the Muse Urania, had found meaning in the sky by hearing the *logoi*—stories or songs of the heavens.

All nine Muses, guardian spirits of Plato's Academy, energize the mind through the ear. Sometime after Plato, the Greeks gave each of them a specialized jurisdiction. They reign over three kinds of poetry, two kinds of drama, choral song and dance, sacred hymns, history, and astronomy; they are restricted to the sphere of eloquence, the arts confined to words and music and profoundly related to memory. As goddesses of expressive energy conveyed by sound, they have nothing to do with the arts that work through the eye, and the visual artist waits in vain for inspiration by an authentic Muse. The Graces, cousins of the Muses, preside over the visual arts.

In earliest times, the Muses, eloquent daughters of Memory and the granddaughters of Mother Earth, were heard in the music of running streams, until people identified them as the goddesses of song. Memory, the mother of the Muses, was conceived in the primeval mating of Earth and Sky and is older than Time. She emerged from the belly of Mother Earth before the birth of the Titans—in the same generation with great cosmic beings such as Ocean and the ancestors of Sun and Moon, as well as Order. All-wise Zeus, son of the youngest Titan, Cronos, united with his aunt Memory, generating nine lovely daughters all of one mind, with spirits free of care and eternally dedicated to song, who give the world relief from evil and sorrow. The Muses keep Olympus full of music and delight. On earth, they pour sweet dew on singing tongues, making humans they love into poets and musicians, or they inspire eloquent discourse, causing wise and gracious words to fill the minds of bards and kings.[15] Hesiod, probably writing early in the seventh century B.C., not long after Homer, tells how they changed him from a gross shepherd, who was nothing but a belly, into a bard inspired to sing about the past and the future with the divine voice they breathed into him. The Muses also confided to Hesiod that even though they know how to speak falsehoods that seem true, they know how to speak the truth as well. Each Muse controls a sphere of eloquence. Among them, Calliope rules over epic poetry, honoring the glory of kings; Clio over history, celebrating the deeds of men; and Urania over astronomy, the mythic lore of the skies.

Memory and her daughters filled the ground with meaning and feeling. Ancestral memories inspired ritual, drama, and rhetoric to hallow the bones of the dead and the places that contained them. The funeral oration that celebrated the fame of the dead grew into a traditional speech in praise of the city, linking the greatness of the place to its departed spirits.

The Academy held a pit where Athenian officials offered sacrifice to the souls of ancestral heroes, an immemorial custom that contributed to the solemnity of the place.[16] Near the Academy, the road from the Double Gate of the city held the tombs of celebrated men, including soldiers who fell in battle. Thucydides described the processions to this location, "the most beautiful suburb of the city," and how the Athenians chose their most eminent citizen to offer a panegyric over the remains of departed heroes. In this way, he introduced the most famous speech in Greek literature—the funeral oration attributed to Pericles.[17]

The Pericles speech celebrated the self-sufficient freedom of the citizens and the power of the city, naming Athens the school of Greece, and declared the excellence of Athenian institutions. Plato, responding to the great speech several decades later, offered a different approach—an encomium of the city that declared the excellence of the ground. In a brief dialogue, *Menexenus*, Plato corrected the form and content of standard funeral panegyrics modeled on the Periclean oration. The ancients took Plato's dialogue very seriously, and Cicero wrote that the Athenians heard it recited every year. On the surface of the dialogue, Socrates pokes fun at the platitudes of patriotic speeches, and a number of commentators have dismissed this dialogue as little more than an attack on rhetoric.[18] Under the surface, however, the *Menexenus* contains another expression of the Socratic doctrine of place. As usual, Socrates is most interesting when he speaks half-seriously, and his levity concerning the rhetoric of men contrasts dramatically with the respect he gives the eloquence of a place. He expresses the doctrine of place by setting a mood or tone and by a sequence of images.

Socrates remains silent about the military and political power of the city, implicitly repudiating the imperialism of Pericles. The other striking difference between the speeches of Socrates and Pericles concerns the importance of urban mythology. In the speech reported by Thucydides, Pericles ignores the ancient legends of Athens, but Plato has Socrates mention these old stories. The Periclean silence about the ancient myths, the *logoi* of the city, sacrifices a valuable element in the Athenian heritage. James Oliver explains, "Whereas Thucydides sought to escape from myths, Plato sought to reinterpret them. For him and for many Greeks thereafter the myths were not literally true but represented the accumulated wisdom of an ancient people. Where no suitable myths existed, Plato in other dialogues invented them."[19]

Whereas Pericles calls the earth the sepulcher of famous men, Socrates claims that the earth is literally their mother. Calling the earth a mother is not merely a metaphor, for in conception and generation the earth does not imitate women. On the contrary, in this respect, women literally follow the earth.

The land of Attica, then, is both the mother and the receptacle or *chora* of Athens. This identification of *chora* with mother went a long way in Greek thought after Plato, and Byzantine theology praised Mary as the mother and *chora* of God, the receptacle of the *Logos*.[20] In Plato's *Menexenus*, Socrates praises the *chora* named Attica as a good mother to the Athenians. According to the local myth, in primeval time she chose to give birth to the first humans instead of generating wild animals. The test of motherhood is in the milk she gives her children, and the countryside of Attica also brought forth the first human food, namely the grain of wheat and barley, the noblest and best nourishment. Mother country brings forth her children, nourishes them with food from the same soil and, when they die, receives them again to rest in their own dwelling places.

The myth of autochthony—imagining the indigenous citizens as products of the soil—proclaimed the natural superiority of Athens to other cities such as Thebes and Sparta, which were founded, according to their own legends, by wandering barbarians who settled on Hellenic ground. Born and reared in their original *chora*, the Athenians were the true and ideal Hellenes, who by their nature resisted barbarian influences. Plato represents Athens as an ideal state and eternal model of good society. Instead of the imaginary cities of the *Republic* and the *Laws*, in the *Menexenus* Plato idealizes the real Athens.

The formal speech in praise of Athens, which probably had its beginnings in the funeral oration in which Pericles expressed the dream of making Athens the mother of all Greece, grew into the familiar Panathenaic discourse associated with the city's most important festival. This customary oration would claim the primacy of Athens and celebrate the benefits that the entire community of Greek people owed to the Athenians.[21] Around 165 A.D., Aelius Aristides wrote a Panathenaic discourse that became a model not merely for speeches about Athens but for an important literary genre later known as the *encomium urbis*—the speech or poem composed to praise a city. Aristides is an important writer for other reasons as well; to his surviving work we owe a great deal of what we know about what life was like in his time, the high point of the Roman Empire. Although not an original thinker, he was a distinguished orator, well educated in the entire literature of archaic and classical Greece. The ideas, tone, and images in his Panathenaic discourse show the continuing vital influence of the Platonic doctrine of place.

Familiar themes that Aristides absorbed from the philosophical movement of Middle Platonism remain prominent in his picture of Athens: attention to ancient legends as important local possessions; exploring the deeper meaning of myths; praise of Attica as the first mother of humans; exaltation of Athens as the source of an ideal Hellenism; and so forth. He describes Athens as the mother and nurse of civilization, the great *chora* or receptacle of seeds and models deposited by the gods—not only the germs of plants, but also the seeds of justice, the arts, and civilized life. Athens is also a receptacle in another sense, as the asylum and comforter of refugees and settler of homeless wanderers. She is their place of rest, welcoming the unfortunates of the world who claim no places of their own. In the third century, Menander the rhetorician selected this discourse of Aristides as his principal model to teach the proper way of praising a city.

The ancients recognized two ways to edify: one with stones and the other with words. Similarly, the lovers of display know two ways to glorify a city: one by erecting splendid buildings, and the other by composing eulogies. Innumerable works of praise in prose and poetry from ancient times through the Middle Ages have followed the standard form of urban panegyric. They describe in exalted language the location of the city; the topography and visual impression; the tale of its origin with special attention to founding myths; the illustrious deeds of its inhabitants; the unique beauty or impressive size of the city; the look of its sacred and secular buildings; the characteristics of its principal rivers; and so forth. The continuity of this tradition of urban rhetoric is impressive, and the same formula remained unchanged for millennia. Leonardo Bruni, writing the best-known eulogy of Florence around 1403, chose the Panathenaic discourse of Aristides as the artistic model for his work.[22]

Like the periegetes, who produced guidebooks, the writers of encomia gave a picture of the city as a whole. Moreover, in Western consciousness, these innumerable eulogies with all their exaggerated perceptions and interpretations have called attention to details in the physique and morale of urban experience. To the naked eye, only a vestige of the literary tradition survives in the homespun stanzas composed by town boosters, the oratory of city officials, the verses in guidebooks, the introductions to local histories. But some traces still remain in familiar ideals such as the Garden City or the Radiant City— even in the most utopian forms proposed by modern architects and planners. The encomia have left a deposit in the unconscious strata of topistic experience. They have helped to shape the ideal of a city and the way we still grasp the qualities of a place.

The Renaissance encomiasts developed some new approaches not found in the ancient city orations. Bruni's eulogy of Florence, for example, presented a new way "to reproduce the total view of a city from both a geographical and historical perspective."[23] And the new linear perspective invented by the painters changed the view of the city held in the eye and grasped by the mind, capturing the features that are rational, symmetrical, and available for mathematical calculation. The bird's-eye view replaced the old medieval picture of the city grasped by the artist on the ground, who knew the city with his legs. Bruni's *Laudatio* anticipated the ideal of the radiant city and the urban utopia, expressing "the geometric spirit of the Renaissance." Nevertheless, on another level, Bruni's representation compared Florence to ancient Athens and Rome, and it still contained elements of the Middle Platonism he inherited from Aristides.

However, the most important tradition conveying the old knowledge of grounded energies was transmitted at the very foundation of the Renaissance by Petrarch, who initiated "a new era in city literature." He expressed the glory of the city in the praise of its ruins. After Petrarch, the encomia acknowledged ruins as places, as locations of feeling. The ruin contained experience that was ended, yet not completed. Once again ruins were experienced as places—as active receptacles of shapes, powers, and feelings—and I identify this meaning with Plato's hidden doctrine of place. It is part of what I call "grounded Platonism."

Aristotle and other ancient writers mentioned Plato's "unwritten opinions," and historians of thought keep discovering hidden doctrines in his work, but they do not agree about them. Some want to identify them with the unwritten mathematical teachings, such as the astronomical problem of Eudoxus, recorded by Simplicius. Others want to associate them with the mystical side of Plato and the mysterious reference in the *Seventh Letter* to his own deepest philosophical insight, which he refused to publish in writing. He explained that this insight, from much discussion and sustained attention, as well as from a common life of inquiry shared with other philosophers, suddenly "like a light kindled from a leaping flame" springs up in the soul and thenceforth nourishes itself.[24]

I am suggesting neither the mathematical nor the mystical side of Plato by his "hidden doctrine of place." Expressed in written dialogues such as *Phaedrus*, *Timaeus*, and *Menexenus*, this doctrine was openly professed in Middle Platonism and in Neoplatonism. Then it passed from medieval writing into the modern period, hidden in a number of different traditions such as the work of some periegetes and the formulas that eulogized cities. It was hidden, yet effective—often remote from explicit awareness, yet surviving in the way we grasp and express a grounded sense of place.

C O N C L U S I O N

To recover archaic *theoria* means to experience a place as a whole through feeling, imagination, and memory, together with intellect and the senses. The human environment is a world of places. If we exclude expressive energies when we build the human environment, we make a world of dead places. Previous chapters explored several causes of dead places. The first topomorphic revolution, creating both settlement and wilderness, connected certain organisms that eventually spread plague, until a later topomorphic change liberated towns from pestilence.

The topomorphic revolution of the late eighteenth century built exclusions, enclosures, and dissociations that cut off the common expressive life of towns. As a result, the modern city is full of barriers, both material and intangible, which conceal or deny that people with different social identities defined by class or by ethnic characteristics dwell in the same town. This segregation saps the vitality of places.

Slums and suburbs are products of topistic differentiation, and this process makes different kinds of slum and suburb. Stereotypes obscure the range of experience in those places. While some slums are good places to dwell—warm and lively environments with a rich and complex social life—others are cacotopes, generating misery in the households and death in the streets. And while some suburbs remain interesting, nourishing communities, others are dead places, where nothing moves but station wagons and lawn sprinklers.

Towns may die for all sorts of reasons, but expressive vitality depends on how a place engages the imagination. A place is dead if the physique does not support the work of imagination, if the mind cannot engage with the experience located there, or if the local energy fails to evoke ideas, images, or feelings. The desert is a dead landscape for many Europeans but an exciting place for Aborigines. The link between imagination and place is no trivial matter. The existential question, "Where do I belong?" is addressed to the imagination. To inhabit a place physically, but to remain unaware of what it means or how it feels, is a deprivation more profound than deafness at a concert or blindness in an art gallery. Humans in this condition belong no *where*.

In modern thinking, people tend the environment to protect themselves. Some of them regard the environment as a mechanism. They want to keep the machine in good order to defend themselves against polluted air, toxic rivers, and poisoned soil. Their most revealing metaphor is "spaceship Earth." For them, the earth is merely a life-support system providing the ingredients they need. Others regard the environment as an organism but still think in terms of controlling objects outside of themselves. In contrast, this book has considered the human environment as a structure of experience.

In the course of the inquiry, we explored three doctrines. One is the idea of selective support, and I have shown how we build the world we suppose by expressing or suppressing specific features of experience. Appearance (or the world we suppose), according to Xenophanes, is built on everything. We have seen that his original words emphasize *built*. We build not only to shelter the body but also to support a structure of consciousness. By construction and demolition we ratify meanings we take for granted. As we rebuild the world, we rebuild ourselves. Another doctrine is the idea of mutual immanence. The structure of mutual immanence includes all the effective presences influencing one another that abide together in a place. Local presences exist as components in one another's natures.[1] To say it in a biblical idiom, they are members of one another. It follows, then, that you cannot destroy the location of their mutual immanence without affecting their inner natures. Finally, we considered Plato's doctrine of Place as the active receptacle of shapes, powers, feelings, and meanings, organizing the qualities within it, energizing experience.

In contrast, Aristotle's doctrine of place, as we have seen, declares the separability of beings from places. His doctrine remains the topistic assumption, the silent premise, for the policy of dislocation implied in slum clearance and urban renewal programs. It supports the idea that people can be removed from places without any harm to their experience, and it assumes that the qualities of their lives may be improved by giving them new containers anywhere. Urban renewal programs have received ample criticism from familiar points of view, but I am suggesting that we look at the topistic assumptions, which often go unnoticed, of both remedial housing and renewal programs. It is obvious that people get emotional about places, and that places have an emotional effect on people. Yet this feature of experience is consistently excluded from the modern processes that make, represent, and destroy places.

C-1. Demolition
(Photo by author)

Today the massive programs of demolition, taken for granted in the 1960s, are considered serious mistakes. The *London Observer* refers to the British program as "the Great Bulldozer Scandal."[2] No one will deny the power of the profit motive or the economic forces that made those urban changes. However, the public that consented to them took for granted certain theoretical assumptions about the human environment that I challenge in this book. A new theoretical perspective must assume the reality of expressive space. This frame of mind would not support topoclasm—the effect of such demolitions.

In England, the *Manchester Evening News* continually reports neighborhood responses to impending demolition. In 1976, for example, the residents of Ladybarn demonstrated in the Manchester town hall, and the story, entitled "The World That Would Not Die," reported that the place did not appear picturesque but looked like ordinary terraced housing. Yet "the street's very ordinariness is the feature that excites affection among its people."[3] In the same year, an association to save

C-2. Slum Clearance
(SHELTER Picture Library)

C-3. Ruins
(SHELTER Picture Library)

Mickelhurst, a community proud of its "village atmosphere," organized
to defend 350 stone terraced cottages against a clearance scheme, and
the newspaper called the effort, "Fight for a Village's Soul." The association secretary observed, "Some of the places they have redeveloped in
Manchester are completely soulless because they have destroyed the
community."[4] The feeling, the atmosphere, the soul of Ladybarn and
Mickelhurst mean a great deal in the idiom that represents dwelling in a
place, but they often remain frivolous irrelevancies to the rationalized
process of clearance and reconstruction.

In opposition to the dominant trends of soulless construction and
ruthless demolition, however, one may detect a growing movement of
topistic concern. All sorts of writers in Europe and America are preoccu-
pied with the feelings of place. They include environmental conserva-
tionists, geographers, architects, and a leader of the American Indian
movement.

In 1971 David Brower, president of Friends of the Earth, urged a revival of the human sense of place. He observed, "The places that we have roots in, and the flavor of their light and sound and feel when things are right in those places, are the wellsprings of our serenity." In the same vein Alan Gussow, a conservationist and landscape artist, wrote: "The environment sustains our bodies. But as humans we also require support for our spirits, and this is what certain kinds of places provide. . . . A place is a piece of the whole environment that has been claimed by feelings. Viewed simply as a life-support system, the earth is an environment. Viewed as a resource that sustains our humanity, the earth is a collection of places."[5]

Vine Deloria—lawyer, political leader, and theologian of the American Indian movement—explains that "American Indians hold their lands—places—as having the highest possible meaning." Both heritages, he writes, European and American Indian, need "an acknowledgement of the reality of places."[6] Christian Norberg-Schulz, a Norwegian architectural theorist and historian, writes: "We are no longer satisfied with making our buildings functional, but want them also to be 'meaningful.' . . . Human life cannot take place anywhere, it presupposes a space which is really a small cosmos, *a system of meaningful places.*"[7]

The meaning of place in personal identity is explored sensitively in recent drama. One of the most important films of the 1950s, *Hiroshima Mon Amour*, identifies the two leading characters with their places, never uttering their names. The film concludes:

She: Hi-ro-shi-ma.
        Hi-ro-shi-ma. That's your name.
He: That's my name. Yes. Your name is Nevers.
        Ne-vers-in France.

The synopsis explains: "They simply call each other once again. . . . Nevers, Hiroshima. For in fact, in each other's eyes, they *are* no one. They are names of places, names that are not names. It is as though, through them, *all of Hiroshima was in love with all of Nevers.*"[8]

In *Equus*, one of the most successful plays of the mid-1970s, Martin Dysart, the psychiatrist, exclaims: "Look! Life is only comprehensible through a thousand local Gods. And not just the old dead ones with names like Zeus—no, but living Geniuses of Place and Person! And not just Greece but modern England! Spirits of certain trees, certain curves of brick wall, certain chip shops, if you like, and slate roofs . . ."[9]

The critique of the built environment, now concerned with the quality of places, has shifted from physique to morale. The poets laureate have left a tradition of expressive protest about the transformations of England. In 1831, during the first stage of the industrial revolution, Robert Southey lamented the impact of steam engines and cotton mills on the environment.[10] Half a century later, Tennyson complained about factory smoke and the polluted air. But in the 1970s, John Betjeman protested, "Places cease to have names, they become areas with a number. Houses become housing, human scale is abandoned."[11] His complaint is not about physical deformity and pollution but about meaning and the loss of identity.

In a recent history of the English home, Harold Priestley observes that the housing problems caused by the industrial revolution and the wartime blitz are still not solved for the entire population. However, where the problem is solved in a material and technical sense, a new riddle of morale has emerged in the housing estates, the new towns, and the suburbs. Among the snug buildings full of amenities and automatic machinery, something has happened to vitality. He observes "the loneliness of the old, the malaise of the middle-aged and the discontent of the young."[12] The companion to this loneliness, malaise, and discontent is boredom. "The curse of America," Kipling predicted to William James in 1896, "sheer hopeless, well-ordered boredom . . . is going some day to be the curse of the world."[13]

In 1845, Friedrich Engels called attention to the widespread devastation and the hideous buildings in Manchester, the world's first industrial city. In 1975, the bishop of Manchester attacked the planners who redesigned it for building a city without a soul.[14] Some months earlier in the same year, two thousand communist demonstrators in France greeted the president of the republic and his cabinet when it met in the new town of Evry. They sounded not at all like Engels in 1845, but rather like the bishop of Manchester in 1975. They protested the "soullessness" of the place and its feeling of emptiness.[15]

In the nineteenth century, the problematic of places was conceived as the problem of housing, the solution found in rationalization. The central problem of the slum, then, was diagnosed as insufficient control and planning of construction, and it was associated with the speculative anarchy of early capitalism. In 1845 Engels wrote of stinking rivers, cellar dwellings, crowded beds, filth, ruin, and people living in houses not fit for habitation. He called Manchester a planless, flung-together chaos of houses and identified the absence of planning as one of the major causes of the terrible conditions he saw in all the factory towns. H. G. Wells reflected on his boyhood experience in the London of the 1880s and criticized "the complete irrational scrambling planlessness of which all of us who had to live in London were the victims. . . . Nowhere was there, nowhere is there yet, an intelligent preparation of accommodation for the specialized civilians in the endless variety rendered inevitable by the enlarging social body."[16]

But the astonished observer who considers the morale of places wonders now if the "intelligent preparation of accommodation for the specialized civilians" is perhaps the predicament instead of the solution, and today critical writers register eloquent scepticism about rational planning. The critique of planning is no longer a response peculiar to conservatives, and in my fieldwork on two continents I found radical populists working in tenant organizations and communities of the poor uniformly identifying planners as enemies of the people, along with the "faceless bureaucrats" who administer the plans. Nevertheless, the absence of planning leads nowhere. The real question is what occupies the minds of the planners. Planning is deadly if the planners are topistic Aristotelians who believe that places are inactive containers of amenities.

I have no quarrel with my colleagues who diagnose urban distress as a problem of planning, or of social justice, or of power, or of economic priorities, or of the restless movement of capital. I think they are correct as far as they go. But I argue that even with power, resources, and good intentions, the defective way of thinking about places—the epistemological stumbling block—would frustrate most genuine efforts to make or keep a good place. The way in which people think and write about the obvious world ignores the magic of places, the passions of space.

It is no longer considered romantic to doubt if rationalization can improve the quality of life. Recently the English philosopher, Stuart Hampshire, wrote an essay on "The Future of Knowledge," in which he explores the burdens of rationality. The philosophers of the Enlightenment had thought that the social sciences and social planning would follow the rapid development of physics and engineering after Newton. Hampshire illustrates the disappointments of rationality with several examples drawn from urban experience. He observes, "we still cannot design a new town, or even a housing development, in any happy confident way, as a center of pleasure in living and as a fully human environment." The greatest danger is boredom, "the disease of advanced

industrial civilization: a sense of triviality, a sense that one is a replace-
able part in a mechanism in no way distinct and indispensable." Against
boredom he finds meaning and sanity in historical awareness: "both
local history, the history that is preserved in buildings and in the contours of roads and fields and streets, and also larger national history;
and, lastly, the history that is based on archaeology and that conveys the
weight of the distant past, with its wild improbabilities and its immense
varieties of styles of life." Demolition, Hampshire shows, makes a significant impact on morale: "Every time a street or building that incorporates
a considerable history is destroyed in some improvement or moderniza-
tion, some future happiness is destroyed with it. The effect is subtle and
indirect, but strong: the whole difference between walking down a street
with visible history in the buildings and in the shapes that form it, and a
barely functional street."[17]

This effect of demolition reminds me of a passage in *The Classic Slum*
by Robert Roberts. An old-timer was watching them clear a slum in
Manchester. "They're knocking our life and times away!" he said, and he
spoke in grief. Hampshire, writing about the future of knowledge and
wishing we could design a "fully human environment," thinks the appetite of reason has starved the imagination. In general, he wants to
nourish the imagination in order to support the burden of rationality,
but in particular he wants to satisfy the emotional-symbolic needs of
places.

Urban constructions and demolitions are topistic forces influencing
morale as they change physique. They shape expressive space. In these
times they often build feelings of separation, isolation, and loss of
connection. But it is possible to build differently—to express links
instead of barriers and to acknowledge the ways in which we still dwell
together. I am not suggesting that we can easily reverse the topomorphic
changes of the modern world or that we can at this moment restore the
lively qualities of archaic cities. Nevertheless, it is possible to build in a
new way that recovers the old consciousness—to rebuild the sense of a
town as a common place. When a new paradigm for the human environment emerges, the ruins of our cities may be the seedbeds of the next
topomorphic revolution.

The obstacle to Hampshire's fully human environment is not rationality or rationalization. The obstacle is ungrounded reason and the
absence of topistic awareness. We need to recollect the unity of a place
as a location of experience and a matrix of energies. For that, we need

to entertain notions born in the dark and to open a place for what Plato called bastard reasoning. We also need a restitution of decayed intelligence.

In this book we have explored past and present, looking for traces of grounded intelligence—not the history of detached intellect. We have avoided cerebral chauvinism, the pitfall of conventional "intellectual history." For the mind includes more than intellect. It contains a history of what we learn through our feet. It grasps the world that meets the eye, the city we know with our legs, the places we know in our hearts, in our guts, in our memories, in our imaginations. It includes the world we feel in our bones. How we grasp the world determines what features of experience we "take" for granted. The world changes when people refuse to "take it" any longer. How then should we rebuild the obvious world?

We can start by rebuilding ourselves. The archaic way of seeing, thinking, and caring is not lost. We can bring it to the surface and change its position in the structure of our experience. The energies of a place include a topistic inheritance, conveyed by images and memories—past experience that is not complete because it still influences the present. Ancient people imagined these energies as spirits and dramatized them in local myths. Just as paleoastronomy made the sky intelligible through stories and songs of celestial presences, so the imaginative lore of places gave expressive intelligibility to grounded energies. These stories quickened the mind's local participation, keeping places alive.

By asking fundamental questions we may begin to enlarge public sensibility and to rediscover the expressive intelligibility of human locations. What is improvement? What is renewal? What does it mean to build? In examining the notion of progress, we should ask: what is topistic progress? How do places improve? They do not improve by technical rationalization—not by erecting taller buildings, or by using new materials, or by designing better machines. The Western technique of improving places has gone as far as it can on its own. Now it is time to recover, incorporate, and integrate other modes of thinking, building, and dwelling—archaic and ancient as well as Eastern—to build a more holistic and grounded experience of place.

G L O S S A R Y

Cacotope: A bad place.

Chorophilia: Love of place.

Energy: The capacity to cause changes in interest, feeling, or action.

Expressive intelligibility: Making sense through a whole experience of perceptions, ideas, images, dramatic encounters, and stories; knowledge with its center in the life of feeling.

Expressive space: A specific milieu laden with emotional and symbolic features of experience; a place that contains feelings and meanings, which may be expressed through objects, structures, forms, surfaces, images, stories, myths, memories, and dreams.

Pathetecture: The process of building feelings and meanings by the arrangement of material objects, especially through construction, dilapidation, and excavation.

Periegete: A guide to a place.

Philochoria: Same as *chorophilia*.

Place: A location of experience; the container of shapes, powers, feelings, and meanings.

Ruins: Physical remains shaping a location of experience that is past but not completed.

Structure of mutual immanence: The system of effective presences dwelling together in a place.

Theoria: An ancient way of grasping experience that involves all the senses and feelings.

Therapeia: Close attendance.

Therapeutae: People who give close attendance.

Topistics: A holistic mode of inquiry designed to make the identity, character, and experience of a place intelligible.

Topoclasm: Destruction of a place.

Topomorphic revolution: A fundamental change in the mode of dwelling together in a place.

Topotherapy: The responsive dwelling, close attendance, cultivation, and care of a place.

Wilderness: A location of unsettled experience.

N O T E S

Introduction. The Places of Experience

1. Herberger, *Thread of Ariadne*, p. 16.
2. Barfield, *Saving the Appearances*, p. 109.
3. Richard Verstegen, a writer, printer, and engraver, lived in England under the name of Richard Rowlands and died in Antwerp around 1620. One of his books is *A Restitution of Decayed Intelligence*. The book has little in it to interest us today, but the title is prophetic. He uses the word "intelligence" to mean "information," but I have taken the liberty of changing the sense of his phrase and intend the word to mean "mental activity."
4. Whitehead, *Science and the Modern World*, p. 10.
5. Rykwert, *Idea of a Town*, p. 23.

Chapter 1. Road to Topistics

1. The Metropolitan Studies Unit in the Laboratory of Community Psychiatry at Harvard University.
2. Tawney, *Poverty as an Industrial Problem*, p. 19.
3. I accepted a Simon Senior Research Fellowship in the University of Manchester.
4. Two of my research associates came along to Manchester as well and worked for the summer as participant observers, following my instructions to find the "worst" housing estate in the whole urban area and move in. Later, they completed Ph.D. dissertations based on the comparative research, and I published an essay on housing projects. Forman, *Let Us Now Praise Obscure Women*; Austin, "Poor Women's Sorority"; Walter, "Dreadful Enclosures."
5. Bachelard, *Poetics of Space*, p. 6.
6. Maritain, "Sign and Symbol."
7. Plato, *Sophist* 247e, in *Dialogues of Plato*, trans. B. Jowett, 3:400; Whitehead, *Adventures of Ideas*, pp. 152–53.
8. Bachelard, *Poetics of Space*, p. 7.
9. Knowlton, "The Genii of Spenser," p. 439; Nitzsche, *Genius Figure in Antiquity*, chap. 1.
10. Collingwood and Wright, *Roman Inscriptions of Britain*, 1:671.
11. Focillon, *Life of Forms in Art*, pp. 5–14.

12. Trachtenberg, *Brooklyn Bridge*, pp. 130, 136–37.

13. Barthes, *Eiffel Tower*, pp. 4–6.

14. Heidegger, *Poetry, Language, Thought*, p. 170.

15. Bohm, *Wholeness and the Implicate Order*, pp. xi, xiv.

16. Bachelard, *Poetics of Space*, p. 6.

17. Immerwahr, *Form and Thought in Herodotus*, p. 2.

18. Snell, *Discovery of the Mind*, p. 144.

19. The word *thea*, coming from the same root that gives us the English word, "theater," meant a "view"; *theamata*, "things that are viewed" or "beheld"; *theorein*, "to contemplate" or "to behold"; and *theoria*, "contemplation." In the time of Herodotus, *theoria* also meant sightseeing abroad, and Solon traveled for the sake of vision. According to Herodotus, Croesus, the ruler of Lydia, addressed Solon: "Stranger of Athens, we have heard much of your wisdom and of your travels through many lands, from love of knowledge and a wish to see the world" (Herodotus 1.29–30). As Bruno Snell has put it, Solon is reputed to be "the first to travel round the world for the sake of *theory*."

Dorothy Emmet has shown that it is good to return to *theoria*, not only because it is the root of our familiar word, but because it is a root in another sense. Ancient *theoria*, nourishing visions, ideas, and images, is a "root" from which new theories can grow. See Snell, *Discovery of the Mind*, p. 144; Emmet, "Why Theoria?," pp. 10–19; "Theoria and the Way of Life," pp. 38–52.

Like the English word "contemplation," the term *theoria* could mean regarding things with the mind as well as gazing with the eyes. The Pythagorean astronomy, with its contemplation (*theoria*) of the heavens, used the term in both senses. *Theoria* was also an essential element in the mystery religions, where ritual led up to the dramatic contemplation of sacred objects. This kind of "seeing" was an attached vision, full of emotion, and a participation in the things revealed. Cornford observed that the Orphic cults taught their initiates to achieve a certain emotional state. "The state of mind is that of passionate sympathetic contemplation (*theoria*), in which the spectator is identified with the suffering God, dies in his death, and rises again in his new birth." An entirely different trend moved *theoria* away from feelings toward the ideal of detached thinking. It may have actually started with Pythagoras, who reformed the Orphic way of life, converting it from religion to philosophy, removing the emotions and reinterpreting *theoria* as the passionless contemplation of the immutable, rational truth. He transformed the Orphic quest for salvation into *philosophia*, the pursuit of wisdom. This direction led ultimately to the meaning of *theoria* in the work of Aristotle—the detached contemplation of speculative wisdom. For the Pythagoreans and for one side of Plato, *theoria* became a mathematical way of seeing the world. It was an internal but intellectual experience, which we still acknowledge when we say, "I see your point." See Cornford, *From Religion to Philosophy*, pp. 198–200.

20. The most attractive things to contemplate, with the highest energies to lead

the soul, became known as "wonders" or *thaumata*. By the simplest play with a word, the list of *theamata*, or things to see, turned into a catalog of *thaumata*, or wonders. Later, this trick revealed to the Alexandrian mind a connection between two famous lists: the Seven Wonders of the World and the Seven Sages, suggesting an obvious affinity between exciting places and theorists in search of things to observe.

Chapter 2. Topomorphic Revolutions

1. Geddes, *Cities in Evolution*, p. 400.
2. Southey, *Sir Thomas More*, 1:18–124.
3. Carlyle, *Past and Present*, book 3, chap. 1; Engels, *Condition of the Working Class*, chaps. 1–3.
4. Harleian manuscript no. 603.
5. Wright, *History of Domestic Manners*, pp. 14–15.
6. Traill and Mann, *Social England*, 1:176. This collection of sources was originally edited and published without pictures by Henry Duff Traill in 1893.
7. Phelps, "An Ancient Sculptured Stone in Manchester Cathedral," pp. 194–95.
8. Wormald, *English Drawings*, p. 21.
9. Tselos, *Sources of the Utrecht Psalter Miniatures*; "Defensive Addenda."
10. The most recent example is Branston, *Lost Gods of England*, pp. 21, 43, 53, 99.
11. Malthus, *Essay on the Principle of Population*, pp. 531–32.
12. Froude, *History of England*, 1:50–51.
13. Thompson, *Passages about Earth*, p. 43.
14. Stanton, *Pugin*, pp. 88–91.
15. Carlyle, *Past and Present*, pp. 34, 42.
16. Ibid., pp. 126, 182, 210, 235, 245.
17. Briggs, "Saxons, Normans, and Victorians."
18. Maitland, *Domesday Book and Beyond*, p. 12; Galbraith, *Domesday Book*, p. 151; Finn, *Domesday Book*, p. 1; Tait, review of Maitland, pp. 768–77.
19. Bryant, *Medieval Foundation of England*, pp. 15–16.
20. Dunmore with Carr, *Late Saxon Town of Thetford*; Davison, "Late Saxon Town of Thetford," pp. 189–208.
21. Rogerson and Dallas, *Excavations in Thetford*.
22. Davison, "Late Saxon Town of Thetford," p. 194.
23. Rogerson and Dallas, *Excavations in Thetford*, pp. 198–99.
24. Newman, "Slums," p. 93.
25. Runciman, *Byzantine Civilisation*, pp. 183, 186, 199.
26. *Cambridge Economic History of Europe*, 1:123.
27. Plutarch, *Lives*, p. 999.
28. Dill, *Roman Society*, pp. 97–98, 375.
29. Friedländer, *Roman Life and Manners*, 1:145.

30. See "Domus," in *Dictionary*, 1:664–66.

31. Ford, *Slums and Housing*, 1:18.

32. Mommsen, *History of Rome*, 4:598.

33. Fowler, *Social Life at Rome*, p. 25.

34. Holmes, *Daily Living in the Twelfth Century*, pp. 36–38. The *ribauz* or "ribald" people in France and Italy were called *lecheurs* and *leccores*, meaning "plate lickers" —the source of our word "lecher."

35. Lapidus, *Muslim Cities in the Later Middle Ages*, pp. 83–87.

36. Conversation with Joseph Needham, November 12, 1974.

37. Ariès, *Centuries of Childhood*, pp. 413–15.

38. Szelenyi, "Regional Management and Social Class," pp. 43–45. At the time the paper was written, this author had left Hungary and was living in the West.

Chapter 3. Sick Places

1. We differentiate between bubonic plague, produced by the bacterium *Yersinia pestis*, carried by the fleas of infected rats; typhus, caused by rickettsia organisms carried by both fleas and lice; typhoid fever, caused by the bacillus *Salmonella typhosa*; smallpox, caused by a virus; scarlet fever, produced by hemolytic streptococcus; and the Asiatic or malignant cholera, caused by a *Vibrio* bacillus shaped like a comma, which is usually transmitted in contaminated water.

2. MacArthur, foreword to *Conquest of Plague*, pp. v–vi.

3. Williams and Miles, *Topley and Wilson's Principles*, p. 1958.

4. Evans, *Life on a Little-Known Planet*, chap. 2; Farb, *Living Earth*, pp. 133–34.

5. Pollitzer, *Plague*, pp. 108–9, 132–33.

6. Giedion, *Eternal Present*, 1:486, 493, 2:32.

7. Fitter, *London's Natural History*, p. 2.

8. Hinton, *Rats and Mice*, pp. 27–28.

9. Gill and Bonnett, *Nature in the Urban Landscape*, pp. 47–48.

10. Hinton, *Rats and Mice*, p. 19.

11. McNeill, *Plagues and Peoples*, p. 194.

12. 1 Sam. 5.

13. Shrewsbury, *History of Bubonic Plague*, p. 30.

14. MacArthur, "Old-Time Plague in Britain," p. 361.

15. Shrewsbury, *History of Bubonic Plague*, p. 232.

16. Ibid., p. 4.

17. Rothschild, "Note of an Exhibit," p. 29.

18. MacArthur, "Old-Time Plague in Britain," p. 364.

19. Lehane, *Compleat Flea*, p. 13.

20. I am grateful to Dr. Miriam Rothschild for responding to my inquiry and for

writing me her observations about historical changes in the environment of fleas and plague.

21. Technically, fleas are known as *siphonaptera*, meaning "wingless tubes," and their biological order includes about 2,000 identified species. A fossil flea from around the Baltic Sea, preserved in amber, reveals its specialized, fully developed biological equipment, showing that it lived as a parasite 50 million years ago. Some parasites that live on rodents, such as the flea of the field mouse and another flea common on domestic mice and rats (*L. segnis*), rarely attack humans, even in hunger, and therefore may be dismissed as potential bearers of plague. Others leave dying rats to attack humans and other animals, but not all these promiscuous feeders are efficient vectors. Similarly, the fleas of dogs and cats—like the human flea—are weak vectors. Rat fleas of the genus *Xenopsylla* are not equally dangerous. The species *X. astia* (literally, "urban") is a poor vector, but the two species *X. brasiliensis* and *X. cheopis* are the most efficient—meaning deadly—plague transmitters. Rothschild, "Fleas," p. 44; Hubbert et al., *Diseases*, chap. 7; Pollitzer, *Plague*; Hirst, *Conquest of Plague*; Jellison, "Fleas and Disease"; Smith, *Insects*, chap. 7.

22. The work of Charles Rothschild as an entomologist is described in the biography of his brother (see Rothschild, *Dear Lord Rothschild*). He assembled the world's greatest collection of fleas, which he donated to the British Museum of Natural History in 1913.

23. Hopkins and Rothschild, *Illustrated Catalogue*, 1:xiii; Rothschild, "New Species of Siphonaptera," p. 85; Rothschild, "A Synopsis of Fleas," p. 85.

24. Pollitzer, *Plague*, p. 12; Gibbon, *Decline and Fall of the Roman Empire*, 2:668.

25. McNeill, *Plagues and Peoples*, p. 159.

26. Ibid., p. 164.

27. Doughty, *Travels*, 1:56, 141.

28. Bell, *Great Plague*, pp. 122, 136, 153–54, 186, 194–95, 319.

29. Bell, *Great Fire*, p. 9; Bell, *Great Plague*, p. 55.

30. Creighton, *History of Epidemics*, 1:328–29; Priestley, *English Home*, p. 93; Hole, *English Home Life*, p. 4; MacArthur, "Old-Time Plague in Britain," p. 363.

31. Verstegen, *Restitution of Decayed Intelligence*, pp. 85–87; see above, Intro., n. 3.

32. Boelter, *Rat Problem*, p. 7.

33. Waterton, *Essays on Natural History*, p. 574.

34. Ibid., pp. 237–38, 242.

35. Shrewsbury, *History of Bubonic Plague*, pp. 9, 506.

36. Gregg, *Plague*, p. 53.

37. In the late 1930s, 1,600 plague fleas (*X. cheopis*) were plucked from ten sewer rats in San Francisco.

38. Hirst, *Conquest of Plague*, p. 124.

39. Pollitzer, *Plague*, p. 283. In a recent letter to me, Miriam Rothschild has observed, "[W]hen my father eventually turned up *X. cheopis* in London it was from

rats in the central heating system of *Guys Hospital!* The new type of building with vast internal heating systems may well favour the Black Rat and *X. cheopis* once again."

40. Marks and Beatty, *Epidemics*, p. 147; Hirst, *Conquest of Plague*, p. 95.

41. Creighton, *History of Epidemics*, 1:675.

42. Hubbert et al., *Diseases*, p. 177.

43. See above, p. 56.

44. Bell, *Great Fire*, pp. 186–87.

45. Shrewsbury, *History of Bubonic Plague*, p. 485.

46. Malcolm, quoted in Bell, *Great Fire*, p. 13.

47. Reddaway, *London 1666*, p. 14.

48. Delaune, *Present State of London*, pp. 56, 492.

49. Heberden, *Observations*, pp. 64, 67–77, 96. Dr. Johnson had prematurely called Heberden's father "the last of our learned physicians."

50. Morris, *History of Urban Form*, p. 193.

51. Bell, *Great Fire*, pp. 291, 293.

52. Buer, *Health, Wealth, and Population*, p. 180.

53. The technical name for the flea that once commonly lived on people and pigs is *Pulex irritans*. The bird flea, commonly found on chickens and known in English as the hen flea, is *Ceratophyllus gallinae*.

54. Hosie, "Observations," pp. 415–20.

55. Miriam Rothschild, letter to author, Jan. 10, 1985.

56. Hubbert, *Diseases*, p. 149.

57. Nelson and Smith, "Ecology of Sylvatic Plague," pp. 273–75.

58. Pollitzer, *Plague*, p. 268.

Chapter 4. Sacred Places

1. Harrison, *Prolegomena*, p. 212.

2. Hesiod, *Works and Days* 90; I am following Jane Harrison's interpretation of the passage (*Prolegomena*, p. 169).

3. Onians, *Origins of European Thought*, p. 369. Conventional etymology derives "sphinx" from *sphingein*, which means "to bind," probably referring to her hyphenated nature as well as to her magical powers. The Greeks conceived a magic spell as a knot, and even an incantation was binding.

4. Edmunds, "The Sphinx in the Oedipus Legend," p. 155; Apollodorus 3.5.8.

5. Hesiod, *Theogony* 326.

6. Pausanias, *Guide*, 1:363. When I visited Greece in 1985, Pausanias in hand, I traced the journey of Oedipus from Corinth to Delphi to Thebes to Colonus. In Thebes I went searching for the mythical place of the Sphinx, but a confusing geographical description in Frazer's commentary on Pausanias started me in the

wrong direction. Fortunately, I paused to question local Thebans, and they insisted that she belongs on "Mt. Sphingion." It makes sense, for Oedipus encountered the Sphinx on his journey from Delphi, before he reached the outskirts of Thebes. Some contemporary maps do read "Mt. Sphingion," but the official name of the hill— almost six hundred meters high—is Mt. Phagas, which means a "great eater" or "glutton."

7. Cohn, *Shape of Sacred Space.* I have also benefited from an unpublished paper by Alan D. Cogswell, "Sacred Places in the Old Testament" (1981).

8. Adams, *Education*, p. 385.

9. Phillips, "Discovery of a Tumulus," pp. 120–22; G. C. Williams, *Book of Amber*, pp. 82–83. The cup is still on display in the Brighton Museum.

10. Ovid, *Metamorphoses*, p. 59.

11. Marshack, "Art and Symbols," pp. 32–34.

12. Simson, *Gothic Cathedral*, pp. 8–9.

13. *Boston Globe*, July 8, 1979, p. 19.

14. Ibid., January 3, 1979, p. 15.

15. Eusebius, *History of the Church*, p. 397.

16. Norberg-Schulz, *Meaning in Western Architecture*, p. 140.

17. Lethaby, *Architecture*, p. 149; Rouham, *Canterbury*, p. 1.

18. Athanasius, *Life of St. Anthony*, p. 865 (my translation). The enormously influential *Life of St. Anthony* was written by Athanasius soon after Anthony's death in 356.

19. See the Greek text and the notes in Butler, *Lausiac History*, 2:100.

20. See Walter, "Heavenly City."

21. Chrysostom, "Second Homily," p. 349.

22. The Seven Wonders of the World—an Alexandrine idea—were all colossal structures.

23. Waddell, *Desert Fathers.* This book is a treasure and a delight to read.

24. Breuil, *Four Hundred Centuries of Cave Art.*

25. Levy, *Gate of Horn*, p. 11.

26. See Bird, *Divining Hand.*

27. Loewe and Blacker, *Oracles and Divination*, p. 162.

28. Luther and Melanchthon, "Deutung Papstesels," pp. 371–85.

29. Frankfort, *Art and Architecture.*

30. Eliade, *Shamanism*, pp. 98, 479, 481; Giedion, *Eternal Present*, 1:465.

31. Freeman and Echegaray, "El Juyo," pp. 16–18; Pfeiffer, "Inner Sanctum," p. 68.

32. Giedion, *Eternal Present.*

Chapter 5. Ungrounded Self

1. Plutarch, *Demetrius* 46.4; Bates, *Sophocles*, p. 72.

2. Gould, "Hiketeia," p. 90.

3. Rose, "Sophocles' *Philoctetes*," pp. 63–64.

4. Ibid., p. 103.

5. Segal, *Tragedy and Civilization*, pp. 11, 224.

6. Freud, *Basic Writings*, p. 181.

7. Ibid., pp. 306–9.

8. Freud, *Letters of Freud and Zweig*, p. 106.

9. Jones, *Life and Work*, 2:11; Bernfeld and Bernfeld, "Freud's Early Childhood," p. 109.

10. McGuire, *Freud/Jung Letters*, p. 260; Ransohoff, "Sigmund Freud," p. 109.

11. Freud, *Origins of Psycho-analysis*, pp. 223–24.

12. For a prosaic note on the place name, see Bernfeld and Bernfeld, "Freud's Early Childhood," p. 108. My Czech informants say that it is impossible to establish with any certainty the original meaning of medieval Czech place names. However, there is a ruined castle in Příbor. It was a seat of the Žerotin family, whose dominion survived the Thirty Years' War (1618–1648), presumably because they were Catholic. Most of the great noble families were Protestant and were therefore replaced by Austrian Catholics.

13. Doolittle, *Tribute to Freud*, p. 17.

14. Freud, "Letter to the Burgomaster of Příbor (1931)," in *Standard Edition*, 21:259.

15. Bernfeld, "Freud and Archeology," p. 113; Jones, *Life and Work*, 2:380.

16. See the fascinating photographic study, commentary, and essay on Freud's home (Engelmann, *Berggasse 19*).

17. Freud, *Origins of Psycho-analysis*, pp. 264, 304, 311, 317.

18. Jones, *Life and Work*, 3:84.

19. Ibid., 2:24.

20. Ibid., 2:16.

21. For the history of models in Freud's work, see Gill, "Topography and Systems."

22. Jones, *Life and Work*, 2:54, 56, 381, 393, 405.

23. Engelman, *Berggasse 19*, p. 138.

24. Ransohoff, quoted ibid., pp. 57–58.

25. Doolittle, *Tribute to Freud*, pp. 154, 141.

26. Ransohoff, quoted in Engelman, *Berggasse 19*, p. 67.

27. Freud, *Collected Papers*, 3:314.

28. Pfeiffer, *Freud and Andreas-Salomé Letters*, p. 230.

29. Engelman, *Berggasse 19*, p. 47.

30. Ibid., p. 23.

31. Scully, *Earth, Temple, and Gods*, pp. 1–2.

32. Schur, *Freud: Living and Dying*, pp. 273–74.

33. Freud, *Standard Edition*, 12:342–44. The quotations in the following paragraphs are taken from this edition.

34. Parke, *Festivals of the Athenians*.

35. Rykwert, *Idea of a Town*, p. 189.

36. Ibid., pp. 188–90.

37. Freud, *Civilization and Its Discontents*, pp. 15–18.

38. Symonds, *Revival of Learning*, p. 104.

39. Petrarca, *Le Familiari*, 2:54; *Rerum familiarium*, pp. 291–95.

40. MacKendrick, "A Renaissance Odyssey," p. 135.

41. Symonds, *Revival of Learning*, p. 112.

42. Bernfeld, "Freud and Archeology," p. 110.

43. Freud, "Constructions in Analysis," in *Collected Papers*, 5:358–71.

44. Bernfeld, "Freud and Archeology," p. 127; Ransohoff, "Sigmund Freud," p. 107.

45. Jones, *Life and Work*, 2:13–14.

46. Freud, "Screen Memories," in *Standard Edition*, 3:312.

47. Bernfeld, "Freud and Archeology," p. 113.

48. Ibid., p. 119.

Chapter 6. The Energies of Places

1. Geography did not require artistic skill because anyone could draw simple lines and make notes to show positions and general outlines. And chorography did not need mathematics, which was crucial to geography. The methodological difference between representing the earth and representing a place then boiled down to quantitative and qualitative perspectives. Ptolemy, *Geographikes Uphegesis*, 1.1. For present purposes, I use my own translation, but I have consulted *Geography of Claudius Ptolemy*, trans. Stevenson; and Rylands, *Geography of Ptolemy*; as well as the version by Drabkin and Cohen included in Lukermann, "The Concept of Location," p. 51.

2. Boyle, *Journey to the Surface of the Earth*.

3. In the ancient world, the Greek word *nomós*, with the accent on the last syllable, meant a place that was allotted or portioned out for use, such as a pasture, while *nómos*, with the accent on the first syllable, meant custom, institutions, or the way of life allotted to a certain people. Here we find what Whitehead called philosophic truth in the presuppositions of language. Within the structure of a word, the Greek language expressed the bond between ways and places.

4. Tuan, "Space and Place," p. 234.

5. Relph, *Place and Placelessness*, p. 6.

6. Needham, *Science and Civilisation in China*, 3:503.

7. Seaton, "Marlowe's Map," p. 16.

8. Parsons, *Map of Great Britain*, pp. 13–14.

9. In Tuan, *Topophilia*, the author borrowed the term from Bachelard; see above, chap. 1.

10. Sophocles, *Oedipus at Colonus* 22, 1520.

11. Aristotle, *Physics* 209a.

12. Whitehead, *Adventures of Ideas*, p. 172.

13. Plato, *Timaeus* 49a.

14. Ibid. 52b.

15. Kirk and Raven, *Presocratic Philosophers*, p. 422; Freeman, *Pre-Socratic Philosophers*, p. 309.

16. Taylor, *Commentary on Plato's Timaeus*, p. 343.

17. Plato, *Timaeus* 49a.

18. Ibid. 50c.

19. Ibid. 51a.

20. Plato, *Timaeus* 52b (my translation). See also Taylor, *Commentary on Plato's Timaeus*, pp. 312–55.

21. Cornford, *Plato's Cosmology*, p. 199.

22. Plato, *Timaeus and Critias*, p. 184.

23. Cassirer, *Philosophy of Symbolic Forms*; Frankfort et al., *Intellectual Adventure of Ancient Man*, chap. 1.

24. Cassirer, *Philosophy of Symbolic Forms*, 2:95.

25. Plato, *Timaeus* 52e, in Cornford, *Plato's Cosmology*, p. 198.

26. Whitehead, *Essays in Science and Philosophy*, pp. 61, 73, 86.

27. Aristotle, *Physics* 209b.

28. See Taylor, *Commentary on Plato's Timaeus*, pp. 346, 666.

29. Aristotle, *Physics* 208a, in *Basic Works*, p. 269.

30. Aristotle, *Physics* 212a.

31. Aristotle, *Basic Works*, p. 270.

32. Taylor, *Commentary on Plato's Timaeus*, pp. 675–76.

33. *Energos* is used as an adjective by Herodotus and Plato, but it is a hapax legomenon, appearing only once in the work of each. In Herodotus, *Histories* 8.26, it characterizes some men who want to be "employed," and in Plato, *Laws* 2.674b, it refers to magistrates "on duty." See also Lindsay, *Blast Power*, p. 15.

34. Plotinus, *Enneads* 3.1.

35. Plato, *Timaeus* 52c, in *Timaeus and Critias*, p. 171.

36. More, *Psychodia*.

37. Panofsky, *Abbot Suger*.

38. Knowles, *Energy and Form*.

39. Scully, *Pueblo*.

40. Macaulay, *Essays*, pp. 104, 277–78.

41. Plato, *Timaeus* 88d.

42. Taylor, *Commentary on Plato's Timaeus*, p. 625.

43. Plato, *Laws* 790d.

44. Whitehead, *Adventures of Ideas*, p. 241.

45. Knights, *Explorations*, p. 125.

46. Giedion, *Space, Time and Architecture*.

Chapter 7. Grasping the Sense of Place

1. Rapoport, "Australian Aborigines," p. 43.

2. Lewis, "Observations on Route Finding," p. 255.

3. Lee, "Conception of the Self," p. 58.

4. Bloomer and Moore, *Body, Memory, and Architecture*, pp. 34–36, 44.

5. Gibson, *Senses Considered as Perceptual Systems*, pp. 97, 129, 123.

6. Ibid., p. 134.

7. Stanner, "The Dreaming," pp. 269–77; Rapoport, "Australian Aborigines," p. 44.

8. Stanner, *Aboriginal Religion*, p. 51 (italics in the original).

9. Baglin and Moore, *People of the Dreamtime*, p. 10.

10. Stanner, *Aboriginal Religion*, p. 152.

11. Lewis, "Observations on Route Finding," p. 252.

12. Berndt and Berndt, *Man, Land and Myth*, p. 18.

13. Gould, *Yiwara*, p. 128.

14. Tucci, *Built in Boston*, pp. 27–30.

15. Hurlbut, *Minerals and Man*, p. 51.

16. Holmes, *Poems*, pp. 130–32.

17. Giedion, *Eternal Present*.

18. Scully, *Earth, Temple, and Gods*, pp. 19, 21.

19. Pausanias, *Guide to Greece*, 1:14; Graves, *Greek Myths*, 1:131–32.

20. Cassirer, *Philosophy of Symbolic Forms*, 3:63, 2:92.

21. Cassirer, *Essay on Man*, pp. 66, 71.

22. Santillana and von Dechend, *Hamlet's Mill*, p. 327.

23. Castaneda, *Separate Reality*, pp. 12–13.

24. Whitehead, *Modes of Thought*, p. 123.

25. Ruskin, *Seven Lamps of Architecture*, p. 7.

26. Lethaby, *Form in Civilisation*.

27. Diels, *Fragmente der Vorsokratiker*, 21.B34.

Chapter 8. Expressive Space

1. Parry, "Landscape," p. 19.

2. Plato, *Phaedrus* 238d.

3. De Vries, *Commentary on the Phaedrus*, p. 88.

4. McCann, "Nostalgia," p. 165.

5. Plato, *Phaedrus* 265b.

6. Ibid. 247–48.

7. Ibid. 278b.

8. De Vries, *Commentary on the Phaedrus*, pp. 264–65; Helmbold and Holther, "Unity of the 'Phaedrus,'" p. 391.

9. Plato, *Phaedrus* 230b.

10. Oliver, *Shelter, Sign, and Symbol*, p. 12.

11. The basic idea behind the word is distribution, and the original Indo-European root, **ai-*, means to give or to allot. Conceptually, then, the word for "diet" remains close to *nómos*, the word for custom, law, or the allotted way of a people.

12. Mumford, *City in History*, p. 299.

13. The Greek words are *astynomous orgas* (Sophocles, *Antigone* [trans. Wyckoff] 355). Vincent Scully, the architectural historian, thinks that the Parthenon, standing out against the mountains, stated "the fact of the city" and expressed the "feelings that make the town" (*Earth, Temple, and Gods*, p. 171).

14. Mailer, "Faith of Graffiti"; Glazer, "Subway Graffiti," pp. 3–11.

Chapter 9. Ominous Space

1. Bottéro, "Symptômes," p. 100.

2. Ibid., p. 101.

3. Oppenheim, "Interpretation of Dreams," p. 242; Saggs, *Greatness That Was Babylon*, pp. 321–24.

4. Oppenheim, *Ancient Mesopotamia*, p. 220; Jastrow, *Religion of Babylonia and Assyria*, p. 405; *Assyrian Dictionary*, 7:37; Weisberg, "Old Babylonian Forerunner," pp. 87–104.

5. Jacobsen, *Toward the Image of Tammuz*, p. 38.

6. Gadd, "Some Babylonian Divinatory Methods," p. 26.

7. Gadd, *Ideas of Divine Rule*, pp. 57, 93; Roux, *Ancient Iraq*, pp. 154, 327.

8. Neugebauer, "Exact Science in Antiquity," p. 30.

9. Mair, *Hesiod*, p. 105.

10. Young, *Doubt and Certainty in Science*, p. 162.

11. Lettvin, "The Gorgon's Eye," p. 135.

12. Marshack, *Roots of Civilization*; idem, "Art and Symbols," pp. 32–41.

13. Giedion, *Eternal Present*, 1:88.

14. See Lindsay, *Origins of Astrology*, p. 420.

15. Barfield, *Saving the Appearances*, p. 20.

16. Young, *Doubt and Certainty in Science*, pp. 61–66.

17. Cassirer, *Philosophy of Symbolic Forms*, 3:72.

18. Ibid., p. 65.

19. Whitehead, *Symbolism*, p. 84.

20. Ibid., p. 8.

21. Saggs, *Greatness That Was Babylon*, p. 324; Oppenheim, *Ancient Mesopotamia*, pp. 206–12; idem, "Interpretation of Dreams," p. 241; idem, "Perspectives on Mesopotamian Divination," pp. 35–43; Gadd, "Some Babylonian Divinatory Methods," pp. 21–34.

22. Leichty, "Teratological Omens," p. 133.

23. Frankfort, *Birth of Civilization*, pp. 51–52, 59, 77; idem, *Problem of Similarity*, p. 17; idem, "Archetype," p. 173.

24. Finkelstein, "Mesopotamian Historiography," p. 466.

Chapter 10. Riddles and Problems

1. Harrison, *Prolegomena*, pp. 207–12.

2. Abrahams, *Jewish Life in the Middle Ages*, pp. 384–86; see also *Jewish Encyclopedia*, 10:408.

3. Contenau, *Everyday Life in Babylon and Assyria*, p. 168.

4. Torcszyner, "Riddle in the Bible," p. 134.

5. Steinthal, "Legend of Samson," pp. 396–98.

6. Santillana and von Dechend, *Hamlet's Mill*, pp. 175–76.

7. Ibid., p. 177.

8. Plato, *Republic* 479c.

9. Burnet, *Greek Philosophy*, p. 222.

10. Plato, *Republic* 527d.

11. Dijksterhuis, *Mechanization of the World Picture*, pp. 15–16.

12. Hanson, *Constellations and Conjectures*, p. 43.

13. Guthrie, *History*, 4:451.

14. Plato, *Epinomis* 987–88.

15. Kahn, "Early Greek Astronomy," pp. 109, 116.

16. Duhem, *To Save the Phenomena*, chap. 1; Vlastos, *Plato's Universe*, pp. 60, 110.

17. The first time this word appeared in Greek literature, it described a mythological rescue. Herodotus wrote that according to Egyptian legend, the goddess Leto "rescued" and hid Apollo from the primeval monster Typhon, and consequently the Egyptians called her his savior or preserver.

18. Plato, *Laws* 821b.

19. Plato, *Phaedo* 97d–98b; idem, *Apology* 26d; Xenophon, *Memorabilia* 4.7.5–6.

20. Plato, *Laws* 908–12.

21. Plato, *Phaedrus* 246c; Cornford, *Plato's Cosmology*, p. 139.

22. Plato, *Timaeus* 40b.

23. Hanson, *Constellations and Conjectures*, p. 23.

24. Mourelatos, *Route of Parmenides*, pp. 118–19.

25. Ibid., pp. 17–25.

26. Farrington, *Greek Science*, pp. 94–95.

27. Plato, *Timaeus* 19e.

28. Ibid., 40c–d.

29. See Foucault, *Birth of the Clinic*, chap. 9.

30. Van Doren, *Portable Walt Whitman*, p. 266.

31. Milton, *Paradise Lost*, 8.79–82.

32. Fraser, *Ptolemaic Alexandria*, 1:385.

Chapter 11. The Ground of Platonism

1. Sterrett, "Torch-Race," p. 418; Frazer, *Pausanias's Description of Greece*, 2:392.

2. Plato, *Laws* 776b.

3. Thompson, "Athenian Twilight"; Frantz, "From Paganism to Christianity"; Cameron, "Last Days of the Academy," pp. 7–29.

4. Bede, *Ecclesiastical History*, 4:1; Cameron, "Last Days of the Academy"; Frantz, "From Paganism to Christianity"; Cameron, "Agathias on the Sassanians."

5. Slater, *Glory of Hera*, p. xxiii.

6. Burnet, *Platonism*, pp. 118–19.

7. Pausanias, *Guide to Greece*, 1:89; Herodotus, *Histories* 7.152.

8. *Athens Annals of Archaeology* (1968): 101–7; Travlos, *Pictorial Dictionary*, p. 42. In Athens, a shard found in the Agora shows a figure with the name *Hekademos*, from the second quarter of the sixth century B.C.

9. Plutarch, *Lives*, p. 20; Graves, *Greek Myths*, 1:362–69.

10. An aristocratic enemy of the tyrants and a successful general of Greek forces against the Persian king, Cimon rose to prominence in Athens, where he encouraged the arts and increased the amenities—expanding the water supply, building roads and temples, and enhancing the splendor of the city with public works of all kinds.

11. Frazer, *Pausanias's Description of Greece*, 2:389; Wycherly, "Peripatos."

12. Aelianus, *Various History*, p. 176. St. Basil, who apparently knew the spot in the fourth century A.D., liked to think of Plato as an ascetic, suggesting that he chose the site for his school precisely because it was unhealthy. Too much health was bad for philosophy, he presumed, and St. Basil enjoyed preaching about the spiritual perils of a healthy body. These sentiments appear in St. Basil's sermon on the Christian utility of pagan books, numbered differently in various collections of his homilies. Plato's esteem in the Christian imagination as an ascetic saint declined when the cult of Plato and the religious appeal of Neoplatonism began to rival the appeal of Christianity.

13. Soldiers, sailors, and travelers, often in need of rescue, especially worshiped savior gods, who included a number of founding heroes and deified mortals as well as Olympian gods. The divine saviors who protected human life anticipated Chris-

tian saints, and in the Hellenistic world the list extended to include not only Zeus, the Heavenly Twins (Castor and Pollux), and Serapis, but also a number of deified humans, such as the Egyptian monarch Ptolemy I and his wife.

14. Diogenes Laertius, *Lives of Eminent Philosophers* 3.45.

15. Hesiod, *Theogony* 53–100.

16. Dyer, *Ancient Athens*, p. 492.

17. Thucydides 2.34–36.

18. Guthrie, *History*, 4:312–23. Modern rationalists find little to interest them in the *Menexenus*. Karl Popper called it a "sneering reply" to the oration of Pericles. Jowett and his editors refused to write an introduction to the dialogue because it lacks an analytical "train of philosophical argument" (*Dialogues of Plato*, trans. B. Jowett, 1:677 [n. 1]). Nevertheless, in the absence of explicit *logos*, grounded Platonism gets expressed in Socratic *logoi*.

19. Oliver, *Civilizing Power*, p. 10.

20. Ibid., p. 42.

21. Ibid., p. 17.

22. Burgess, *Epideictic Literature*; Hammer, *Latin and German Encomia of Cities*; Schlauch, "Old English Encomium Urbis." Bruni's *Laudatio Florentinae Urbis* is studied in Baron, *Crisis of the Early Italian Renaissance*.

23. Baron, *Crisis of the Early Italian Renaissance*, pp. 196–201.

24. Plato, *Seventh Letter*, in *Works*, 7:531; Guthrie, *History*, 4:1.

Conclusion

1. Whitehead, *Adventures of Ideas*, p. 172.

2. *London Observer*, 7 December 1975.

3. *Manchester Evening News*, 8 March 1976.

4. Ibid., 7 January 1976.

5. Gussow, *Sense of Place*, pp. 15, 27.

6. Deloria, *God Is Red*, pp. 74, 75, 296.

7. Norberg-Schulz, *Meaning in Western Architecture*, pp. 223, 226–28.

8. Duras, *Hiroshima Mon Amour*, pp. 13, 83.

9. Shaffer, *Equus*, p. 71.

10. Southey, *Sir Thomas More*, pp. 158, 174.

11. John Betjeman, foreword to *Rape of Britain*, by Amery and Cruickshank.

12. Priestley, *English Home*, p. 199.

13. Mumford, *City in History*, p. 494.

14. *Manchester Evening News*, 8 November 1975.

15. *Manchester Guardian*, 27 February 1975.

16. Wells, *Experiment in Autobiography*, 1:275–76.

17. Hampshire, "Future of Knowledge," p. 14.

BIBLIOGRAPHY

Abrahams, Israel. *Jewish Life in the Middle Ages*. New York: Meridian, 1958.

Adams, Henry. *The Education of Henry Adams*. Boston: Houghton Mifflin, 1961.

Aelianus, Claudius. *Various History*. Translated by Thomas Stanley. London: Dring, 1665.

Amery, Colin, and Cruickshank, Dan. *The Rape of Britain*. London: Paul Elek, 1975.

Apollodorus. *The Library*. Translated by J. G. Frazer. 2 vols. Loeb Classical Library. 1921.

Ariès, Philippe. *Centuries of Childhood*. Translated by Robert Baldick. New York: Knopf, 1962.

Aristotle. *The Basic Works of Aristotle*. Edited by Richard McKeon. New York: Random House, 1941.

————. *Works*. Loeb Classical Library. 1926–35.

————. *Works*. Edited by W. D. Ross. 12 vols. London: Oxford University Press, 1927–54.

Assyrian Dictionary. Chicago: University of Chicago, Oriental Institute, 1956–.

Athanasius. *Life of St. Anthony*. Vol. 26 of *Patrologia Graeca*. Paris: Migne, 1887.

Austin, June P. "Poor Women's Sorority: Social Life among Women in Low-Income Public Housing." Ph.D. dissertation, Boston University, 1981.

Bachelard, Gaston. *The Poetics of Space*. Translated by Maria Jolas. Boston: Beacon Press, 1969.

Baglin, Douglass, and Moore, David R. *People of the Dreamtime*. New York: Weatherhill, 1970.

Banham, Reyner. *Guide to Modern Architecture*. London: Architectural Press, 1962.

Barfield, Owen. *Saving the Appearances*. New York: Harcourt, Brace and World, 1957.

Baron, Hans. *The Crisis of the Early Italian Renaissance*. Princeton, N.J.: Princeton University Press, 1966.

Barthes, Roland. *The Eiffel Tower and Other Mythologies*. Translated by Richard Howard. New York: Hill and Wang, 1979.

Bates, William N. *Sophocles*. New York: Russell and Russell, 1969.

Bede. *Ecclesiastical History of the English People*. Edited by B. Colgrave and R. A. B. Mynors. London: Oxford University Press, 1969.

Bell, Walter G. *The Great Fire of London in 1666*. 2d ed. London: John Lane, 1920.

————. *The Great Plague in London in 1665*. London: John Lane, 1924.

Bennett, Steven J. "Patterns of the Sky and Earth: A Chinese Science of Applied Cosmology." *Chinese Science* 3 (1978): 1–26.

Berndt, Ronald M., and Berndt, Catherine H. *Man, Land and Myth in North Australia.* East Lansing: Michigan State University Press, 1970.

Bernfeld, Siegfried and Bernfeld, Suzanne C. "Freud's Early Childhood." *Bulletin of the Menninger Clinic* 8 (1944): 107–15.

Bernfeld, Suzanne C. "Freud and Archeology." *American Imago* 8 (1951): 107–28.

Berry, Wendell. *The Unsettling of America.* New York: Avon, 1978.

Besant, Walter. *London.* London: Chatto and Windus, 1898.

Bird, Christopher. *The Divining Hand.* New York: Dutton, 1979.

Bloomer, Kent C., and Moore, Charles W. *Body, Memory, and Architecture.* New Haven, Conn.: Yale University Press, 1977.

Boelter, W. R. *The Rat Problem.* London: Bale, 1909.

Bohm, David. *Wholeness and the Implicate Order.* London: Routledge and Kegan Paul, 1980.

Bottéro, Jean. "Symptômes, signes, écritures en Mésopotamie ancienne." In *Divination et Rationalité*, edited by J.-P. Vernant. Paris: Editions du Seuil, 1974.

Boyle, Mark. *Journey to the Surface of the Earth: Mark Boyle's Atlas and Manual.* Cologne, London, Reykjavik: Hansjorg Mayer, 1970.

Branston, Brian. *The Lost Gods of England.* New York: Oxford University Press, 1974.

Breuil, Henri. *Four Hundred Centuries of Cave Art.* Translated by M. E. Boyle. Paris: Windels, 1952.

Briggs, Asa. "Saxons, Normans, and Victorians." In *The 1066 Commemorative Series*, no. 5. Hastings and Bexhill Hill Branch of the Historical Association, 1966.

Bryant, Arthur. *The Medieval Foundation of England.* New York: Collier, 1968.

Bryce, James B. *Studies in Contemporary Biography.* New York: Macmillan, 1903.

Buer, Mabel C. *Health, Wealth, and Population in the Early Days of the Industrial Revolution.* London: Routledge, 1926.

Burgess, Theodore C. *Epideictic Literature.* Chicago: University of Chicago Press, 1902.

Burnet, John. *Greek Philosophy: Thales to Plato.* London: Macmillan, 1928.

———. *Platonism.* Berkeley: University of California Press, 1928.

Butler, Dom Cuthbert. *The Lausiac History of Palladius.* 2 vols. Cambridge: Cambridge University Press, 1898–1904.

Cambridge Economic History of Europe. 2 vols. Cambridge: Cambridge University Press, 1966.

Cameron, Alan. "The Last Days of the Academy at Athens." *Proceedings of the Cambridge Philological Society*, n.s., no. 15 (1969): 7–29.

Cameron, Averil. "Agathias on the Sassanians." *Dumbarton Oaks Papers*, nos. 23–24 (1969–70): 167–74.

Carlyle, Thomas. *Past and Present.* 1843. Reprint. London: Chapman and Hall, 1896.

Cassirer, Ernst. *An Essay on Man.* New York: Anchor, 1953.

————. *The Philosophy of Symbolic Forms.* Translated by Ralph Manheim. 3 vols. New Haven, Conn.: Yale University Press, 1955–57.

Castaneda, Carlos. *A Separate Reality.* New York: Touchstone, 1971.

Chrysostom, John. "Second Homily on the Statues." In *Works of St. John Chrysostom.* Vol. 10 of Select Writings of the Nicene and Post-Nicene Fathers. New York: Christian Literature Company, 1889.

Cipolla, Carlo M. *Cristofano and the Plague.* Berkeley: University of California Press, 1973.

Cogswell, Alan D. "Sacred Places in the Old Testament." Unpublished paper, Boston University, 1981. Typescript.

Cohn, Robert L. *The Shape of Sacred Space.* Chico, Calif.: Scholars Press, 1981.

Collingwood, Robin G., and Wright, R. P. *The Roman Inscriptions of Britain.* Oxford: Clarendon Press, 1965.

Contenau, Georges. *Everyday Life in Babylon and Assyria.* London: Arnold, 1954.

Cornford, Francis M. *From Religion to Philosophy.* New York: Harper Torchbooks, 1957.

————. *Plato's Cosmology.* New York: Liberal Arts Press, 1957.

Creighton, Charles. *A History of Epidemics in Britain.* 2d ed. New York: Barnes and Noble, 1965.

Davison, Brian K. "The Late Saxon Town of Thetford." *Medieval Archaeology* 2 (1967): 189–208.

Defoe, Daniel. *A Journal of the Plague Year.* 1722. Reprint. New York: Heritage Press, 1968.

Delaune, Thomas. *The Present State of London.* London: Prosser and How, 1681.

Deloria, Vine, Jr. *God Is Red.* New York: Delta, 1973.

De Vries, Gerrit J. *A Commentary on the Phaedrus of Plato.* Amsterdam: Hakkert, 1969.

Dictionary of Greek and Roman Antiquities. 2 vols. London: Murray, 1901.

Diels, Hermann. *Die Fragmente der Vorsokratiker.* 7th ed. 3 vols. Berlin-Charlottenburg: Weidmannsche Verlagsbuchhandlung, 1954.

Dijksterhuis, Eduard J. *The Mechanization of the World Picture.* Translated by C. Dikshoorn. London: Oxford University Press, 1961.

Dill, Samuel. *Roman Society from Nero to Marcus Aurelius.* New York: Meridian, 1957.

Diogenes Laertius. *Lives of Eminent Philosophers.* Translated by R. D. Hicks. Loeb Classical Library. 1958.

Doolittle, Hilda. *Tribute to Freud.* New York: Pantheon, 1956.

Doughty, Charles M. *Travels in Arabia Deserta.* New York: Dover, 1979.

Duhem, Pierre. *To Save the Phenomena.* Translated by E. Doland and C. Maschler. Chicago: University of Chicago Press, 1969.

Dunmore, Stephen, with Carr, Robert. *The Late Saxon Town of Thetford.* East Anglian Archaeology Report no. 4. Dereham: Norfolk Archaeological Unit, 1976.

Duras, Marguerite. *Hiroshima Mon Amour.* Translated by Richard Seaver. Text for the film by Alain Resnais. New York: Grove Press, 1961.

Edmunds, Lowell. "The Sphinx in the Oedipus Legend." In *Oedipus: A Folklore Casebook,* edited by Lowell Edmunds and Alan Dundes. New York: Garland, 1983.

Eliade, Mircea. *Shamanism.* Translated by W. R. Trask. Princeton, N.J.: Princeton University Press, 1972.

Emmet, Dorothy. "Theoria and the Way of Life." *Journal of Theological Studies,* n.s. 17, pt. 1 (1966): 38–52.

———. "Why Theoria?" *Theoria to Theory* 1 (1966): 10–18.

Engelman, Edmund. *Berggasse 19: Sigmund Freud's Home and Offices, Vienna 1938.* New York: Basic Books, 1976.

Engels, Friedrich. *The Condition of the Working-Class in England.* Translated by F. Wischnewetsky. St. Albans: Panther, 1974.

Eusebius. *The History of the Church from Christ to Constantine.* Translated by G. A. Williamson. New York: New York University Press, 1966.

Evans, Howard E. *Life on a Little-Known Planet.* New York: Dutton, 1968.

Farb, Peter. *Living Earth.* London: Constable, 1960.

Farrington, Benjamin. *Greek Science.* Harmondsworth, Eng.: Penguin, 1949.

Finkelstein, J. J. "Mesopotamian Historiography." *Proceedings of the American Philosophical Society* 107 (1963): 464–72.

Finn, R. Weldon. *Domesday Book: A Guide.* London: Phillimore, 1973.

Fitter, R. S. R. *London's Natural History.* London: Collins, 1946.

Focillon, Henri. *The Life of Forms in Art.* 2d ed. Translated by C. B. Hogan and George Kubler. New York: Wittenborn, 1948.

Ford, James. *Slums and Housing.* Cambridge, Mass.: Harvard University Press, 1936.

Forman, Rachel Z. *Let Us Now Praise Obscure Women: A Comparative Study of Publicly Supported Unmarried Mothers in Government Housing in the United States and Britain.* Washington, D.C.: University Press of America, 1982.

Foucault, Michel. *The Birth of the Clinic.* Translated by A. M. S. Smith. New York: Pantheon, 1973.

Fowler, William W. *Social Life at Rome in the Age of Cicero.* New York: Macmillan, 1909.

Frankfort, Henri. "The Archetype in Analytical Psychology and the History of Religion." *Journal of the Warburg and Courtauld Institutes* 21 (1958): 166–78.

———. *The Art and Architecture of the Ancient Orient.* Harmondsworth, Eng.: Penguin, 1977.

———. *The Birth of Civilization in the Near East.* London: Benn, 1951.

———. *The Problem of Similarity in Ancient Near Eastern Religions.* London: Oxford University Press, 1951.

Frankfort, Henri; Frankfort, H. A.; Wilson, John A.; Jacobsen, Thorkild; and Irwin, William A. *The Intellectual Adventure of Ancient Man.* Chicago: University of Chicago Press, 1946.

Frantz, Alison. "From Paganism to Christianity in the Temples of Athens." *Dumbarton Oaks Papers*, no. 19 (1965): 187–205.

Fraser, P. M. *Ptolemaic Alexandria.* 3 vols. London: Oxford University Press, 1972.

Frazer, James G. *Pausanias's Description of Greece.* 6 vols. London: Macmillan, 1913.

Freeman, Kathleen. *The Pre-Socratic Philosophers.* 3d ed. Cambridge, Mass.: Harvard University Press, 1966.

Freeman, Leslie G., and Echegaray, J. Gonzalez. "El Juyo: A 14,000-year-old Sanctuary from Northern Spain." *History of Religions* (August 1981): 1–19.

Freud, Ernst, ed. *The Letters of Sigmund Freud and Arnold Zweig.* London: Hogarth Press, 1970.

Freud, Sigmund. *The Basic Writings of Sigmund Freud.* Translated by A. A. Brill. Modern Library. 1938.

———. *Civilization and Its Discontents.* Translated by Joan Rivère. London: Hogarth Press, 1955.

———. *Collected Papers.* 5 vols. London: Hogarth Press, 1950.

———. *The Origins of Psycho-analysis: Letters to Wilhelm Fliess.* New York: Basic Books, 1954.

———. *Standard Edition of the Complete Psychological Works of Sigmund Freud.* Translated by J. Strachy. 24 vols. London: Hogarth Press, 1978.

Friedländer, Ludwig. *Roman Life and Manners under the Early Empire.* Translated by L. A. Magnus. London: Routledge and Kegan Paul, 1965.

Froude, James A. *History of England from the Fall of Wolsey to the Death of Elizabeth.* 12 vols. New York: Scribner, 1871.

Gadd, Cyril J. *Ideas of Divine Rule in the Ancient East.* London: British Academy, 1948.

———. "Some Babylonian Divinatory Methods." In *Rencontre assyriologique, La divination en Mésopotamie ancienne.*

Galbraith, V. H. *Domesday Book.* Oxford: Clarendon Press, 1974.

Gauldie, Sinclair. *Architecture.* London: Oxford University Press, 1969.

Geddes, Patrick. *Cities in Evolution.* New ed. London: Benn, 1968.

Gibbon, Edward. *The Decline and Fall of the Roman Empire.* 3 vols. Modern Library. 1932.

Gibson, James J. *The Senses Considered as Perceptual Systems.* Boston: Houghton Mifflin, 1966.

Giedion, Sigfried. *The Eternal Present.* 2 vols. Bollingen Series. New York: Pantheon, 1962–64.

————. *Mechanization Takes Command.* New York: Norton, 1969.

————. *Space, Time and Architecture.* 5th ed. Cambridge, Mass.: Harvard University Press, 1976.

Gill, Don, and Bonnett, Penelope. *Nature in the Urban Landscape.* Baltimore, Md.: York Press, 1973.

Gill, M. M. "Topography and Systems in Psychoanalytic Theory." *Psychological Issues* 3, no. 10 (1963).

Glazer, Nathan. "On Subway Graffiti in New York." *The Public Interest,* no. 54 (1979).

Gould, John. "Hiketeia." *Journal of Hellenic Studies* 93 (1973).

Gould, Richard A. *Yiwara.* New York: Scribner's, 1969.

Graves, Robert. *The Greek Myths.* 2 vols. Harmondsworth, Eng.: Penguin, 1955.

Greenwood, Major. *Epidemics and Crowd-Diseases.* New York: Macmillan, 1937.

Gregg, C. T. *Plague.* New York: Scribner's, 1978.

Gussow, Alan. *A Sense of Place.* San Francisco: Friends of the Earth, 1971.

Guthrie, William K. C. *A History of Greek Philosophy.* 6 vols. Cambridge: Cambridge University Press, 1962–81.

Hammer, William. *Latin and German Encomia of Cities.* Chicago: University of Chicago Libraries, 1937.

Hampshire, Stuart. "The Future of Knowledge." *New York Review of Books,* 31 March 1977.

Hanson, Norwood R. *Constellations and Conjectures.* Dordrecht, Neth.: Reidel, 1973.

————. *Patterns of Discovery.* Cambridge: Cambridge University Press, 1969.

Harleian Manuscript No. 603. Western Manuscripts Division, The British Library.

Harrison, Jane. *Prolegomena to the Study of Greek Religion.* New York: Meridian, 1957.

Heberden, William. *Observations on the Increase and Decrease of Different Diseases, and Particularly of the Plague.* London: T. Payne, 1801. Reprinted in *Population and Disease in Early Industrial England.* Brookfield, Vt.:Gregg International Publishers, 1973.

Heidegger, Martin. *Poetry, Language, Thought.* Translated by Albert Hofstadter. New York: Harper and Row, 1975.

Heisenberg, Werner. *The Physicist's Conception of Nature.* Translated by A. J. Pomerans. New York: Harcourt, Brace, 1958.

Helmbold, W. C., and Holther, W. B. "The Unity of the 'Phaedrus.'" *University of California Publications in Classical Philology* 14 (1952).

Herberger, Charles F. *The Riddle of the Sphinx.* New York: Vantage Press, 1979.

————. *The Thread of Ariadne.* New York: Philosophical Library, 1972.

Herodotus. *Histories.* Translated by George Rawlinson. Modern Library. 1942.

Hesiod. *The Homeric Hymns and Homerica.* Translated by Hugh G. Evelyn-White. Loeb Classical Library. 1914.

Hinton, M. A. C. *Rats and Mice as Enemies of Mankind*. 3d ed. London: British Museum, 1931.

Hirst, Leonard F. *Conquest of Plague*. London: Oxford University Press, 1953.

Hole, Christina. *English Home Life*. London: Batsford, 1947.

Holmes, Oliver Wendell. *Poems*. Boston: Ticknor, Reed and Fields, 1848.

Holmes, Urban T., Jr. *Daily Living in the Twelfth Century*. Madison: University of Wisconsin Press, 1952.

Hopkins, G. H. E., and Rothschild, Miriam. *An Illustrated Catalogue of the Rothschild Collection of Fleas in the British Museum*. London: British Museum, 1953.

Hosie, G. "Observations on the Occurrence of *Ceratophyllus gallinae* around New Housing Estates in the West of Scotland." In *Fleas*, edited by Robert Traub and H. Starcke. Rotterdam: Balkema, 1980.

Hubbert, W. T. *Diseases Transmitted from Animals to Man*. 6th ed. Springfield, Ill.: Thomas, 1975.

Hurlbut, Cornelius S., Jr. *Minerals and Man*. New York: Random House, 1968.

Immerwahr, Henry R. *Form and Thought in Herodotus*. Cleveland: Western Reserve University Press, 1966.

Jacobsen, Thorkild. *Toward the Image of Tammuz*. Cambridge, Mass.: Harvard University Press, 1970.

Jacoby, Felix. *Atthis*. Oxford: Clarendon Press, 1949.

Jastrow, Morris. *The Religion of Babylonia and Assyria*. Boston: Ginn, 1898.

Jellison, W. L. "Fleas and Disease." *Annual Review of Entomology* 4 (1959): 389–414.

Jencks, Charles, and Baird, George. *Meaning in Architecture*. New York: Braziller, 1969.

Jones, Ernest. *The Life and Work of Sigmund Freud*. 3 vols. New York: Basic Books, 1943.

Kahn, C. H. "On Early Greek Astronomy." *Journal of Hellenic Studies* 90 (1970): 99–116.

Kirk, G. S., and Raven, J. E. *The Presocratic Philosophers*. Cambridge: Cambridge University Press, 1963.

Knights, Lionel C. *Explorations*. New York: Stewart, 1947.

Knowles, Ralph L. *Energy and Form*. Cambridge, Mass.: MIT Press, 1974.

Knowlton, E. C. "The Genii of Spenser." *Studies in Philology* 25 (1928).

Lapidus, Ira M. *Muslim Cities in the Later Middle Ages*. Cambridge, Mass.: Harvard University Press, 1967.

Lee, Dorothy. "Notes on the Conception of the Self among the Wintu Indians." *Explorations* 2–4 (1954–55).

Lehane, Brendan. *The Compleat Flea*. London: John Murray, 1969.

Leichty, Erle. "Teratological Omens." In Rencontre assyriologique, *La divination en Mésopotamie ancienne*.

Lethaby, William R. *Architecture Mysticism and Myth*. 1891. Reprint. New York: Braziller, 1975.

————. *Form in Civilisation*. London: Oxford University Press, 1922.

Lettvin, Jerome Y. "The Gorgon's Eye." In *Astronomy of the Ancients*, edited by K. Brecher and M. Freitag. Cambridge, Mass.: MIT Press, 1979.

Levy, Gertrude R. *The Gate of Horn*. London: Faber and Faber, 1963.

Lewis, David. "Observations on Route Finding and Spatial Orientation among the Aboriginal Peoples of the Western Desert Region of Central Australia." *Oceania* 46 (1976): 249–82.

Lindsay, Jack. *Blast Power and Ballistics*. New York: Harper and Row, 1974.

————. *Origins of Astrology*. New York: Barnes and Noble, 1971.

Loewe, Michael, and Blacker, Carmen, eds. *Oracles and Divination*. Boulder, Colo.: Shambhala, 1981.

Lukermann, F. "The Concept of Location in Classical Geography." *Annals of the Association of American Geographers* 51 (1961).

Luther, Martin, and Melanchthon, Philip. "Deutung Papstesels zu Rom und Munchkalbs zu Freyberg funden." In *D. Martin Luthers Werke*. Weimar: Bohlhaus, 1900.

MacArthur, William P. Foreword to *The Conquest of Plague*, by L. F. Hirst. London: Oxford University Press, 1953.

————. "Old-Time Plague in Britain." *Transactions of the Royal Society of Tropical Medicine and Hygiene* 19 (1925–26).

Macaulay, Thomas B. *Essays, Critical and Miscellaneous*. Boston: Phillips, Sampson, 1854.

McCann, W. H. "Nostalgia: A Review of the Literature." *Psychological Bulletin* 38 (1941).

McGuire, William, ed. *The Freud/Jung Letters*. Princeton, N.J.: Princeton University Press, 1974.

MacKendrick, Paul. "A Renaissance Odyssey: The Life of Cyriac of Ancona." *Classica et Mediaevalia* 13 (1952).

McNeill, William H. *Plagues and Peoples*. New York: Anchor, 1976.

Mailer, Norman. "The Faith of Graffiti." In *Watching My Name Go By*, by Mervyn Kurlansky and Jon Naar. London: Mathews, Miller, Dunbar, 1974.

Mair, A. W. *Hesiod*. London: Oxford University Press, 1908.

Maitland, Frederic W. *Domesday Book and Beyond*. Cambridge: Cambridge University Press, 1907.

Malthus, Thomas R. *An Essay on the Principle of Population*. 2d ed. London: J. Johnson, 1803.

Maritain, Jacques. "Sign and Symbol." *Journal of the Warburg and Courtauld Institutes* 1 (1937–38): 1–11.

Marks, Geoffrey, and Beatty, W. K. *Epidemics*. New York: Scribner's, 1976.

Marshack, Alexander. "The Art and Symbols of Ice Age Man." *Human Nature* 1 (1978): 32–41.

_____. *The Roots of Civilization*. New York: McGraw-Hill, 1972.

Milton, John. *Paradise Lost: An Authoritative Text*. Edited by Scott Elledge. New York: Norton, 1975.

Mommsen, Theodor. *The History of Rome*. Translated by W. P. Dickson. 4 vols. New York: Scribner, 1891.

More, Henry. *Psychodia or a Platonicall Song of the Soul*. Cambridge: Daniel, 1642.

Morris, A. E. J. *History of Urban Form*. London: George Godwin, 1972.

Mourelatos, Alexander P. D. *The Route of Parmenides*. New Haven, Conn.: Yale University Press, 1970.

Mumford, Lewis. *The City in History*. New York: Harcourt, Brace and World, 1961.

Needham, Joseph. *Science and Civilisation in China*. Vol. 3, *Mathematics and the Sciences of the Heavens and the Earth*. Cambridge: Cambridge University Press, 1970.

Nelson, B. C., and Smith, C. R. "Ecology of Sylvatic Plague in Lava Caves at Lava Beds National Monument, California." In *Fleas*, edited by Robert Traub and H. Starcke. Rotterdam: Balkema, 1980.

Neugebauer, Otto E. "Exact Science in Antiquity." In *Studies in Civilization*, edited by Alan J. B. Wace. Philadelphia: University of Pennsylvania Press, 1941.

Nitzsche, Jane C. *The Genius Figure in Antiquity and the Middle Ages*. New York: Columbia University Press, 1975.

Norberg-Schulz, Christian. *Meaning in Western Architecture*. New York: Praeger, 1975.

Oliver, James H. *The Civilizing Power*. Transactions of the American Philosophical Society, n.s. 58, pt. 1, 1968.

Oliver, Paul. *Shelter, Sign, and Symbol*. Woodstock, N.Y.: Overlook Press, 1977.

Onians, Richard B. *The Origins of European Thought*. Cambridge: Cambridge University Press, 1951.

Oppenheim, A. Leo. *Ancient Mesopotamia*. Chicago: University of Chicago Press, 1964.

_____. *The Interpretation of Dreams in the Ancient Near East*. Transactions of the American Philosophical Society, n.s. 46 (1956).

_____. "Perspectives on Mesopotamian Divination." In Rencontre assyriologique, *La divination en Mésopotamie ancienne*.

Ovid. *Metamorphoses*. Translated by M. M. Innes. Harmondsworth, Eng.: Penguin, 1955.

Paley, Morton. *Energy and the Imagination*. London: Oxford University Press, 1970.

Panofsky, Erwin, ed. *Abbot Suger on the Abbey Church of St.-Denis and Its Art Treasures*. Princeton, N.J.: Princeton University Press, 1946.

Parke, Herbert W. *Festivals of the Athenians*. London: Thames and Hudson, 1977.

Parry, Adam. "Landscape in Greek Poetry." *Yale Classical Studies* 15 (1957).

Parsons, E. J. S. *The Map of Great Britain circa A.D. 1360 Known as the Gough Map*.

Oxford: Bodleian Library, 1970.

Pausanias. *Guide to Greece.* Translated by Peter Levi. 2 vols. Harmondsworth, Eng.: Penguin, 1971.

Petrarca, Francesco. *Le Familiari.* Edited by V. Rossi. Firenze: Sansoni, 1934.

———. *Rerum familiarium libri I–VIII.* Translated by A. S. Bernardo. Albany: State University of New York Press, 1975.

Pfeiffer, Ernst, ed. *Sigmund Freud and Lou Andreas-Salomé Letters.* Translated by W. and E. Robson-Scott. New York: Harcourt Brace Jovanovich, 1972.

Pfeiffer, John. "Inner Sanctum." *Science 82* 3 (1982): 66–68.

Phelps, Joseph J. "An Ancient Sculptured Stone in Manchester Cathedral." *Transactions of the Cheshire and Lancashire Antiquarian Society* 23 (1906).

Phillips, Barclay. "Discovery of a Tumulus at Hove, Near Brighton." *Sussex Archaeological Collections* 9.

Plato. *The Dialogues of Plato.* 4th ed. Translated by B. Jowett. 4 vols. London: Oxford University Press, 1969.

———. *Platonis Opera.* Edited by John Burnet. 5 vols. Oxford: Clarendon Press, 1972–77.

———. *The Timaeus and the Critias.* Translated by Thomas Taylor. New York: Pantheon, 1944.

———. *Works.* Translated by R. G. Bury. 12 vols. Loeb Classical Library. 1929.

Plutarch. *Lives.* Translated by John Dryden. Modern Library. 1967.

———. *The Parallel Lives.* Translated by G. Perrin. Loeb Classical Library. 1914–20.

Pollitzer, R. *Plague.* Geneva: World Health Organization, 1954.

Priestley, Harold E. *The English Home.* London: Frederick Muller, 1970.

Ptolemy, Claudius. *Geographikes Uphegesis.* Edited by C. Muller. Paris: Didot, 1883.

———. *Geography of Claudius Ptolemy.* Translated by E. L. Stevenson. New York: New York Public Library, 1932.

Pugin, Augustus W. N. *Contrasts.* 1836. Reprint. New York: Humanities Press, 1969.

Ransohoff, Rita. "Sigmund Freud, Collector of Antiquities, Student of Archaeology." *Archaeology* 28 (1975): 102–11.

Rapoport, Amos. "Australian Aborigines and the Definition of Place." In *Shelter, Sign, and Symbol,* edited by Paul Oliver. London: Barrie and Jenkins, 1975.

Reddaway, T. T. *London 1666: Fire and Rebuilding.* London: Bedford College, 1965.

Relph, Edward. *Place and Placelessness.* London: Pion, 1976.

Rencontre assyriologique internationale, 14th, Strassbourg, 1965. *La divination en Mésopotamie ancienne.* Paris: Presses universitaires de France, 1966.

Roberts, Robert. *The Classic Slum.* Harmondsworth, Eng.: Penguin, 1973.

Rogerson, Andrew, and Dallas, Carolyn. *Excavations in Thetford 1948–59 and 1973–80.* East Anglian Archaeology Report no. 22. Dereham: Norfolk Archaeological Unit, 1984.

Rose, Peter W. "Sophocles' *Philoctetes* and the Teachings of the Sophists." *Harvard Studies in Classical Philology* 80 (1976): 49–105.

Rossbach, Sarah. *Feng Shui, the Chinese Art of Placement*. New York: Dutton, 1983.

Roszak, Theodore. *Where the Wasteland Ends*. New York: Anchor, 1973.

Rothschild, Miriam. *Dear Lord Rothschild: Birds, Butterflies and History*. Philadelphia: Balaban, 1983.

————. "Fleas." *Scientific American* 213, no. 6 (1965).

————. "Note of an Exhibit." *Proceedings of the Royal Entomological Society of London*, ser. C, vol. 38, no. 7 (1973).

Rothschild, Miriam, and Clay, Theresa. *Fleas, Flukes and Cuckoos*. London: Collins, 1957.

Rothschild, Nathaniel Charles. "New Species of Siphonaptera from Egypt and the Soudan." *Entomologist's Monthly Magazine*, 2d ser., vol. 14 (1903).

————. "A Synopsis of Fleas Found on Mus Norwegicus Decumanus, Mus Rattus Alexandrinus and Mus Musculus." *Bulletin of Entomological Research* 1, pt. 2 (1910).

Rouham, Sally. *Canterbury: The Story of a Cathedral*. Canterbury: Christ Church, 1975.

Roux, Georges. *Ancient Iraq*. Harmondsworth, Eng.: Penguin, 1976.

Runciman, Steven. *Byzantine Civilisation*. London: Arnold, 1933.

Ruskin, John. *The Seven Lamps of Architecture*. London: Smith, Elder, 1849.

Rykwert, Joseph. *The Idea of a Town*. London: Faber and Faber, 1976.

Rylands, T. G. *The Geography of Ptolemy Elucidated*. Dublin: Ponsonby and Weldrick, 1893.

Saggs, H. W. F. *The Greatness That Was Babylon*. New York: Hawthorn, 1962.

Santillana, Giorgio de, and von Dechend, Hertha. *Hamlet's Mill*. Boston: Godine, 1977.

Schlauch, Margaret. "An Old English Encomium Urbis." *Journal of English and Germanic Philology* 40 (1941): 14–28.

Schur, Max. *Freud: Living and Dying*. New York: International Universities Press, 1972.

Scully, Vincent. *The Earth, the Temple, and the Gods*. Rev. ed. New York: Praeger, 1969.

————. *Pueblo: Mountain, Village, Dance*. London: Thames and Hudson, 1975.

Seaton, Ethel. "Marlowe's Map." *Essays and Studies by Members of the English Association* 10 (1923).

Segal, Charles. *Tragedy and Civilization*. Cambridge, Mass.: Harvard University Press, 1981.

Shaffer, Peter. *Equus*. New York: Avon, 1975.

Shrewsbury, John F. D. *A History of Bubonic Plague in the British Isles*. Cambridge: Cambridge University Press, 1970.

Simson, Otto von. *The Gothic Cathedral*. 2d ed. New York: Pantheon, 1962.

Skinner, Stephen. *The Living Earth Manual of Feng-Shui*. London: Routledge and Kegan Paul, 1982.

Slater, Philip E. *The Glory of Hera*. Boston: Beacon, 1968.

Smith, K. G. V., ed. *Insects and Other Arthropods of Medical Importance*. London: British Museum, 1973.

Snell, Bruno. *The Discovery of the Mind*. Translated by T. G. Rosenmeyer. New York: Harper Torchbooks, 1960.

Sophocles. *Antigone*. Translated by E. Wyckoff. Chicago: University of Chicago Press, 1959.

————. *The Plays and Fragments*. Edited and translated by R. C. Jebb. 2 vols. Cambridge: Cambridge University Press, 1899.

Southey, Robert. *Sir Thomas More: Or, Colloquies on the Progress and Prospects of Society*. 2d ed. 2 vols. London: John Murray, 1831.

Stanner, W. E. H. "The Dreaming." In *Reader in Comparative Religion*, edited by W. A. Lessa and E. Z. Vogt. 3d ed. New York: Harper and Row, 1972.

————. *On Aboriginal Religion*. Oceania Monograph no. 11. Sydney: Australasian Medical Publishing Company, 1960.

Stanton, Phoebe. *Pugin*. New York: Viking, 1972.

Steinthal, H. "The Legend of Samson." In *Mythology among the Hebrews*, edited by Ignaz Goldziher and translated by R. Martineau. New York: Cooper Square, 1967.

Sterrett, J. R. Sitlington. "The Torch-Race." *American Journal of Philology* 22 (1901): 393–419.

Symonds, John A. *The Revival of Learning*. London: John Murray, 1923.

Szelenyi, Ivan. "Regional Management and Social Class: The Case of Eastern Europe." Centre of Environmental Studies, London, 1975. Mimeographed paper.

Tait, James. Review of Maitland. *English Historical Review* 12 (1897): 768–77.

Tawney, Richard H. *Poverty as an Industrial Problem*. London: Ratan Tata Foundation, 1913.

Taylor, Alfred E. *A Commentary on Plato's Timaeus*. Oxford: Clarendon Press, 1928.

Thompson, Homer. "Athenian Twilight: A.D. 267–600." *Journal of Roman Studies* 49 (1959): 61–72.

Thompson, William I. *Passages about Earth*. London: Rider, 1975.

Thucydides. [no title]. Translated by B. Jowett. 2 vols. London: Oxford University Press, 1881.

Tocqueville, Alexis de. *The Old Regime and the French Revolution*. Translated by Stuart Gilbert. New York: Anchor, 1955.

Torcszyner, Harry. "The Riddle in the Bible." *Hebrew Union College Annual* 1 (1924).

Trachtenberg, Alan. *Brooklyn Bridge*. Chicago: University of Chicago Press, 1979.

Traill, Henry D., and Mann, J. S., eds. *Social England: A Record of the Progress of the People*. 6 vols. London: Cassell, 1901–4.

Traub, Robert, and Starcke, H. *Fleas*. Proceedings of the International Conference on Fleas, Ashton Wold, June 1977. Rotterdam: Balkema, 1980.

Travlos, John. *Pictorial Dictionary of Ancient Athens*. New York: Praeger, 1971.

Tselos, Dmitri. "Defensive Addenda to the Problem of the Utrecht Psalter." *Art Bulletin* 49 (1967): 334–49.

_____. *The Sources of the Utrecht Psalter Miniatures*. Minneapolis: n.p., 1955.

Tuan, Yi-Fu. "Place: An Experiential Perspective." *Geographical Review* 65 (1975).

_____. "Space and Place: Humanist Perspective." In *Progress in Geography*, edited by C. Board et al. Vol. 6. New York: St. Martin's Press, 1975.

_____. *Topophilia*. Englewood Cliffs, N.J.: Prentice-Hall, 1974.

Tucci, Douglass S. *Built in Boston*. Boston: Little, Brown, 1978.

Valéry, Paul. *Collected Works*. Vol. 10, *History and Politics*. Translated by D. Folliot and J. Mathews. New York: Bollingen, 1962.

Van Doren, Mark, ed. *The Portable Walt Whitman*. New York: Viking, 1945.

Verstegen, Richard. *A Restitution of Decayed Intelligence*. Antwerp: Robert Bruney, 1605.

Vlastos, Gregory. *Plato's Universe*. Seattle: University of Washington Press, 1975.

Waddell, Helen. *The Desert Fathers*. Ann Arbor, Mich.: Ann Arbor Paperbacks, 1957.

Walter, Eugene Victor. "Dreadful Enclosures: Detoxifying an Urban Myth." *European Journal of Sociology* 18 (1977): 151–59.

_____. "The Heavenly City of the Fourth-Century Hermits." *Comparative Civilization Review*, No. 2 (Spring 1979): 1–17.

_____. "Pauperism and Illth: An Archaeology of Social Policy." *Sociological Analysis* 34 (1973): 239–54.

Waterton, Charles. *Essays on Natural History*. Edited by Norman Moore. London: Warne, 1871.

Weisberg, David B. "An Old Babylonian Forerunner to Summa Alu." *Hebrew Union College Annual* 40–41 (1969–70): 87–104.

Wells, Herbert George. *Experiment in Autobiography*. London: Jonathan Cape, 1969.

Welty, Eudora. *Place in Fiction*. New York: House of Books, 1957.

White, Lynn, Jr. *Machina ex Deo*. Cambridge, Mass.: MIT Press, 1968.

Whitehead, Alfred North. *Adventures of Ideas*. New York: Macmillan, 1933.

_____. *Essays in Science and Philosophy*. New York: Philosophical Library, 1948.

_____. *Modes of Thought*. New York: Free Press, 1966.

_____. *Science and the Modern World*. New York: Macmillan, 1946.

_____. *Symbolism*. New York: Putnam's, 1959.

Williams, G. C. *The Book of Amber*. London: Benn, 1932.

Williams, Graham S., and Miles, A. A. *Topley and Wilson's Principles of Bacteriology and Immunity*. 5th ed. Baltimore: Williams and Wilkins, 1964.

Wormald, Francis. *English Drawings in the Tenth and Eleventh Centuries.* London: Faber and Faber, 1952.

Wright, Thomas. *A History of Domestic Manners and Sentiments in England during the Middle Ages.* London: Chapman and Hall, 1862.

Wycherly, R. E. "Peripatos: The Athenian Philosophical Scene—II." *Greece and Rome,* 2d ser., vol. 9 (1962): 2–21.

Xenophon. *Memorabilia.* Translated by E. C. Marchant. Loeb Classical Library. 1923.

Young, John Z. *Doubt and Certainty in Science.* London: Oxford University Press, 1951.

I N D E X

Omens, 160–64, 171–72, 185, 187. *See also* Divination
Oxyrhyncus, 81

Paleoastronomy, 165–69, 182–83, 198, 213
Palladius, 80–81
Panathenaea, 128, 151, 190, 201
Parmenides, 185
Pathemata, 150
Pathetecture, 143–44
Pausanius, 19, 193
Pericles: funeral oration of, 199–200, 201
Periegesis, 19
Periegetes, 19, 21
Pestilence. *See* Plague
Peter the Chanter, 80
Petrarch, Francesco, 110, 203
Phelps, Joseph, 28
Philochoria, 146
Philochoriac, 10, 19–20
Philoctetes, 98, 99
Philo of Larissa, 197
Pintupi, 132–33
Plague: defined, 44–45; causes and symptoms of, 44–45, 52; pneumonic, 45; bubonic, 45, 46, 48, 49, 52, 53, 64; spread of, 45–46, 47–56, 221 (n. 21); sylvatic, 46, 47, 48, 65–66; as disease of place, 46–67; decline of, 56–67
Plato, 20, 21, 190, 226 (n. 33); and Aristotle, 4, 12, 121–26, 191, 205; and *theoria*, 4, 218 (n. 19); *Phaedrus*, 10, 120, 129, 146–50, 193, 203; sees place as active receptacle, 12, 121–24, 126, 130, 205; use of word *chora* by, 120, 121–24, 126, 130, 133, 136, 150, 192, 200; on grasping of place through bastard reasoning, 121–25, 129, 130–31, 133, 135–36, 192, 203, 213; *Timaeus*, 123–24,

125, 126, 127, 129, 130, 150, 186–87, 203; *Menexenus*, 129, 200, 201, 203, 231 (n. 18); *Laws*, 130, 184, 185, 201; use of word *topos* by, 147, 148; and invention of the problem, 176, 181–82, 183–85, 186–87; and ungrounded Platonism, 176, 183, 188; on riddles, 181; and astronomy, 181–85, 186–87, 189, 198; *Republic*, 182, 201; and Socrates, 184; and the Academy, 188–89, 191, 196–97, 230 (n. 12); and myths, 193, 198, 201; *Lysis*, 196; as healer of souls, 197–98; and Pericles' funeral oration, 199–200, 231 (n. 18); *Seventh Letter*, 203. *See also* Grounded Platonism
Plotinus, 127
Polemo, 197
Pollution, 2
Poor: places of, vs. places of the rich, 26–33, 37–43, 150–52
"Popedonkey," 86–89
Přibor (Freiberg), 100–101, 113, 224 (n. 12)
Problem(s): and riddles, 176, 181, 182; Plato's invention and use of, 176, 181–82, 183–85, 186–87
Psalm 111/112, 26–30, 33
Psychagogy, 146–50
Ptolemy, Claudius, 115–16, 118, 119, 120–21; *Geographic Guide*, 115
Pueblo Indians, 128–29
Pugin, A. W. N., 31–32
Pugin's Medieval Court (Great Exhibition of 1851), 31
Pulex irritans (human flea), 51–52, 64
Pythagoreans, 186, 218 (n. 19)

Rapoport, Amos, 132, 141
Rats: and plague, 45–47, 48–60, 62, 63–64, 65–67, 221 (n. 21), 221–22 (n. 39)
Rattus norvegicus (sewer rat), 56–60